ROUTLEDGE LIBRARY EDITIONS:
INDUSTRIAL RELATIONS

Volume 21

INDUSTRIAL RELATIONS
IN THE PUBLIC SERVICES

INDUSTRIAL RELATIONS IN THE PUBLIC SERVICES

Edited by
R. MAILLY, S.J. DIMMOCK
AND
A.S. SETHI

Routledge
Taylor & Francis Group

LONDON AND NEW YORK

First published in 1989 by Routledge

This edition first published in 2025
by Routledge
4 Park Square, Milton Park, Abingdon, Oxon OX14 4RN

and by Routledge
605 Third Avenue, New York, NY 10158

Routledge is an imprint of the Taylor & Francis Group, an informa business

British Library Cataloguing in Publication Data
A catalogue record for this book is available from the British Library

ISBN: 978-1-032-81770-5 (Set)
ISBN: 978-1-032-81961-7 (Volume 21) (hbk)
ISBN: 978-1-032-81964-8 (Volume 21) (pbk)
ISBN: 978-1-003-50224-1 (Volume 21) (ebk)

DOI: 10.4324/9781003502241

Publisher's Note
The publisher has gone to great lengths to ensure the quality of this reprint but
points out that some imperfections in the original copies may be apparent.

Disclaimer
The publisher has made every effort to trace copyright holders and would
welcome correspondence from those they have been unable to trace.

Industrial Relations in the Public Services

Edited by
R. Mailly, S.J. Dimmock
and
A.S. Sethi

ROUTLEDGE

First published 1989 by Routledge
11 New Fetter Lane, London EC4P 4EE

Printed and bound in Great Britain by
Biddles Ltd, Guildford and King's Lynn

British Library Cataloguing in Publication Data

Industrial relations in the public services.
1. Great Britain. Public services. Industrial
relations
I. Mailly, R. II. Dimmock, Stuart J.
III. Sethi, Amarjit Singh
331'.041363'0941

ISBN 0-415-00416-0

CONTENTS

List of contributors   vii

Preface   ix

List of abbreviations   xi

1   The politics of industrial relations
     in the public services
     R. Mailly, S. J. Dimmock and A. S. Sethi   1

2   Public service trade unionism in the
     twentieth century
     R. H. Fryer   17

3   New managerialism in the Civil Service:
     industrial relations under the Thatcher
     administrations 1979-86
     R. Blackwell and P. Lloyd   68

4   Industrial relations in the National
     Health Service since 1979
     R. Mailly, S. J. Dimmock and A. S. Sethi   114

5   Bargaining strategies in local government
     I. Kessler   156

6   Industrial relations in the school sector
     R. V. Seifert   199

7   Some conclusions
     R. Mailly, S. J. Dimmock and A. S. Sethi   259

Index   273

LIST OF CONTRIBUTORS

R. Blackwell
Senior Lecturer
Department of Business Management Studies
Coventry Polytechnic

S. J. Dimmock
Director of Organisation and Manpower Development
Basildon and Thurrock Health Authority
    (formerly Lecturer in Personnel Management and
    Industrial Relations,
    Nuffield Institute, Leeds University)

R. H. Fryer
Principal
Northern College
Barnsley

I. Kessler
Senior Lecturer
Personnel Management
Bristol Polytechnic

P. Lloyd
Associate Director
Charles Barker Human Resources Consultancy

R. Mailly
Industrial Relations Adviser
Trent Regional Health Authority
    (formerly Lecturer in Labour Law,
    Nuffield Institute, Leeds University)

R. V. Seifert
Senior Lecturer and Associate Director
Centre for Industrial Relations
Keele University

A. S. Sethi
Associate Professor
Faculty of Administration
University of Ottawa

PREFACE

This book provides a survey of the 'politics' of industrial relations in the public services between 1978 and 1987. It is both historical and analytical in its approach and attempts to understand how politics has affected the conduct of industrial relations during this period. Developments occur so fast in this field that, since the completion of the contributory chapters, industrial action has occurred in the NHS and a widespread debate has commenced in the media over the funding and structure of the NHS persuading the Prime Minister to establish a Cabinet committee to review its future. This would not have been predicted six months ago, although the more radical programme for reform of the Civil Service announced recently was perhaps more predictable. Thus the book is concerned with a highly volatile area although assessments of development over the past eight years may give us pointers for future developments.

The contributors to this book have therefore coped with delays and redrafts to adjust to the increasing pace of developments with good humour and patience and for that the editors are grateful. In addition, the editors would wish to thank Pam Mathews for her accurate work in completing the final version of the manuscript and the many others who helped along the way. The editors, of course, take full responsibility for the completed work and any errors that may remain.

R. Mailly
S. J. Dimmock
A. S. Sethi

LIST OF ABBREVIATIONS

ACAS	Advisory Conciliation and Arbitration Service
ACC	Association of County Councils
ADC	Association of District Councils
AEU	Amalgamated Engineering Union
AGSRO	Association of Government Supervisors and Radio Officials
AMA	Association of Municipal Authorities
AMMA	Assistant Masters and Mistresses Association
APT&C	Administrative, Professional and Technical and Clerical (Bargaining Group in Local Authorities)
ASLEF	Associated Society of Locomotive Engineers and Firemen
ATTI	Association of Teachers in Technical Institutions
AUT	Association of University Teachers
BMA	British Medical Association
CCMA	Contract Cleaners and Maintenance Association
CLEA/ST	Committee of Local Education Authorities School Teachers Section
COCSU	Council of Civil Service Unions
COHSE	Confederation of Health Service Unions
CPSA	Civil and Public Services Association
CSU	Civil Service Union
DES	Department of Education and Science
DHA	District Health Authority
DHSS	Department of Health and Social Security
EIS	Education Institute of Scotland
FBU	Fire Brigades Union
FDA	Fire Division Association
FMI	Financial Management Initiative
GCHQ	General Communications Headquarters
GLCSA	Greater London Council Staff Association

List of Abbreviations

GMBATU	General and Municipal Brickworkers and Allied Trades Union
HVA	Health Visitors Association
HCSA	Hospital Consultants Specialist Association
IHSM	Institute of Health Service Management
IPCS	Institute of Professional Civil Servants
IRSF	Inland Revenue Staff Association
FMI	Financial Management Initiative
LACSAB	Local Authority Conditions of Service Advisory Board
LEA	Local Education Authorities
MPU	Medical Practitioners Union
NAHA	National Association of Health Authorities
NAHT	National Association of Head Teachers
NAS/UWT	National Association of Schoolmasters/ Union of Women Teachers
NALGO	National Association of Local Government Officers
NATFHE	National Association of Teachers in Further and Higher Education
NBPI	National Board of Prices and Incomes
NCU	National Communications Union
NHS	National Health Service
NUPE	National Union of Public Employees
NUR	National Union of Railwaymen
NUT	National Union of Teachers
PAT	Professional Association of Teachers
PESC	Public Expenditure Survey Committee
POA	Prison Officers Association
PSBR	Public Sector Borrowing Requirement
RAWP	Regional Allocative Working Party
RCN	Royal College of Nursing
RHA	Regional Health Authority
RTA	Remuneration of Teachers Act
SHA	School Heads Association
SSTA	Scottish Secondary Teachers Association
TSSA	Transport Salaried Staff Association
TUC	Trades Union Congress

Chapter 1

THE POLITICS OF INDUSTRIAL RELATIONS IN THE PUBLIC SERVICES

R. Mailly, S. J. Dimmock and A. S. Sethi

This book provides an analysis of the politics of industrial relations in the public services since 1979. This is likely to prompt two questions in the reader: first, why the public services? Secondly, why 1979? It is the purpose of this introduction to attempt to provide answers to both these questions. Defending the proposition that industrial relations in the public services are distinctive and deserve separate analysis leads us to a definitional problem. What, indeed, are the public services? An analysis which begins with the problems of definition inevitably runs the dangers either of becoming bogged down in disputation or of adopting a definition which other interested parties find inadequate, incomplete or insufficiently discriminatory.

Probably, the most orthodox or common sense definition of public services in Britain would include those services provided by Local Government, the National Health Service (NHS) and the Civil Service (or at least parts of it). Immediately we face severe difficulties in the definition of the boundaries of each of these three huge areas of employment. First, where do contractors <u>within</u> each service fit? Second, what about employment in public agencies, such as the Tourist Boards? Third, this apparently straightforward approach would automatically exclude consideration of workers in the gas industry (privatised since 1979), in electricity supply, water and the railway industries and in the postal service. Some approaches to the study of public services attempt to delineate the area under consideration by reference to the 'non-trading' aspects of public service employment. Indeed, at one time, such an approach was reflected in the national bargaining machinery for local

1

authorities. However, a moment's reflection will immediately call to mind all those anomalous examples which do not fall comfortably within such a definition. Thus, there are many small areas of trading with local authority work, within the NHS and even within central government employment.

An alternative approach is that which claims to advance not only beyond simple empirical description but also to the kind of initial categorisation briefly touched upon above. This attempt at a full-blown <u>theoretical</u> perspective locates public service and most public sector employment within an analysis of the state in contemporary society or, more particularly, of the capitalist state. Not only is the state to be seen in both its national and local forms (Cockburn, 1977) but, more importantly, it is to be understood in terms of its relations with capitalism and the manner in which its relative autonomy is deployed to reproduce, regulate and even modify capitalist social relations (Poulantzas, 1968 and 1978). In these complex and specifically historical processes, different aspects or apparatus of the state not only play quite different roles, but they also shift through time in detailed forms relatively independently of each other. Their key relation is to the particular balance of class forces obtaining generally within a given society's historical conjuncture as well as to the more narrow relations within that society. Seen in this way, different aspects of state employment, for example education or the NHS, can be understood in terms of the ideological, economic and social functions they perform in capitalist society. Rather than seeing developments in the state as either further manifestations of the growth of a monstrous leviathan as, for example, in classical liberal theory and more recently refined in the 'crowding out' thesis (to be discussed below); or else as evidence of the social progress of welfare provisions as, for example, in Fabian or social democratic perspectives; this approach locates the study of the state and the work of state employees firmly within the class struggle. It follows that within the state are to be found precisely those divisions of class position and class affiliation which prevail throughout society. This gives rise, according to some authors, to the opportunity for state workers to be both 'in' and 'against' the state and able to seek alliances both against particular developments within state forms and state policies but also with groups struggling outside the

2

state who are also subordinated to it (CSE, 1979a and 1979b). In so far as such workers also seek to hitch trade union organisation and action to the cause of the struggle, it might be claimed that such state workers were also promising to transcend the conventional limitations of economistic trade unionism, with its emphasis upon regulating and expressing capitalist social relations rather than challenging and replacing them (see Lenin, 1947; Anderson, 1967; Fryer, 1979).

This theoretical perspective, although initially attractive, has serious drawbacks. First, it seems that the processes and categories are so vague and open-ended as to allow an all too easy application of the theory: in consequence, as theory, it lacks a sharp cutting edge. Indeed it appears that only the most scant knowledge of any particular aspects of state work and trade unionism is required to be able to fit them into a general framework. Secondly, as has often been remarked in criticism of both Poulantzas and Althusser's schema, it is not immediately evident where the boundary lies between the 'state' and 'society'. If this is true then we are back to our initial problems of definition and differentiation in the empirical world which greater theoretical sophistication might reasonably have been expected to help resolve. Finally the theory fails to illuminate what might be the role of management within the public services and how managerial strategy may contrast or reflect management strategy in the private sector.

In summary, although this theory of the state is useful in shedding light on the reasons for conflict within the state, and the fact that various aspects of the state serve social and economic functions, it does little to help us understand why industrial relations in the public services might be distinctive. Although it provides pointers as to why trade unionism may be of a different complexion than the private sector, there is little in the theory to suggest that management in the public services may be driven by different imperatives or have to respond to different contingencies than in the private sector.

MANAGEMENT AND INDUSTRIAL RELATIONS IN THE PUBLIC SERVICES

The dearth of material on the study of management in industrial relations which became so apparent during

3

R. Mailly, S. J. Dimmock and A. S. Sethi

the 1970s has been somewhat ameliorated in the last decade. Analysts on both sides of the Atlantic have suggested that management has some choice as to the labour relations strategy they follow and that labour relations strategies may be subordinated to other imperatives or may not exist at all in some British firms (Gospel and Littler, 1983; Sissons and Purcell, 1983; Thurley and Wood, 1983; Dimmock and Sethi, 1986; Sethi and Dimmock, 1987). The majority of studies of management in British industrial relations have examined the private sector or publicly owned manufacturing bodies (see for example Marsden et al., 1985). The important exception to this trait has been the study of the Post Office by Batstone, Ferner and Terry (1984). Subsequent studies have expanded upon their interesting findings (Ferner, 1985 and 1987). These studies provide some insights into how and for what reasons industrial relations in state owned enterprises may differ from those in the private sector. In particular what are the imperatives which influence managerial strategy in state owned enterprises? They conclude that there are a number of contingencies which will influence managerial strategy in both the public and private sectors, but by far the most important contingency in publicly owned enterprises is the 'political contingency'. This describes the shifting influences of changes in government economic and social policy and the rules they set for the conduct of their enterprise: management may be able to subtly modify such policies during their implementation but their room for discretion is limited.

> Management's ability to evade government short-term economic measures was particularly limited. In other areas, management could win greater discretion by shaping and forestalling possible political pressures although in doing so it was still constrained by the rhetoric associated with the political contingency . . . (op. cit., 36-7).

Although Ferner has postulated a 'continuum' of state influence in industrial relations, ranging from the private sector where the state will provide the rules under which firms operate, to the other extreme at which an organisation's operation may be almost entirely determined by the state (Ferner, 1985), Batstone et al. suggested that the relation-ship is not an immutable one. Their research

4

revealed that the political contingency had to be studied in an historical context. 'At times the contingency may impose on management an imperative for action as forceful as that facing a private firm in the midst of a profits crisis' (op. cit., 288).

It is postulated here that the nature of the political contingency applying to the public services is a crucial influence upon the conduct of industrial relations. Further, the position of the three services on Ferner's continuum makes them particularly sensitive to changes in economic and social policy; and that 1979 marked a decisive turning point in such policies which was to have a profound impact upon industrial relations in this sector. The distinctiveness of industrial relations in these services is directly related to their position upon this continuum, with the Civil Service situated at one extreme, with government as the employer; the NHS being placed marginally further along the continuum, with the responsibility for government policies being 'carried' (Ferner, 1987: 52) by health authorities, who are the employers, but who are funded from the Exchequer; and local authorities at the further end of the continuum, having power to raise a proportion of their own finance as well as being employers.

To explain how and in what ways the political contingency has changed since 1979, it is first of all necessary to examine the pattern of industrial relations existing prior to that date.

THE TRADITIONAL PATTERN OF INDUSTRIAL RELATIONS

The traditional pattern of industrial relations in the public services which existed until the late 1960s is one of highly centralised collective bargaining, with local industrial relations under-developed compared with the private sector and relatively undisturbed by disputes (Winchester, 1983). This system was underpinned for a large proportion of employees by a highly developed system of personnel policies - most marked in the Civil Service - supporting job security, incremental salaries, internal promotion and internal labour markets. These sets of policies have been labelled 'bureaucratic paternalism' by some commentators (Littler, 1982). The policies were most consistently applied to the white collar employees in the public sector. However, the espousal of the 'good employer' image became synonymous with working for the public services and in particular the Civil Service. It was further defined by the Priestly Commission in 1957:

> The good employer is not necessarily one who offers the highest rates of pay - he seeks rather to provide stability and continuity of employment and consults with representatives of his employees upon changes that affect their remuneration and their conditions of work. He provides adequate facilities for training and advancement and carries on a range of practices which today constitute good management, whether they be formalised in joint consultation along Civil Service lines or not. Such employees are likely to be progressive in all aspects of management policy. (Beaumont, 1981)

Beaumont is more specific in detailing the employment policies of a 'good employer': positive support for equal opportunities for all employees and potential employees, a support for union organisation, a belief that terms and conditions of employment whilst not the best should be among those who pay somewhat above the average; and adherence to due procedure in the termination of people's employment (Beaumont, 1981).

These personnel policies were largely kept intact during these years, Beaumont argues, because of a felt moral 'duty' on the part of the government to treat its own employees 'fairly' and secondly to act as a good example to the private sector. The image was certainly more closely intact in the Civil Service than in the other services where the obligation was perhaps not felt so strongly and other pressures bore upon it (see MacIntosh, 1955; Clegg and Chester, 1957). Beaumont notes, however, that there was a perception amongst civil servants that their relative wage levels had deteriorated at this time. Data on civil service wage levels during this period is not conclusive but the perception of employees and trade unions is an important indicator that the 'good employer' image had begun to be eroded. Winchester (1983) suggests that the impact of incomes policies on pay in the public services during the 1970s was crucial in the public sector's growing reputation as a major source of instability in British industrial relations.

THE END OF COMPARABILITY

Pay and pay determination, therefore, were the major reasons for a slow erosion of the good employer principle in the late 1970s. However, Beaumont was not equivocal in asserting that the rest of the principles remained in place at the end of that decade. They too were about to come under severe pressure in the next few years.

The dual role of government as manager/financier in the public services and manager of the economy put the traditional pattern of industrial relations during the 1970s under some strain. A series of incomes policies beginning in the mid 1960s and continuing to the end of the 1970s were to rely heavily on controlling monies in the public sector and particularly in the public services. This in turn was to place pressure on the notion of 'comparability' enshrined in the Priestly Commission Report of 1957. Comparability took different forms within the Civil Service, the NHS and local authorities. Within the Civil Service it was loosely based upon the Priestly definition, while in the other two services comparisons within the private sector were difficult to identify or largely non-existent. It followed that comparisons were found internally within the three public services: for example, NHS ancillary workers were linked with local authority manual workers and NHS administrators with non-industrial civil servants. Internal relations were important also in all three services, but the notion of 'comparability' was the driving force behind many pay claims during the 1970s, which culminated in the rash of disputes labelled the 'winter of discontent' in the winter of 1978/79.

There is no doubt that <u>all</u> sectors of the public services suffered relative wage deprivation during the 1970s (Heald, 1983: 224). This overall picture must be refined by the fact that during periods of severe control pay generally lagged seriously behind the private sector and enjoyed 'booms' or catching-up periods when controls were relaxed; as for example in the period of pay reviews from between 1974 and 1975. The interaction between pay in the public services and incomes policies led to a crisis in public service pay when the Labour government attempted to impose a five per cent limit on wage rises in 1978. After a series of protracted disputes involving most workers in the three public services, the government appointed

Professor Hugh Clegg as Chairman of the Standing Commission on Pay Comparability. Professor Clegg and his team were given the difficult task of 'establishing acceptable bases of comparison for most of the public services sector'. The very terms of reference, therefore, accepted that comparability was a legitimate method of determining pay in the public services. Although hampered by shortage of time, the committee did make a systematic attempt to analyse and apply the concept of comparability. Clegg found the concept more difficult to apply in practice than it appeared in theory. However, the Commission accepted the principle of comparability as a valid one for determining public services pay, although Clegg argued that more sophisticated methods may need to be used than in the past (Clegg, 1982).

The incoming Conservative government of 1979 acted swiftly to abolish the Standing Commission, after reluctantly accepting its findings. This was not surprising as the Conservatives had entered office committed to a change in policy over methods of deciding public sector pay, hence 'affordability' was to be the primary criterion not comparability (Conservative Manifesto, 1979). The system of pay determination in the public services had been under great and increasing strain in the last decade, but this change of policy was to prove the first decisive break with traditional criteria. Further pressure was to be placed upon that system through the way the Conservatives' economic and social policies were to impact upon the public sector.

PUBLIC EXPENDITURE - GOOD OR BAD?

Public expenditure expanded rapidly in the post-war years, particulary between 1960 and 1980. The bulk of this growth was in the 'core' elements of the welfare state (education, libraries and arts, health and personal social services, social security, and housing). Expenditure on these services grew from 48.07 per cent in 1966 to 54.68 per cent of public spending in 1981 (Heald, 1983). Governments of both political persuasions had, under a broad Keynesian consensus, increased the public sector borrowing requirements (PSBR) since 1945 and public expenditure was seen as a 'good thing'. In the 1970s the Keynesian interpretation of the role of public expenditure came under increasing criticism from differing perspectives. Commentators

8

criticised the economic theory for failing to take
account of budget constraints upon a government
(Burrows, 1979), others claimed it ignored the
inevitability of a 'fiscal crisis' if the state
inexorably increased public borrowing (Offe, 1984).

The strain placed upon the economy by high
public spending led to the economic crisis of
1975/76. Following unprecedentedly high inflation
and a balance of payments crisis, Dennis Healey, the
Chancellor of the Exchequer, turned to the
International Monetary Fund for financial assistance
and restrictions on public spending were
subsequently introduced, through the regime of cash
limits.

The system of planning expenditure which
existed prior to 1976 was one in which the Cabinet
determined the volume of resources and their
distribution between spending departments. There
was no predetermined limit on cash expenditure;
estimates were based upon current pay and prices and
any increases in costs which arose during the
financial year were met through supplementary votes
in Parliament. As Thompson and Beaumont note (1978:
123), this system, linked with a method of pay
determination based primarily upon comparability, at
a time of high inflation, failed to provide a
realistic control over government expenditure.

After the intervention of the International
Monetary Fund cash limits were set for the budgets
of the Civil Service, the NHS and local authorities,
with external financial limits being set for the
loans and grants to nationalised industries
(Winchester, 1983). Initially cash limits provided
administrative support for the Labour government's
income policy. Indeed it has been argued that cash
limits and incomes policy neatly complemented each
other (Heald, 1983: 226). However, this twin-
pronged policy came to a halt with the collapse of
the Social Contract in 1978. Henceforth, under the
Conservative government from 1979 onwards cash
limits were to be used as the cutting edge for an
implicit public sector pay policy.

Cash limits served another important purpose
under the Labour government - assisting the squeeze
on public expenditure. There is considerable
controversy about the nature and extent of 'cuts' in
public expenditure during these and subsequent years
(Winchester, 1983). Heald notes (1983: 194) that an
'inflation factor' would be set by the Treasury
within the cash limit, but significantly below
actual inflation rates, so squeezing the volume of

expenditure without making explicit how large cuts were to be planned. It is argued by Winchester (op. cit., 172) that the reductions in expenditure which took place in the years 1976 to 1979 were primarily in capital expenditure, with some marginal cuts in planned growth. The nature of the reductions in public expenditure was to change significantly in the years following 1979.

In 1979, the Conservatives came to power electorally committed through their manifesto to reducing the size of the public sector. In contrast to all other post-war governments, they proceeded to set out in the annual review of public expenditure plans through reductions in real terms (Wright, 1981) by the Public Expenditure Survey Committee (PESC). In addition, in 1982/83 they replaced the system of 'volume' planning with 'cash' planning. This system allowed further squeezes to be made in spending, in the form of shortfalls on inflation allowances which could be planned for each year, rather than revaluation taking place at the end of each financial year. As Heald notes: 'Cash planning, even more so than cash limits, is a blunt instrument of great appeal to those attaching priority to <u>less</u> rather than <u>better</u> public spending' (1983: 196).

This policy, combined with the view that 'affordability' should be the main determinant of pay in the public services, indicated a profound change in how the public services were to be viewed. However, the government's policy was not derived from the simplistic notion that too much money was being spent upon the state but from a combination of an ideology and economic policy which saw the public services as something of an anathema.

MONETARISM AND THE PUBLIC SERVICES

The forces within the Conservatives which had grouped around Margaret Thatcher had been re-evaluating the experiences of the Heath government in opposition. They had rejected the long-run post-war policies and adopted a different approach to economic and social issues. Central to the new philosophy of the Conservatives was the need to reduce the role of state intervention. Reduction in public spending and a strict control of money supply, which had initially been tried by Edward Heath, was not reasserted as a cornerstone of government policy. Borrowing on the ideas of Milton

Friedman the role of the state was no longer seen as economically and socially beneficial, but a corrosive element which acted to reduce individualism within the market place and to encourage the denial of personal responsibility within the social affairs of the community. In consequence a reduction both in the role of the state in the economy and in the size of state ownership were deemed necessary. The reduction of state interference within the economy, particularly in regard to wage bargaining, would encourage the re-emergence of the laws of the market.

Wage settlements that could not be supported by increased productivity would pay the price exacted by the market place. Without the possibility of government support to ease them through hard times, employers within the private sector would stand firm against excessive demands and take steps necessary to increase productivity. The prospect of increased unemployment which had stimulated all previous post-war governments to intervene in the economy was viewed more sanguinely by the Conservatives. For the long term it was preferred to continuing inflation and unsound money. Indeed unemployment in the long term was unavoidable unless government took action to reduce the money supply. The primary aim, even if this led to an increase in temporary unemployment, must again become the stability of the value of money (Hayek, 1976).

As Heald notes (1983: 35) it is sometimes difficult to determine where economic theory finishes and ideological statements begin when reading monetarist theorists. Indeed, the importance of ideology within Conservative policy should not be underestimated (Hall, 1983). The marriage of free market liberalism with 'organic patriotic Toryism' - 'the translation of a theoretical ideology into a populist idiom' (op. cit., 28) - stands as a major political achievement.

The re-emphasis on the market and the unrestricted interplay of supply and demand marked the end of corporatism (Crouch, 1977 and 1979) as an element within official Conservative thinking. It reduced the need for government intervention both in the field of economic and industrial planning and in wage determination within the private sector. It also removed the pressure for government to attempt to maintain a dialogue with the TUC over these issues. The principal area of intervention in trade union affairs would necessarily be designed to ensure the proper functioning of the market, by

R. Mailly, S. J. Dimmock and A. S. Sethi

restricting the ability of unions to exercise undue
influence in collective bargaining and in the wider
political process.   To this end the programme of
trade union reform would be incremental rather than
holistic.   Moreover, in following through the
philosophy of market individualism, it would be
aimed at reducing the collective power of trade
unions in favour of the individual member.   The
Employment Acts of 1980 and 1982 and the Trade Union
Act of 1984 served to undermine the ability of trade
unions to take effective collective action and to
assert state control over their organisation and
rule-making functions.   Moreover, the Conservatives'
economic policies resulted in high levels of
unemployment which increased worker insecurity and
eroded union membership levels.
        The disputes in the public sector during the
winter of 1978/79 not only provided an ideal
platform for Margaret Thatcher to attack trade
unionism, but also as a populist base upon which to
launch an attack upon the state and in particular
the Civil Service.   The Prime Minister's own dislike
for bureaucracy and for the 'consensus' politics
epitomised by Whitehall was possibly one of the most
important factors behind an anti-state policy which
was supported by monetarist economists who had
turned their attention to the role of the public
sector during the 1970s, and formulated the
crowding-out thesis.
        According to this thesis, the public sector is
viewed as wasteful and inefficient and a burden on
the private sector (Bacon and Eltis, 1976).   In
fact, two distinct types of crowding out have been
put forward by theorists.   Physical or direct
crowding out, they argued, occurs when the state
pre-empts real resources from the private sector
such as manpower and materials.   Bacon and Eltis
(op. cit.) argued that public employment growth had
been directly at the expense of the (predominantly
private) market sector.   Monetarist writers tend to
emphasise financial or indirect crowding out.   They
postulate that higher public borrowing will mean
higher interest rates which will have a doubly
damaging effect upon the economy.   Investment in
such things as house building and consumer durables
will be reduced and higher domestic interest rates
will attract an inflow of capital, thus putting up
exchange rates.   Heald (1983) notes that some of the
assumptions upon which the crowding-out thesis is
based are questionable.   For example, direct
crowding-out assumes that the market sector would

12

want all the manpower that the public sector has absorbed and that much of the growth in public sector employment during the 1970s was part-time and female. Equally it is hard to find a conclusive answer to the question of whether high public expenditure stimulates the economy to such an extent as to cancel out the 'indirect' effects of public spending described above. However, the influence of the theory is important, for as Heald (1983: 16-41) notes:

> If it is believed that the macro economic effects of public spending are damaging and short-run changes for stabilisation purposes viewed as worthless, if not perverse, an important pillar supporting the post-war role of public expenditure crumbles.

THE IMPACT OF MONETARISM ON THE PUBLIC SERVICES

The clearest indication that the Conservative government's policies on the public services were not developed out of a rigid economic dogma was the rejection of some of the central tenets of monetarism during their first term. The control of the money supply through monetary targets, espoused as the foundation of sound economic policy at the beginning of the Thatcher government, were dropped in 1982 after Sterling M3 went out of control in 1980/81. Equally, the commitment to lower public spending in real terms was reappraised in 1982. There was an initial sharp tightening of budgetary policy in the years 1979-81 and then a marked loosening. The main areas to suffer reductions were health and education, but it soon became clear that these sensitive areas could only suffer reductions in real terms for a short period before tangible effects upon the quality of service began to prove politically unpopular. The government then turned to the use of 'efficiency' as a by-word for producing the same level of services with less money. Measures introduced included tighter budgetary control, exemplified by the Financial Management Initiative in the Civil Service (see Chapter 3). In addition, services were to be scrutinised to see if they gave 'value for money' (Rayner Scrutinies, see Chapters 3 and 4). The Audit Commission was used to scrutinise local authorities' expenditure (see Chapter 5). In the second term of the Thatcher government every area of the public services was scrutinised to see if it was possible to introduce privatisation. Where it was politically expedient to do so services were contracted out to the private sector or tested against commercial bids (see Chapters 3, 4 and 5).

Each of these policy changes had a profound impact upon the conduct of each of the services, not least in the area of industrial relations. The following chapters analyse that impact, looking at changes in bargaining structure, managerial strategy, the response of the trade unions and impact upon local industrial relations. These chapters are preceded by an analysis of the nature of trade unions in the public services, examining developments before and after 1979.

REFERENCES

Anderson, P. (1967) 'The Limits and Possibilities of Trade Union Action', in Blackburn, R. and Cockburn, A. (eds.) The Incompatibles: Trade Union Militancy and the Consensus, Penguin, Harmondsworth, pp. 263-80

Bacon, R. W. and Eltis, W. A. (1976) Britain's Economic Problem: Too Few Producers, (1st edn), Macmillan, London

Batstone, E., Ferner, A. and Terry, M. (1984) Consent and Efficiency: Labour Relations and Management Strategy in the State Enterprise, Blackwell, Oxford

Beaumont, P. (1981) Government as Employer - Setting an Example?, Royal Institute of Public Administration, London

Burrows, P. (1979) 'The Government Budget Constraint and the Monetarists - Keynesian Debate', in Cook, S. T. and Jackson, P. M. (eds.) Current Issues in Fiscal Policy, Martin Robertson, Oxford

Clegg, H. A. (1982) 'How Public Pay Systems Have Gone Wrong Before', in Gretton, J. and Harrison, A. (eds.) How Much Are Public Servants Worth?, Blackwell, Oxford

Clegg, H. A. and Chester, T. E. (1957) Wage Policy and the Health Service, Blackwell, London

Cockburn, C. (1977) The Local State, Pluto Press, London

Conservative Manifesto (1979) Conservative Central Office, London

Crouch, C. (1977) Class Conflict and the Industrial Relations Crisis, Heinemann, London

Crouch, C. (1979) The Politics of Industrial Relations, Fontana, London

CSE (1979a) In and Against the State, CSE, London

CSE (1979b) Struggle Over the State, CSE, London

Dimmock, S. J. and Sethi, A. S. (1986) 'The Role of Ideology and Power in Systems Theory', Industrial Relations, 41(4)

Ferner, A. (1985) 'Political Constraints and Management Strategies: The Case of Working Practices in British Rail', British Journal of Industrial Relations, XXIII(1), March 1985

Ferner, A. (1987) 'Industrial Relations and the Meso-Politics of the Public Enterprise', British Journal of Industrial Relations, XXV(1), March 1987

Fryer, R. H. (1979) 'British Trade Unions and the Cuts', Capital and Class, 8, pp. 94-112

Gospel, N. and Littler, C. (1983) Managerial Strategies and Industrial Relations, Heinemann, London

Hall, S. (1983) 'The Great Move Right Show', in Hill, S., and Jacques, M. (eds.) The Politics of Thatcherism, Lawrence & Wishart, London

Hayek von, F. A. (1976) Law, Legislation and Liberty, Vol. 2, 'The Mirage of Social Service', Routledge & Kegan Paul, London

Heald, D. (1983) Public Expenditure: Its Defence and Reform, Martin Robertson, Oxford

Lenin, V. I. (1947) What Is To Be Done?, Progress, Moscow

Littler, C. (1982) The Development of the Labour Process in Capitalist Societies: A Comparative Study of the Transformation of Work Organisation in Britain, Japan and the USA, Heinemann, London

McIntosh, M. (1955) 'The Negotiation of Wages and Conditions for Local Authority Employees', Public Administration, XXIII

Offe, C. (1984) Contradictions of the Welfare State, Hutchinson, London

Poulantzas, M. (1968) Political Power and Social Classes, Verso, London

Poulantzas, M. (1978) State, Power and Socialism, Verso, London

Sethi, A. S. and Dimmock, S. J. (1987) 'A Transactional Model of Industrial Relations', Labour and Society, 12(2), International Labour Organisation, Geneva

R. Mailly, S. J. Dimmock and A. S. Sethi

Sissons, K. and Purcell, J. (1983) in G. S. Bain
   (ed.) Industrial Relations in Great Britain,
   Blackwell, Oxford
Thompson, A. W. J. and Beaumont, P. B. (1978)
   Public Sector Bargaining, Saxon House,
   Farnborough
Thurley, K. , and Wood, S. (eds.) (1983) Managerial
   Strategy and Industrial Relations, Cambridge
   University Press, Cambridge
Winchester, D. (1983) in G. S. Bain (ed.)
   Industrial Relations in Great Britain,
   Blackwell, Oxford
Wright, M. (1981) Big Governments in Hard Times,
   Martin Robertson, Oxford

Chapter 2

PUBLIC SERVICE TRADE UNIONISM IN THE TWENTIETH CENTURY

R. H. Fryer

UNION GROWTH IN THE PUBLIC SERVICES

The most striking feature about public service unionism in Britain has been its remarkable growth throughout the present century. In 1911, the total union membership within the services listed in Table 2.1 was less than half a million. Strictly speaking, some of the services included in the table were still very much in the private sector in 1911. But the major areas of trade unionism listed, in local government, education, posts and tele-communications, were most clearly 'public'. By 1979, since when trade unionism in Britain has experienced a sharp decline, the same public services included just short of five million trade unionists. By 1986, according to the latest estimate by IDS, public sector unionists affiliated to the TUC totalled a little over four and a quarter million workers. In addition, there was a further group of 641,000 public sector trade unionists outside the TUC (IDS, 1987). Given that the public corporations by 1986 employed a little over 1.1 million workers and that union density of membership in that branch of the public sector stood at an estimated minimum of 80 per cent, public service unionism by 1986 probably stood at just short of four million members.

In 1911, public service unionism (as defined by Table 2.1) constituted some 14.3 per cent of trade unionism in all industries and services in Britain. That proportion grew steadily over the decades that followed, with a particular spurt during the 1920s when unions outside the public sector suffered heavy membership losses. By 1979, public service unionism constituted 37.4 per cent of all trade unionism and the proportion appears to have held steady and even

17

Table 2.1 Public Service Union Membership (000s) and Union Density (%) Great Britain 1911-1979

	1911		1921		1931		1951		1961		1965		1971		1974		1979	
	UM	UD	UM	UD	UM	UD	UM	UD	UM	UD	UM	UD	UM	UD	UM	UD	UM	UD
Local govt and education	179.9	39.3	415.9	59.3	484.5	51.1	906.5	67.3	1130.3	65.5	1288.8	65.7	1568.1	65.4	1831.6	67.9	2232.0	77.5
Health services	32.4	19.8	41.0	27.9	51.7	31.5	255.2	42.7	293.1	37.4	300.7	33.8	477.7	45.8	626.9	55.1	971.2	73.7
National government	18.2	21.0	116.6	57.2	110.0	75.4	403.7	64.4	423.5	79.7	438.3	79.0	546.2	94.0	593.2	100	583.8	91.3
Gas	17.9	20.2	63.9	56.4	27.4	21.7	112.0	76.1	98.7	77.7	86.6	69.1	93.8	77.3	91.6	86.0	95.5	90.3
Electricity	0.4	2.2	14.4	33.4	21.9	25.3	124.4	67.5	160.1	73.5	174.2	71.6	188.8	89.6	190.0	100	179.9	99.1
Water	1.3	8.3	2.5	11.3	4.7	14.5	17.6	52.2	21.1	53.8	24.1	54.0	38.4	85.9	47.1	98.5	56.2	92.7
Railways	98.8	16.9	410.6	59.1	320.1	55.3	424.8	84.8	351.6	85.1	284.1	83.9	224.1	91.2	207.2	92.8	204.2	97.8
Posts and telecommunications	94.9	59.2	140.9	64.2	148.3	62.4	270.1	81.2	301.6	85.3	324.3	84.0	374.0	84.9	378.2	85.8	427.6	99.9
All above services	443.8	28.2	1205.8	56.2	1168.6	50.4	2514.3	63.7	2780	66.4	2921.1	64.3	3511.1	69	3965.8	73.1	4760.4	81.7
All industries services	3219	19.0	6512	37.9	4569	24.3	9266	44.7	9518	43.2	9742	42.6	10518	47.0	11226	49.2	12702	53.6

Sources: Price and Bain, 1976
Bain and Price, 1980
Bain and Price, 1983
Price and Bain, 1983

slightly increased during the next seven years. Whilst public sector unionism accounted for some 44.4 per cent of all TUC membership by 1986, when non-TUC affiliates are included, public sector unionism constituted some 51 per cent of all trade unionism. (The largest non-TUC affiliates are found in the public sector, especially in the health and local government branches of the public services). Overall, by 1986, union density in the public sector stood at 70 per cent when only TUC affiliates were included and at 81 per cent when non-TUC affiliates were also considered. In the private sector, density based upon TUC affiliates was only 35 per cent and this increased marginally to 38 per cent when non-TUC affiliates were included (IDS, 1987). Ironically, privatisation in such areas as British Telecom, British Gas and British Shipbuilders, which all have had historically high levels of union density, will have boosted private sector union density, at least in the short term.

Between 1911 and 1979, as trade union membership in Britain grew four-fold, the growth in public service unionism was an astonishing ten-fold. But that overall growth masks significant variations within the public services. Thus, for example, the rate of membership growth in posts and telecommunications union membership was only slightly higher than for the economy as a whole (perhaps not surprisingly in view of its high density already in 1911 and the only modest increase in employment in this sector; in 1911 total employment or potential union membrship was 160,304 and by 1979 that had risen to 428,028). By contrast, membership in railways grew only two-fold over the period as a whole, although by 1951 the increased membership had already reached more than four times its number in 1911. Since 1951, a sharp decline in railway employment has cut away at trade union membership there, despite the maintenance of high levels of union density by the NUR, ASLEF and TSSA. At the other extreme, union membership in health and in local government and education showed an enormous increase over the period. Union membership in health multiplied thirty-fold and in local government and education by twelve-and-a-half. These enormous increases reflect not only the very rapid increase in employment in these areas of the public services, especially since the 1960s (as illustrated in Table 2.2), but also the successful establishment of high levels of union density amongst the rapidly growing workforce.

Table 2:2 Public Sector Employment in Great Britain 1950-1986 (000s)

| | CENTRAL GOVERNMENT | | | | Local Authorities | Public Corporations |
	Total	of which HM Forces	Civilian	(of which NHS)		
1950	1831	690	1141	-	1419	2474
1955	1904	803	1101	-	1493	2632
1960	2160	518	1642	(575)	1737	1861
1965	1796	423	1373	(650)	2040	2023
1970	1909	372	1537	(741)	2500	1921
1975	2262	336	1926	(1042)	2993	2012
1980	2393	323	2070	(1174)	2956	2038
1985	2360	326	2034	(1223)	2958	1262
1986	2337	322	2015	(1215)	3010	1169

Source: Economic Trends, 1987

But even these comparisons mask other differences both within areas of employment and between unions. Thus, for example, within the Civil Service, employment overall appeared to have remained more or less constant throughout the 1970s expressed as full-time equivalents. In 1970, the total was 700,800 but, after rising to 747,600 in 1976 fell back to 705,100 in 1980. However, whereas in 1970 non-industrial civil servants had constituted 70.4 per cent of the total, by 1980 this had risen to 77.7 per cent. In 1970, industrial civil servants totalled 207,800, but by 1980 this had fallen by 24.2 per cent to 157,400. Employment in some of the civil departments had grown faster than others during the 1970s and some had actually contracted. Thus, growth had occurred in Customs and Excise, Inland Revenue, Employment (especially), the Home Office and the DHSS. In contrast, transport and environment, defence, foreign and commonwealth and education all experienced falls in staffing. Nor, of course, were increases or decreases common across all grades.

By October 1986, the total employed in the Civil Service had dropped substantially to 598,800 and industrial civil servants now comprised only 94,300 or 15.7 per cent of that total, or more than a halving of their proportion within the Civil Service since 1970. Staffing levels in environment, education and science as well as defence continued to decline, whilst Employment (including the MSC) continues to show the most marked growth followed by the Home Office (CSO, 1981 and 1986; Wilkinson, Elliot and Travers, 1982).

Bearing in mind the mixed pattern of trade unionism in the Civil Service, with organisation based on a combination of department (IRSF), grade-based (CPSA, SCPS, FDA and CSU partially) and occupational recruitment (IPCS and CSU partially), these changes in the internal pattern of Civil Service staffing carry different implications for each of the unions involved and, within them, for their respective arrangements for section, group and departmental organisation and representation.

Individual union growth
Turning to growth in individual unions, the changes in employment briefly touched upon above need to be borne in mind. As may be seen from Table 2.3, since 1970 there has been substantial and sustained union growth in local government, the National Health Service and overall in posts and telecommunications

21

Table 2.3 Growth of Selected TUC-Affiliated Public Service Unions 1970-1985 (000s).
Index: 1970 = 100

	Union	1970 (Index)	1975 (Index)	1980 (Index)	1985 (Index)
Public services generally	NALGO	439.89 (100)	625.16 (142)	782.34 (178)	752.13 (171)
	NUPE	372.72 (100)	584.49 (157)	699.16 (188)	663.78 (178)
NHS	COHSE	89.55 (100)	167.20 (187)	216.48 (242)	212.98 (238)
	HVA	5.43 (100)	8.60 (158)	13.65 (251)	15.95 (294)
	RCN (not TUC affiliated)		1976 101.00	1979 161.96	1984 245.00
Civil Service	CPSA	184.94 (100)	224.72 (122)	216.42 (117)	146.54 (79)
	SCPS	59.00 (100)	99.94 (169)	108.84 (184)	86.85 (147)
	IPCS	92.42 (100)	103.50 (112)	98.75 (107)	89.24 (96)
	IRSF	49.74 (100)	60.58 (122)	62.34 (125)	55.12 (111)
	CSU	35.25 (100)	46.78 (133)	45.62 (129)	31.21 (89)
	FDA			8.17	7.62
	POA	13.66 (100)	19.73 (144)	21.37 (156)	23.78 (175)
Education	NUT	310.54 (100)	281.86 (91)	232.40 (75)	207.65 (67)
	NAS/UWT	56.90 (100)	82.71 (145)	124.28 (218)	127.61 (224)
	NATFHE	29.74 (100)	59.75 (201)	67.86 (228)	77.39 (260)
	EIS		28.69	47.49	43.28
	AUT			31.92	31.23
Other local government	FBU	30.00 (100)	30.00 (100)	30.00 (100)	43.83 (146)
	GLCSA	14.10 (100)	19.77 (140)	17.07 (121)	15.45 (110)
Posts and tele-communications	NCU	116.56 (100)	124.68 (107)	130.98 (112)	161.32 (138)
	UCW	209.48 (100)	185.00 (88)	202.29 (97)	194.23 (93)

Source: Certification Officer Reports 1970, 1975, 1980 and 1985

although, since privatisation, the majority of both NCU and UCW members have been transferred to the private sector.

NALGO recruits white collar clerical, administrative and managerial staff in local government, the NHS, gas, electricity supply and water as well as in universities. With more than three-quarters of a million members in 1985, NALGO is now officially recorded as the fourth largest union affiliated to the TUC after the TGWU, AEU and GMBATU. In view of the huge losses in manufacturing jobs and the consequential large arrears in subscriptions in the engineering industry, it is probable that NALGO is, more accurately, the third largest TUC union. Of course, the union only affiliated to the TUC in 1964 after a long saga of campaigns and membership ballots (see Spoor, 1967; Newman, 1982). Between 1970 and 1980 the union's membership grew by 78 per cent and, despite cuts in public expenditure during the 1980s, membership losses have so far been very limited and the union in 1985 still stood at 71 per cent above its membership level of 1970.

A similar picture emerges when NUPE is examined. Where NALGO focuses attention upon white collar workers, the bulk of NUPE's membership is manual, especially in local government and the NHS, although the union also organises workers in the water industry and universities. As far as can be seen from figures available but not published, NUPE can justifiably claim to be the largest of Britain's local government unions, as well as being officially the sixth largest TUC affiliate. As in the case of NALGO, the union can probably claim more members 'in benefit' than in the AEU where arrears subscriptions have become extremely serious. NUPE's growth rate since 1970 has been very close to that of NALGO, although it grew slightly faster up to 1980, by which time it had increased membership over the decade by 78 per cent. Cuts and membership losses appear to have had a slightly greater effect upon NUPE than NALGO, with somewhat greater losses from an initially slightly lower total.

To some extent, by concentrating on the period since 1970, the account understates the remarkable and sustained growth rates of both NALGO and NUPE. For example, in 1950 NALGO had only 197,056 members and NUPE only 140,054. If 1950 is taken as a baseline, then over the last 35 years NALGO's growth amounts to 282 per cent and NUPE's to 374 per cent

23

R. H. Fryer

and the picture would have been even more impressive
if pre-war membership figures had been used as the
baseline.
Elsewhere in local government, trade union
membership has also grown. Mention has already been
made of the two giant general unions, GMBATU and
TGWU, who recruit manual workers, as well as of the
principal craft and occupationally specialist
organisations. Trade unionism has also grown
amongst teachers and lecturers, although the
fortunes of the different unions have varied.
Whilst NUT membership has fallen by about 100,000
from just over 300,000 in 1970, the NAS/UWT has more
than doubled. Similarly, NATFHE has grown markedly,
although in part this reflects the merger of ATTI
and ATCDE to create one college lecturers' union
which has continued to grow since the merger in
1976. Other local government unions, the FBU and
Greater London Council Staff Association, also
manifested membership growth over the last 15 years.
In all likelihood, the return of a constant
membership figure of 30,000 by the FBU for several
years actually masked some growth; but, by 1985
membership had grown by 46 per cent over the 1970
figure. GLCSA membership growth was slower, by only
10 per cent over the period as a whole although up
to 1975 the Association had achieved a 40 per cent
increase over its 1970 membership, but this fell
away as rival campaigns were mounted to recruit
white collar workers in the capital to NALGO and, to
a lesser extent, to NUPE. This was achieved not so
much by 'poaching' existing members but by
recruiting new employees, a process greatly
facilitated by the high levels of labour turnover
obtaining in local government, especially amongst
lower clerical and manual workers.
By contrast with local government unionism,
growth in Civil Service and government service trade
unionism since 1970 has been more modest and has
suffered more serious reverses since 1980. Thus,
for example, the CPSA which organises principally
clerical work grades in the Civil Service and allied
public services, saw an increase in membership in
the first five years from 1970 of 40,000 or 22 per
cent. After that membership fell back slightly to
1980 and then, with the transfer of membership in
telecommunications to the NCU in 1985 and a decline
in density of organisation, there was a further fall
to just 146,540 in 1985 or just 79 per cent of the
membership level 15 years earlier. A similar,
fluctuating membership pattern has been evident in

24

the CSU which recruits principally amongst manual workers and certain technical and occupational specialisms in the Civil Service. During the 1970s, especially the first five years, the CSU also experienced substantial membership increases, with no less than a 33 per cent increase in the five years to 1975. After that, membership declined slightly but then, from the 1980s onwards, the union was badly hit by cuts and privatisation of services and membership slumped to 89 per cent of its 1970 level. The IPCS, organising qualified technical and scientific staff, especially in the Ministry of Defence and associated organisations, has also lost membership since the mid 1970s, although on nothing like the scale of the CSU and CPSA. Even so, since 1975 the union has lost 14,260 members or 14 per cent of its 1975 membership. By 1985, membership of the IPCS had fallen marginally below its pre-TUC affiliation total of 92,418, despite its merger with AGSRO which recorded a membership of 11,595 in 1980.

A somewhat better initial picture emerges when the other two large Civil Service unions are concerned. The Society of Civil and Public Servants, which organises lower, middle and some senior administrative and managerial grades, grew sharply in the early 1970s, thanks especially to mergers with separate staff associations in Customs and Excise and the Department of Employment. Growth continued to 1980 and then fell away at a rapid rate to 1985. In the five years from 1980, 21,900 members were lost, or 20 per cent. In the circumstances described, whatever the general advantages of further merger and amalgamation to promote stronger, unified unionism in the Civil Service, the abortive merger between SCPS and CPSA in 1985 and the agreement for merger between SCPS and CSU after membership ballot in 1987 take on the clear aspect of necessary defensive actions. Even the rather special, departmentally-based IRSF has not managed to escape the widespread loss of membership over the past five years. Over the decade of the 1970s, the IRSF managed to increase membership by 25 per cent but again the last five years have seen a drop of 7,220 or 11.6 per cent. Even so, at 55,120 the IRSF membership in 1985 still stood at 11 per cent above the Federation's membership for 1970. Finally, the FDA, organising top civil servants, also saw a fall in membership from 1980 to 1985. One very important consequence of these widespread reductions in Civil Service membership is the loss of direct representation on

the TUC General Council under the 'automaticity'
arrangement which provides for a seat on the General
Council to organisations with 100,000 members. This
is especially critical for both the IPCS and SCPS
whose earlier membership figures would have
qualified them for a seat each.

Whereas there are a number of large trade
unions with sizeable memberships in both local
government and the Civil Service, a quite different
picture arises in considering the NHS. Whilst NALGO
and NUPE both have substantial membership interests
in white collar and ancillary staffs respectively,
the general picture is of more than 40 organisations
seeking representation amongst the NHS staff of 1.3
million full-time equivalents in 1985. Amongst
these organisations four stand out, for quite
different reasons. The first is COHSE, which
proclaims itself to be a 'specialist' health
workers' union and which recruits especially amongst
nurses and ancillary staff. COHSE's roots go back
deep into the organisation of Asylum and Poor Law
Institution workers (see Carpenter, 1980, 1985a,
1985b). From 1970 onwards the union has experienced
substantial growth, with only a slight decline in
the 1980s. Despite COHSE's temporary expulsion from
the TUC following its refusal to 'deregister' under
the provisions of the 1971 Industrial Relations Act,
membership increased by 87 per cent to 1975 and by a
further 29.5 per cent to 1980.

Although in competition with NUPE for both
nursing and ancillary membership in the NHS, COHSE's
main rival, the RCN, remains unaffiliated to the
TUC. It was because of the competition from the RCN
and the advantages which the latter could benefit
from by registering under the 1971 Industrial
Relations Act, that COHSE itself refused to deregister. Membership growth in the RCN has been
spectacular and has increased by 155,000 or 172 per
cent in the last 10 years alone. The RCN enjoys
certain opportunities for organisation and
recruitment amongst student and pupil nurses during
their training and has also turned its mind
seriously to a reorientation of its organisation and
systems of representation in recent years. Even so,
its fortunes contrast quite sharply with those of
unions in the Civil Service and, over the past five
years, with its rivals which also organise in local
government, the water industry, universities, gas
and electricity.

The third notable organisation is much smaller,
the Health Visitors Association. The union is, as

its name implies a specialist occupational
organisation and it has a distinguished record in
its campaigns for health education and improved
preventative health care in the community. Again,
the NVA has achieved remarkable success in
membership growth over the last 15 years from 5,430
in 1970 to 15,950 by 1985. Finally, there is the
HCSA which organises hospital consultants and
specialists. In 1985 its membership totalled only
2,486 and that was already a decline of 1,200 since
1980. The vast majority of doctors, both in
hospitals and general practice, are not members
either of the NCSA nor of the old MPU which is now
part of the ASTMS. When TUC affiliates meet to
discuss both the health services in general and
doctors in particular, the ghost at the table, so to
speak, is the BMA. Whilst the BMA is not affiliated
to the TUC and does not describe itself in any way
as a trade union (and, in that sense, is not
'unionate'), it clearly carries out many of the
regulatory and representational functions aspired to
by organisations describing themselves as trade
unions or commonly assumed to be so.

Union organisation and democracy
Closely linked to the questions of union growth is
the whole issue of union organisation and democracy
in public service unionism. The relationships are
multiple and complex here and, certainly, no one
influence can, with any confidence, be isolated as
providing the key impetus to the changes and
developments which characterised public service
unionism in the 1970s and early 1980s. Perhaps
chief amongst those changes have been, first, the
very large extension of workplace representation and
shop steward organisation in public service unionism
and, secondly, the decision by several public
service unions to commission, or themselves embark
upon, thorough internal structure reviews and reorganisations.
Although it would be quite easy to assume that
workplace or even shop steward-based representation
was unheard of in the public services before the
1970s, there can be little doubting their enormous
increase during the 1970s and 1980s. Thus, the
research by Fryer et al. in NUPE revealed that:

In 1970 39 per cent of the union's 1,600
branches had no stewards and this had dropped
to only eleven per cent by 1974. An estimate
at the end of 1973 suggested that the union had

27

> just over seven thousand stewards of whom
> nineteen per cent were women . . . In 1974 only
> 29 per cent of union stewards in post had held
> the position for four years or more and 59 per
> cent said that the members they represented had
> not been represented by a union steward before
> they had taken up office. (Fryer, 1983: 38)

Similarly, in a study of NUPE's local government
organisation carried out in 1982, almost two-thirds
of the branches reported that stewards had first
made their appearance between 1970 and 1978. By
1982 three-quarters of NUPE's local government
branches reported that all sections of the workforce
in their main local authority were 'covered' by
stewards (Hayes, Joyce and Williams, 1986: 81).
This is not, of course, the same as saying that
every workplace, establishment or, still less,
workgroup had its own steward or stewards elected
from and responsible to that particular group of
members alone. Because of the highly dispersed,
fragmentary nature of the labour force - by place of
work, occupation, department, function and hours of
employment - the simple notion of a straightforward
link between stewards and workgroups, even if it is
applicable in some parts of manufacturing industry,
is inapplicable in much of the public services.
Again, this is confirmed in the recent Workplace
Industrial Relations survey (which probably
understates the matter because of the sampling frame
chosen): in 1984, in 36 per cent of workplaces
manual workers were represented by a steward from
'elsewhere in the organisation' as against 45 per
cent where representation was by one or more
stewards from the workplace itself. In private
manufacturing, private services and the nationalised
industries, manual workplace representation was
predominantly drawn from the workplace itself.
Amongst white collar workers, perhaps not
surprisingly in view of the importance of large
concentrations of such employees in town halls,
hospitals and Civil Service establishments, the
pattern of representation was much more similar
across the sectors surveyed (op. cit., 80).
    Of course, as the increasing, but still
remarkably limited, research findings have begun to
demonstrate, the number, quality, character,
activities and responsibilities of stewards and
local representatives varies greatly both within
unions and between them, between men and women, from
section to section and department to department,

from type of authority to type of authority and
according to the organisational and institutional
arrangements for representation and negotiation
(see, for example, Somerton, 1977; Fryer et al.,
1978; Drake et al., 1982; Fairbrother, 1982;
Kessler and Winchester, 1982; Marchington and
Armstrong, 1982; Terry, 1982; Hayes et al., 1986;
Kessler, 1986).

Looking across the variety and diversity of
local and workplace representation in the public
services, several salient issues are worthy of note.
First, there has been an enormous and rapid growth
in the number of shop stewards, local
representatives and workplace 'activists' over the
past 15 years. Even bearing in mind the range of
activities embraced within the nomenclature (it is
clearly not enough to declare 'a steward is a
steward is a steward'), this growth is impressive.
Thus, although NALGO'S conference only formally
adopted the steward system in 1977, already by 1978
the union was claiming to have 30,000 'stewards' in
its ranks. According to the data collected in the
Workplace Industrial Relations study, whereas manual
stewards in all establishments fell by 10,000 (or
5.5 per cent) between 1980 and 1984, (with an
especially large drop of 24 per cent in private
manufacturing), they increased by 15,000 or 24 per
cent in the public sector. Although there was an
overall increase in non-manual stewards of some
28,000 (20.7 per cent), this masked a large decline
in the white collar private manufacturing sector of
12,000 (34.3 per cent) and an equally dramatic
increase in white collar stewards in the public
sector of some 30,000 or 34.9 per cent, although the
authors do warn that their research probably
understated public sector steward numbers in 1980
(op. cit., 84-6).

A second feature of shop steward and local
organisation has been the extension of local
consultative and bargaining machinery, including
joint arrangements between workplaces, unions and
departments in local authorities, the Civil Service
and National Health Service. Of course, not all
stewards have been involved in these developments,
but they have gone on alongside the extension of
facilities for stewards, the sophistication of local
procedures and increases in leading stewards,
conveners, and full-time stewards. Between 1980 and
1984 full-time stewards in the public sector
increased from 1,000 to 1,600 with an especially
large increase amongst white collar workers from 500

to 1,000 in that period. As the authors of the Workplace Industrial Relations survey remarked, with notable restraint: 'The stereotype of the trade union representative as a manual shop steward in manufacturing industry evidently needs revision' (op. cit., 86).

Thirdly, steward systems were often 'sponsored' in their development (Fryer et al., 1974) either by the union nationally, by full-time paid officials, by branch officials or by employers (Terry, 1982; Kessler, 1986). This is not to say that steward organisation was not thrown up, in embryonic form at least, by other occurrences such as a national or local dispute and the need to co-ordinate, organise and give local leadership to such initiatives: such was plainly the case in the Dirty Jobs Dispute, the NHS ancillary workers' strike of 1973, the Civil Service disputes of 1979 and 1981 and the 1979 Winter of Discontent. However, even in these circumstances, the resultant representation and forms of organisation, where they lasted, were soon embraced within a framework approved and underpinned by the union's own hierarchy of authority or employer-union agreed negotiating structure. Partly as a result of systematic reviews of union organisation and partly in response to increased local bargaining and militancy, unions revised their rule books to provide for stewards and local representation, issued handbooks and guidelines to stewards on their role and responsibilities and took up increasing numbers on TUC-organised day release shop steward training courses. Again, as might be expected, the increased union training has been most marked amongst non-manual workers in recent years, but whilst manual representative training dropped from 37 per cent of establishments in private manufacturing reporting it in 1980 to 28 per cent in 1984, public service manual steward training was reported in 31 per cent of establishments in 1984 as against 28 per cent four years earlier. Non-manual representative training in the public services increased from 22 per cent of establishments reporting it in 1980 to 30 per cent in 1984 (Millward and Stevens, op. cit., 90). Nor were these developments restricted to organisations affiliated to the TUC. Outside the TUC, it was most notably the RCN which first reviewed and overhauled its structure and then actively promoted local steward representation in the NHS (Tavistock, 1973; Carpenter, 1977).

Fourthly, and closely linked to the previous point, steward growth and organisation was also stimulated by their official recognition in national agreements between employers and trade unions. Needless to say, in some areas stewards already existed and were given de facto local recognition before their status was officially endorsed nationally, but the conclusion of national agreements for local authority manual stewards in 1969 and for stewards in the National Health Service in 1971 not only stimulated growth and changes in union rules but also, crucially, gave legitimacy to the appointment, election and training of stewards and other local representatives (Fryer, 1983). In this respect, the growth of local organisation may seem paradoxical in industries and sectors of the economy long dominated by national and often highly centralised bargaining, especially where the bulk of pay, procedures and conditions of employment are concerned. At the very least, the peculiar articulation of national and local organisation provides a quite different model for that usually assumed to operate although, to cynics, the inclusion of stewards in union rule books and handbooks and their explicit recognition by employers is sufficient evidence in itself of incorporation and, by implication, demobilisation. For this school of thought, unofficialism and informality denote not only independence but also the true, untrammelled spirit of the rank and file. Whatever grains of truth such a perspective contains, the main thrust of its assumptions is plainly a matter of debate and its theoretical shortcomings have been adequately outlined elsewhere (Lane, 1974; Zeitlin, 1982; Hobsbawm, 1984).

Fifthly, the adoption of new rules and agreements to include stewards and their development locally represented an enormous challenge to union structures, even where on an individual basis branch officials, full-time officers and members welcomed the advent of stewards. Irrespective of personal feelings, the problems were three-fold. Could steward systems simply be grafted on to local, especially branch, structures? Would steward systems come to represent alternative centres of power and communication, albeit informally? Would separate steward-based institutions be created, both jointly with employers, within unions and between them, on a formal and constitutional basis, which would effectively bypass branch-based representation

31

and authority? Plainly, if the answer to either of
the latter questions were in the affirmative, as it
was in NUPE, NALGO, COHSE and, in some places in the
Civil Service for CPSA, IPCS, SCPS and the CSU, then
there could be potential difficulties of parallel
organisation and representation in public service
unionism. On the other hand, a grafting operation
especially on to local branches or branch
committees, of whatever degree of sophistication,
might either undermine existing branch organisation
and activity or else stifle the incipient stewards'
movement locally by placing artificial barriers on
numbers, constituencies, authority to elect and
endorse and so on. This last question, for example,
figured very centrally in the SCPS's response to the
review team's proposal that branch executive
committees should be made up exclusively of local
stewards and branch officials. In its response to
the Warwick team's proposals, the SCPS argued that
restricting branch and district committees to
stewards and branch officials:

> . . . could have been disadvantageous in a
> number of cases; for example, where the
> management posting system was deliberately
> operated in order to concentrate known Society
> (i.e. SCPS) activists within a single
> constituency; and also in Branches where
> Society members were performing senior line
> management functions or dealt with industrial
> relations in the office, and were thus unlikely
> to become stewards. (SCPS, 1983: 9)

Again, stewards' numbers and their level of
individual commitment might make unworkable or
impracticable the idea of branch or district
committees comprised of all eligible stewards: on
the other hand, local systems built on only a
proportion of stewards risked introducing hierarchy,
division and possibly a bureaucratisation of rank
and file relationships.

Sixthly, as far as steward development in the
public services is concerned, factors essentially
external to the unions immediately concerned also
stimulated the growth of steward activity within
them. Amongst these were, importantly, the
development of personnel and industrial relations
management specialism within the services (see
Millward and Stevens, op. cit., 40-41). This
brought with it a sophistication of procedures and
processes as well as more local attention to the

detailed substance of agreements which required a response from the unions and which, very often, the managers were happy to see in the form of steward organisation. In addition, there were the developments in government and employer policy on pay, cuts, reorganisation and privatisation which stimulated local, often defensive, strategies including local organisation. Here the link between national and state policy, militancy and union organisation becomes clearest. However, the point can be overstressed, because changes in national policy did not always lead to local resistance and, where it occurred, local resistance did not necessarily entail the transformation of temporary local representation and co-ordination into permanent structures of shop steward representation. Whilst it may frequently be true that strikes are veritable schools of war in raising the consciousness of workers in struggle, thus affecting union structures as much as attitudes to employers, they most certainly should not be mistaken for the war itself, so to speak, as Lenin so cogently argued. Putting local organisation on a sound footing after a dispute and where it had not so existed before, was contingent on many considerations and was by no means a foregone conclusion. Similarly, the development of steward organisation in the public services cannot be divorced from developments elsewhere in the economy and industrial relations. A combination of post-Donovan enthusiasm for formalised local bargaining, revolutionary zeal for rank and file representation and a sheer demonstration effect must certainly have acted as influences upon public service unionism. As redundancy and redeployment also brought in men and women with experience of other unions and industries with stewarding arrangements, this too added to the influences.

Finally, as should be evident by now, although the slow advent of an element of bonus bargaining and policing undoubtedly made a contribution to the development of steward organisation amongst some groups of workers in local government, the NHS (less so) and Civil Service (very much less so), it would be quite wrong to ascribe overmuch importance to this single influence acting alone, as it appears Clegg was inclined to do (Clegg, 1979). Equally important, and maybe more so, were essentially national developments with clear local implications, such as the Health and Safety at Work Act, the ACAS Codes of Practice, and the need for local representation to understand and monitor the changed sick pay regulations when they were introduced. This is not to deny any importance to the initial stimulus provided by productivity bargaining and bonus schemes (including opposition to them), but many groups never had bonus schemes applied and even where they operated, local stewards bargained about and spent their time on much more than just pay and bonus. Thus, Hayes and his colleagues report six main activities of NUPE stewards in local government, including not only negotiating with management, but communicating with members and other stewards, in recruitment and in the distribution of union literature (Hayes et al., 1986: 91). Amongst the negotiating issues raised with management by stewards were holidays, discipline, hours and overtime, health and safety, bonus and work study, paid educational leave, working practices, and redundancy. Individual grievances were cited by most stewards (63 per cent) amongst the three issues most frequently taken up, followed by health and safety (mentioned by 51 per cent), discipline (43 per cent), working practices (31 per cent) and incentive bonus schemes (29 per cent).

As might be expected, the exploration and promotion of local systems of steward and other representation figured very prominently in the reviews unions undertook of their own structures and organisation. Most notable here is the number of public service unions which engaged in such an examination, whether on their own, through specially convened committees or by contracting for some external body to conduct the survey. Two studies of the latter kind were commissioned from the Sociology Department at Warwick University; one of the National Union of Public Employees (Fryer et al., 1974) and, later, one of the Society of Civil and Public Services (Drake et al., 1982a, 1982b). In between times, the Inland Revenue Staff Federation made use of the (now defunct) Behavioural Sciences Research Division of the (equally defunct) Civil Service Department to conduct an extensive review of structures, attitudes and opinions and communication in the Federation (Humphrey et al., 1977, 1977b; IRSF, 1977).

The Tavistock Institute of Human Relations undertook an 'exploratory study' of the RCN membership as early as 1973 (Tavistock, 1973) which, as well as dealing with the position of stewards in the Royal College, looked at branch and area organisation, national boards, section committees and the Council itself. As has already been mentioned, the NALGO Executive established its own working party in 1974 and, in the South West, a detailed investigation was conducted into the desirability and possibility of formally initiating a proper system of local representation by stewards (NALGO, 1974). More recently, both the IRSF and the CPSA have commissioned extensive surveys of membership attitudes and opinions. Thus, the IFF research report has constructed a profile of union membership in the CPSA as well as their attitudes to pay, health and safety, training, promotion, industrial action, representation and union publications (CPSA/IFF, 1986). More recently still, EPIC's research on behalf of the IRSF has produced a detailed analysis of the position of women in the Federation and comparable trade unions, drawing attention especially to the range of policies and special organisational arrangements established to promote greater female participation and sexual equality in the unions (IRSF/EPIC, 1987).

Common themes

A number of these reports have common themes, despite the fact that they are dealing with often quite different patterns of union organisation and representation. The most prominent of these are the related issues of union democracy and the stimulation and promotion of greater membership participation. Whilst not denying the importance of informal, workplace involvement in union matters, again and again the investigations point to the need to institutionalise such participation by the creation of effective and widespread local representation and by the reinvigoration and, if necessary, reorganisation of local branches, sub-branches and membership section meetings. Regular branch meetings are more a feature of unions such as NALGO, NUPE and COHSE than they are of the white collar Civil Service unions, where annual general meetings and conference mandating meetings have traditionally played an extremely important role. Branch organisation has proved a headache for virtually all British unions, especially in so far as membership attendance is concerned. From an organisational point of view, much criticism has been properly attached to geographical branches in which diverse groups of members and individuals from otherwise unrelated workplaces have been expected to participate. One popular solution has been to call for workplace branches. Whilst such an approach

could be adopted in some areas of public service
work (large hospitals and offices and some depots),
widespread membership dispersal - as for example in
schools, residential homes, small local offices and
even where there is no workbase to speak of - makes
this apparently straightforward remedy an unlikely
starter. Members, however, can be grouped on a more
local basis than has often been the case and this,
together with negotiated facility of time for
attendance and the organisation of transport, can
help to boost attendance.

A second common theme of the inquiries has been
how to combine adequate forms of organisation and
representation in the union for legitimate sectional
interests together with integration of these
potentially divergent interests into a common union
perspective. At first glance, it might seem that
the likely difficulties are much less in unions
which largely cover only one employer or even one
department of state, such as the IRSF, but even here
questions of grade, occupational and geographical
representation are important. Unions like NALGO and
NUPE have, in addition to these questions, the task
of providing a relevant structure for members
working for different employers, under a range of
local, regional and national bargaining arrangements
and working alongside a variety of other union
members with their own systems of organisation and
representation. Thus, not only does NALGO organise
staff in local government, the NHS, gas,
electricity, airports, water supply and
universities, but it also represents members at very
different levels of the pay and authority hierarchy
in those several services. The same problems
confront NUPE, only to a slightly lesser extent. On
the other hand, NUPE also recruits white collar and
professional workers who, for ideological reasons or
just plain convenience, prefer membership of NUPE to
one of the other organisations. Where COHSE is
concerned, although the union works predominantly in
the NHS, with the need for organisational
arrangements to cover hospitals, districts and
regions, as well as national bargaining, it also
confronts a service typified by extremes of
divergence in earnings, qualifications, authority
and attitudes to professionalism. This last matter
has also been of importance to teacher unions on the
one hand and bodies deliberately standing outside
the TUC such as the RCN and the much smaller rival
organisations to the main teacher and college
lecturer unions.

The various reviews also turned their attention to the methods of election/appointment of full-time officials. Although methods of election where executives are concerned have now been given a greater degree of uniformity following the 1984 Trade Union Act, there is still plenty of room for variety and conflict over other elections and in relationship to the position of full-time officials. Closely connected to this issue is the whole complexion of factional and political organisation within the unions under review. Characteristically, this necessarily very tricky ground has been largely avoided or trodden upon most gingerly by review teams and internal union working parties alike. This has not always been the case in the unions concerned, where vigorous and overt political campaigning, publicity and mobilisation have become part of the stock in trade of conferences, membership ballots and elections. Most notable, of course, has been the CPSA where campaigns for and against Communist Party membership have a long history and where, over the past 15 years especially, bitter disputes (often involving the courts and the national press) have broken out not just between rival groups on the right and the left but within those groups giving rise to competing Broad Left groups in the union. Although political and factional organisation occurs in all of the other public service unions, it has not reached the level of activity and hatred sometimes expressed in the CPSA. Thus, the International Socialists (later, Socialist Workers' Party) was particularly active in organising hospital workers during the 1970s and Catholic Action has a long history of right-wing organisation in several unions, both of which have attracted press comment. There are signs too that, as in the past, the government is considering the extent to which it should set limits upon the political activities and affiliations of men and women employed in state work.

But the problems of organisation and representation do not end with the tangled matter of political organisation in public service unions. Typically, the unions have turned, or been advised to turn, to matters of minority representation and under-representation within the unions. This has led to a range of 'positive action programmes', for example, for women, black and ethnic minorities. Included in this have been special training and education programmes, reserved seats, seminars and conferences, full-time officials with particular responsibilities to promote the interests of particular groups of members. As the analysis above has shown, women are an especially important section of public service union membership. Given the operation of the labour movement and, in part, the government rules covering migrant workers, there are also large concentrations of black and other ethnic minority employees in the public services, especially in the National Health Service. At branch level, newsletters have been issued in a number of languages and, nationally, anti-racist education and campaign packs have been prepared.

Part of the responsibility for developing these campaigns and educational materials has fallen on the education and research departments of public service unions. Since the 1970s, with increased membership militancy, the growth of stewards' organisation and the waves of government policy detrimental to the interests of public service workers, these head office departments have played an increasingly important role in informing, educating and campaigning for membership mobilisation. Thus, for example, the high quality research publications in response to restriction upon public expenditure played an important part in building up the public service unions' campaign against the cuts in the 1970s (Fryer et al., 1978). Again, the union research departments have developed an impressive intelligence and report-writing expertise in preparing submissions to public enquiries, pay committees and in response to government policy.

Similarly, in recent times, the unions' research departments have also given much thought and imagination to their publicity about the effects of privatisation, not only upon their own members, but on the quality of public services and the risks posed to the continuation. This last aspect of the unions' work has led one union, NUPE, to initiate a pilot scheme of community education, in which the interests and points of view of workers and consumers can be brought together locally to explore areas of agreement and debate. This is plainly a key area in which the public service unions have much work to do, for public opposition to their actions and to the quality of the services their members are engaged in providing can easily lead to political support for demands to 'roll back the state' or 'reduce the bureaucracy and over-protection of workers' said to be inherent in much public sector employment and social provision.

Here, as elsewhere in the consideration of public service union organisation, the need for a close relationship between union organisation and union policy is self-evident. Public service unions, by virtue of their location between the twin forces of the public policy of the state on the one hand and public consumption and reaction on the other, cannot behave simply as pure collective bargaining and representational organisations alone. Their structures and their policies must also be oriented towards these two other social forces. In that sense, if no other, they are forced into an inherently political arena, fraught with difficulties but also rich with possibility. That, of itself, does not automatically lend their actions a political character (as some commentators have assumed) but they do thereby acquire potential political implications. In such circumstances it is easy to understand the decisions of the IRSF and CPSA to hold political fund ballots under the provisions of the 1984 Trade Union Act where they had no such funds previously and where neither union is currently affiliated to the Labour Party. In the event, both organisations secured convincing votes in favour of establishing such funds, in common with every other union that has held such ballots over the past two years (Coates and Topham, 1986; Steele et al., 1986). Ironically, possibly precisely because those unions are not affiliated to the Labour Party, the uses to which their newly established political funds will be chiefly addressed will be political in a more catholic and innovative manner than if a large slice of them were accounted for in affiliation fees. It remains to be seen.

Women and part-time workers

Public service trade unions face specific problems and opportunities regarding membership involvement because of the large percentage of their membership that is female. The main unions under consideration in the public services include in their membership and potential membership, a very large number of women workers, both manual and non-manual. In local government and the National Health Service especially, a large proportion of these women are emloyed on a part-time basis, and just as the 1970s and early 1980s saw a substantial growth in the use of part-time female labour in the economy as a whole, so too their already substantial use in these

areas of public services also grew (Dex and Perry,
1984; Beechey, 1985). Thus, by early 1986, there
were in local authority education employment alone
181,824 part-time teachers and lecturers and 511,338
part-time ancillary staff. The vast majority of the
latter are female as are the majority of the former.
In education ancillary work alone - school and
college meals, cleaning, clerical work, portering,
driving and caretaking - the ratio of part-timers to
full-timers in 1986 was 2.55:1. Similarly, in
social services (the other local authority area of
predominantly female labour), part-timers totalled
215,373 as against 170,842 for full-timers, a ratio
of 1.26:1. Again, the great majority of part-time
workers in social services are women, engaged in
domestic work, home help work, and residential care.
Rather absurdly, the mistakenly named local
authority Manpower Watch statistics, published
regularly in the DE Gazette, do not break down the
departmental staffs according to gender, but some
common sense idea of the situation can be gleaned
from the fact that in local authority construction
there were only 660 part-timers in 1986 as against
129,885 full-time workers. Much the same position
prevails in refuse collection and disposal where
full-time male workers predominate: in England and
Wales (Scotland has a different classification
system) there were only 237 part-timers in 1986.
    Just how significant the public services are
for women's full-time and part-time employment is
demonstrated by the fact that out of 9.337 million
women workers all told in March 1986, 7.55 million
worked in service employment generally. Five and a
quarter million or 69.8 per cent of all women
service workers were employed in the public
services, that is in public administration and
defence, sanitary services, education, medical and
health services and social welfare. For part-time
female workers, the public services were slightly
less important as major employers: in 1986 out of
4.434 millions in total, 3.983 millions worked in
all services and, of those, 1.91 million or 48 per
cent in the public services (Department of
Employment, 1986).
    For sheer reasons of numbers alone, then, the
public services constitute a major arena for trade
union organisation and recruitment amongst women and
part-time paid workers. Gradually over the past 15
years, the trade unions in the public services have
given attention to both the opportunities and the
challenges thus presented to them.

Women in public service unions

Of all the public service unions listed in Table 2.4 NUPE claimed in 1986 the largest number of female members, at just short of 450,000. Indeed, NUPE has more women members than any other British trade union. In 1970 NUPE's female membership constituted 59.2 per cent and by 1980 this had already grown to 66.7 per cent and its peak total of 466,100. By comparison with the growth of male membership in NUPE of 53.4 per cent between 1970 and 1980, female membership in the union had increased by 100 per cent. Even when cuts and privatisation began to reduce jobs and trade unionism in the 1980s, female membership in NUPE fell by only the same 5.1 per cent as males (23,580 as against 11,800).

Substantial female membership is also found in NALGO (391,000), COHSE (167,080), the CPSA (103,140) and the NUT (148,260). Whilst the highest proportion of women members (at 99.4 per cent) was to be found in the relatively small HVA, the lowest proportion, of less than one per cent, was found in another small union, the FBU. In the majority of cases, the proportion of female members in public service unions increased throughout the 1970s and into the 1980s. Exceptions are to be found amongst the CSU (with a drop from 40.8 per cent to 36.4 per cent females from 1980 to 1985) and in the NUT from 73.7 per cent to 71.4 per cent from 1970 to 1985. The sharp growth in the NCU's female membership from 1980 to 1985 was a direct consequence of the transfer of membership from the CPSA in tele-communications.

In examining the figures of female employment and trade union membership in the public services, several other features of women's positions at work also require consideration as well as their situation in wider social relations. First, in addition to predominating amongst part-time workers, women are also enormously over-represented at the bottom of hierarchies of seniority, authority, pay and other conditions of employment. This is as true of women engaged in routine clerical work in local authorities and the Civil Service as it is of manual workers. Secondly, even where women usually have access to professional training and employment in nursing and teaching, men are still over-represented in senior, managerial and supervisory positions. In this regard, all women in public services, including professionals in the health services and education, are likely to work under the control of male managerial employees. Thus, for example, whereas

Table 2.4 Growth of Female Membership of Selected TUC-Affiliated Public Service Unions, 1970-85 (000s)

	Union	1970	(%)	1975	(%)	1980	(%)	1985	(%)
Public services generally	NALGO	167.80	(38.1)	267.22	(42.7)	394.54	(50.4)	N.A.	
	NUPE	220.77	(59.2)	382.64	(65.5)	466.10	(66.7)	442.52	(66.7)
NHS	COHSE	34.07	(38.1)	124.17	(74.3)	168.12	(77.7)	167.08	(78.5)
	HVA	5.43	(100)	8.59	(99.9)	13.60	(99.6)	15.86	(99.4)
Civil Service	CPSA	121.63	(65.8)	153.87	(68.5)	156.46	(72.3)	103.14	(70.4)
	SCPS			16.65	(16.7)	N.A.		N.A.	
	IPCS			7.42	(7.17)	7.40	(7.49)	8.13	(9.1)
	IRSF	28.00	(56.3)	33.72	(55.7)	38.88	(62.4)	33.90	(61.5)
	CSU	9.57	(27.2)	17.68	(37.8)	18.59	(40.8)	11.37	(36.4)
	FDA					N.A.		0.76	(9.9)
Education	NUT	228.86	(73.70)	211.89	(75.18)	166.90	(71.82)	148.26	(71.4)
	NAS/UWT	6.25	(10.98)	16.76	(20.26)	N.A.		N.A.	
	NATFHE	3.83	(12.88)	12.50	(20.92)	15.69	(23.12)	22.78	(29.4)
Other local government	GLCSA	4.70	(33.33)	7.42	(37.53)	6.74	(39.51)	6.69	(42.7)
Posts and tele-communications	NCU	1.86	(1.60)	3.55	(2.85)	3.90	(2.98)	32.14	(19.9)
	UCW	52.37	(25.00)	41.19	(22.27)	N.A.		48.56	(25.0)

Source: TUC Reports, 1971, 1976, 1981 and 1986

women constituted only 2.6 per cent of permanent secretaries in the Home Civil Service in 1985 and 10 per cent of principals, they made up 68 per cent of clerical officers and 74.9 per cent of clerical assistants (EOC, 1986). One especially notable aspect of women's work is the extent they are expected, both formally and informally, to provide supportive action to men at work. This ranges from reminding them of, and helping them with, family birthdays through managing their diaries to clearing up after their mess. Small wonder that much women's paid work is characterised by them as an apparent extension of the content, form and social relationships involved in domestic unpaid labour (Dex, 1985).

Thirdly, and again this obtains even in professional occupations, female pay characteristically lags seriously behind that of their male colleagues. Information collected by the New Earnings Survey for 1986 demonstrates that overall women's average hourly earnings, excluding the effects of overtime, amounted to 73.9 per cent of men's. Amongst registered and enrolled nurses the proportion was higher at 89.6 per cent of men's hourly earnings; amongst general clerks it was 82 per cent of men's hourly earnings; and amongst automatic data processing operators 70.3 per cent of men's hourly earnings.

Fourthly, because of the extensive sexual segregation of labour in the public services as elsewhere and the at least partial construction of skill on the basis of gender, even job-evaluated payment systems still locate the majority of women towards the bottom end of the points system. Thus, for example, the recently concluded extensive job evaluation exercise amongst local authority manual workers has produced the following initial results. (The main gender basis of each occupational group is noted in brackets).

The five top-rated job occupations are school caretaker (mostly male), higher grade (690 points); home help (mostly female) (630); school caretaker (mostly male) (612); cook (mostly female) (606); and social services driver (male and female) (600). At the bottom come domestic assistant (mostly female) (158 points); school cleaner (mostly female) (176 points); gardener (male and female) (176 points); road sweeper (mostly male) (198

points);   and   office   cleaner   (mostly   female)
(200 points).   (<u>Guardian</u>, 1987)

Fifthly,   because   of   employment   interruptions
associated   still   with   marriage,   childbearing   and
raising,   husbands'   job   change   and   earlier
retirement,   women   accumulate   less   pension   rights,
holiday entitlement and sick leave arrangements than
men.   Each of these is related closely to length of
time in the job or employment in question.   Sixthly,
women suffer from some disadvantages and detriments
at   work   not   suffered   by   men   or   only   to   a   limited
extent,   such   as   sexual   harassment,   other   sexual
discrimination   and   the   non-recognition   of
occupationally related ill health (EOC, 1986).
Although this is by no means an exhaustive list
of   additional   problems   faced   by   women   workers   and
trade   unionists,   and   although   they   are   not   limited
to women in the public services, the point is simply
to underline the striking extent of the problems and
the large numbers of women and proportion of female
trade   unionists   in   the   public   services   who,   to   a
greater   or   lesser   extent,   face   these   issues   and
might reasonably expect their trade unions to be
doing something about them.   Indeed, if a lead is to
be given at all, it ought to be so in the public
service unions.   A number of unions in the public
services   have   attempted   to   tackle   some   of   those
matters: firstly,   by   promoting   women's   union
activity   and   the   improvement   of   their   working
conditions   through   collective   bargaining.   NUPE
reacted to reports in the 1970s (Fryer et al., 1974,
1975,   1978),   critical   of   the   lack   of   women's
participation in unions' affairs by the appointment
of more women full-time officials and shop stewards.
By 1984 the union had 42 per cent female shop
stewards   (NUPE,   1984),   even   so   the   NUPE   working
party   reported   continued   under-representation   of
women at all levels in the union and underlined the
pressing   urgency   of   giving   greater   attention   to
collective   bargaining   and   social   issues   of
particular importance to women.
NALGO was amongst the first unions in Britain
to raise the whole issue of sexual harassment of
women   members   at   work   (NALGO,   1981;   Hadjfotiou,
1983).   Thereafter   other   unions   in   the   public
services   drew   attention   to   what   the   TUC's   own
guidelines called 'repeated and unwanted verbal or
sexual   advances,   sexually   explicit   statements   or
sexually   discriminating   remarks'   (TUC,   1983).

Table 2.5 Female Representation in Selected Public Service Unions (%) 1976-85

	MEMBERSHIP 1976	MEMBERSHIP 1985	FULL-TIME (PAID) OFFICIALS 1976	FULL-TIME (PAID) OFFICIALS 1985	EXECUTIVE COUNCILLORS 1976	EXECUTIVE COUNCILLORS 1985	TUC DELEGATES 1976	TUC DELEGATES 1985
COHSE	70	80	12.5	12	3.6	14	0	21
CPSA	68	70	14.3	21	30.8	41	26.7	50
NALGO	43	52	8.9	13	7.6	32	12.5	29
NUPE	65	67	1.7	7	23.1	42	12.1	34
NUT	75	72	7.7	10	14.6	16	3.6	19

Sources: TUC Reports, 1976, 1977 and 1986
TUC Statistical Statements, 1976 and 1985
Ellis, 1981
Labour Research Department, 1986

R. H. Fryer

Public service unions are also becoming more aware
of the equal pay for work of equal value laws and
using them as a bargaining tool in both local
government and the NHS.

Militancy and industrial action

Another prominent feature of public service and
indeed wider public sector unionism over the past 15
to 20 years has been the increase in union militancy
and the incidence of industrial disputes.
Throughout the 1950s and most of the 1960s, when
unofficial strikes and other union action was
catching political and analytical attention in the
mines, dock work, shipbuilding, engineering and
vehicle manufacture, industrial disputes were rare
in the public services other than railways. Even
where disputes occurred, they usually fell short of
stoppages of work and certainly of official strike
action. Some public service unions had rules
forbidding the use of the strike weapon and even
after NALGO had affiliated to the TUC in 1964, most
Civil Service and teachers' unions and their members
remained unaffiliated until later in that decade and
into the 1970s.
    Initially, the chief link between militancy,
TUC membership, the revoking of no-strike union
rules and the advent of strike action was a
succession of government incomes policies which had
especially restrictive effects upon workers in the
public services. In several cases it was a desire
to influence both TUC and government policy on
economic strategy and incomes policy which brought
erstwhile unaffiliated unions into the TUC. Thus
after NALGO followed ATTI (later NATFHE) and the NAS
(later NAS/UWT) in 1967 and the NUT in 1970, the
SCPS in 1976 and the AUT in 1974. Although the
Conservative government's 'pay pause' of 1960/61
affected the public sector, the most notable impact
came first with the incomes policies of the 1964-66
and 1966-70 Labour governments and then with the
Heath Conservative government's 'N Minus One'
formula in the early 1970s followed by its three-
phase pay policy. Thereafter, there ensued the
period of the Social Contract under the 1974-79
Labour government, which eventually broke down in
the so-called 'Winter of Discontent' in 1978/79
after Denis Healey, then Chancellor of the
Exchequer, had first failed to obtain TUC agreement
to a five per cent pay norm and then was proved
unable to impose it. Over the whole of this period,
and especially from 1969 onwards, public service

union responses to incomes policies and their particular application to different groups of workers were largely responsible for the increases in working days lost through stoppages which are recorded in Table 2.6.

Table 2.6 **Average Working Days Lost per 1000 Employees 1967-1985**

Column 1 = All industries and services
Column 2 = Public Administration and Defence 1967-82; Public Administration, Sanitary and Education 1984-85
Column 3 = Professional and Scientific Services 1967-82; Medical and Health 1983-85

YEAR	COLUMN 1	COLUMN 2	COLUMN 3
1967	125	2.5	2.5
1968	200	30.0	2.5
1969	300	125.0	45.0
1970	475	750.0	125.0
1971	600	5.0	15.0
1972	1,100	20.0	35.0
1973	325	125.0	100.0
1974	650	125.0	70.0
1975	275	80.0	10.0
1976	146	39.0	7.0
1977	448	702.0	13.0
1978	414	316.0	6.0
1979	1,291	1,447.0	381.0
1980	531	49.0	48.0
1981	201	682.0	24.0
1982	252	188.0	242.0
1983	180	32.0	4.0
1984	1,277	214.0	17.0
1985	298	265.0	24.0

Source: Department of Employment Gazette

47

From 1969 onwards virtually every section of public service and public sector employment was affected in one way or another by disputes, the majority of them national, officially orchestrated and organised strikes. After local authority refuse workers had taken unofficial strike action in London and Liverpool in 1969, this was followed by the first official national local authority manual workers' strike in 1970 (the 'Dirty Jobs' Dispute). After that came a succession of disputes; first, the bitter and prolonged postal workers' strike in 1971; the first national miners' strike since 1926 in 1972; the first-ever hospital ancillary workers' strikes in 1972 and 1973; the gas workers also in 1973 as well as the first-ever national stoppage in the Civil Service; teachers were on strike in 1973 and 1974 as well as workers in electricity supply in 1972. Miners and nurses and ambulance drivers went on strike in 1974, as well as hospital engineers and these disputes were followed by local authority craftsmen in 1975 and a range of local authority and health authority workers in a relatively quieter 1976. In 1977 there was the huge and very bitter dispute in the fire service and protest strikes in the Civil Service at the suspension of the operation of the Pay Research Unit. Social workers were on strike in 1978 whilst 1978-79 culminated in the Winter of Discontent with workers in local authority, water, the Health Service and, later, civil servants all engaged in strike action (Clegg, 1982; Winchester, 1983).

Overall, the tale of the 1970s is well, if rather crudely, told by Table 2.6 but that gives only the picture of recorded stoppages of work and does not convey the many varied features of the different strikes, near-strikes and other disputes in the various public services over the period. Thus, although incomes policies were a key element in the precipitation of several of the major confrontations, from 1976 onwards especially, restriction upon public expenditure, cash limits, cuts and then privatisation also became increasingly important areas of conflict (Fryer, 1983; Hall, 1983). When the Conservative government of Mrs. Thatcher took power in 1979, although it declared itself officially against formal incomes policy, its tough stance on public expenditure and cash limits, linked with an ill-disguised hostility to the public sector generally, soon brought it into conflict with civil servants in 1981, with workers in the National Health Service in 1982, water workers in 1983 and, most cataclysmically, with the miners in 1984-85 (Beynon, 1985; Goodman, 1985). Teachers and civil servants also came into conflict with government policy again in 1986 and 1987 and, for the teachers in particular, the problem turned on government decisions to dismantle the established machinery of collective bargaining.

Key aspects of public service conflict

Although sufficient justice cannot be done here to the shifts and nuances in successive policies and the range of problems confronting different groups of public service workers and their unions over the period since 1969, several salient aspects of these disputes deserve brief comment. First, it should be noted that, for many groups of workers and their trade unions, these strikes and other disputes represented either their first experience of widespread official industrial action or at least the first experience of such action for a very long time. Secondly, and not surprisingly given the earlier discussion on occupational and membership composition, the strikes drew large numbers of women into industrial action, also often for the first time. Thirdly, for the most part, the strikes were both official and national and so marked a break with the unofficial and fragmented local disputes that had attracted so much political and scholarly attention in the 1960s. Fourthly, the strikes included some of the most bitter confrontations of the period, especially the defeat of the postal workers in 1971 (Foot, n.d.), the fire brigades strike of 1977 when troops were deployed to provide emergency cover, the grave diggers during the Winter of Discontent and the successive defeats of steel workers, civil servants, hospital workers and miners under Mrs. Thatcher's governments.

Fifthly, the strikes often produced innovative organisational elements, including not only the 'flying pickets' in the miners' strikes, but rolling or selective action in Health, local government and the Civil Service, occupations and demonstrations, the withdrawal of emergency services, union communications and information arrangements of military-like precision (especially in the Civil Service) and the extension of disputes into main areas of public policy such as private medicine and pay beds, hospital closures, public expenditure, public ownership, fuel and social policy. Sixthly, especially where direct services to patients, pupils, clients and claimants were concerned, the

most immediate effects of the strikes were felt not
so much by employers or the state as by the general
public, including of course not only other trade
unionists and their families but also some of the
most vulnerable sections of the community. On the
unions' side it did not always prove possible (or
even desirable) to maintain essential or emergency
services and in political circles (not exclusively
Conservative) proposals were voiced for a legal
restriction upon strikes in 'essential services',
possibly in exchange for an agreed formula or
procedure on matters of pay.
        Seventhly, it was precisely around the question
of pay that so many of the difficulties turned.
Throughout the public services pay, and especially
low pay, was inextricably bound up with problems of
comparability with the private sector. For civil
servants a system had been devised following the
Priestly Commission of 1955 (Elliot and Fallick,
1981) for comparability studies to be placed on a
formal footing through the operation of the Pay
Research Unit. It was government interference in,
and even suspension of, the PRU which provoked
disputes in the Civil Service. But the question of
comparability was no less significant for other
groups of public service workers and their unions
where no such official machinery existed (Clegg,
1982). Hence, the issue preoccupied much of the
time and energy of public bodies charged with
overseeing successive periods of incomes policy
including the National Board for Prices and Incomes
(Liddle and McCarthy, 1972), the Pay
('Relativities') Board, the Clegg Comparability
Commission and, in between, a whole host of special
inquiries into the pay of miners in 1972, teachers
and nurses in 1974, firemen in 1978 and culminating
with civil servants in 1982. Liddle and McCarthy
(1972) estimated that the NBPI scrutinised pay
determination procedures and staffing arrangements
in areas covering 48 per cent of public sector
employment as against only 20 per cent of private
industry.
        An eighth feature of these public service and
public sector disputes was closely related to the
question of pay and comparability and that was the
vexed problem of productivity and efficiency in the
public services. Early on in its life the NBPI drew
attention to the link between low pay and poor
productivity in local government, gas, health
services and water (NBPI, 1967). One solution was
to seek to establish work studied incentive schemes

(often at a time when employers in manufacturing industry were attempting to move away from them towards measured day work, as had been accomplished in the mines with the installation of the National Power Loading Agreement in 1966). In industries and unions (not to mention employers) long dominated by different national agreements and national bargaining (in many cases since the initiation of Whitleyism after the First World War), the introduction of locally based incentive schemes presented a challenge to organisation and expertise alike. Despite the fact that such schemes were much slower getting off the ground than the NBPI had hoped, and perhaps partly because they were also fiercely resisted in some quarters (as for example in some hospitals), the advent of local bargaining and local policing of schemes contributed toward the development of local organisation in public service unionism, notably the development of shop stewards systems, and the sophistication of public service management, especially in industrial relations and personnel (Fowler, 1975; Carpenter, 1977; Barnard and Harrison, 1986). Not that the extent of such schemes or their influence over earnings should be exaggerated. As data from the New Earnings Survey makes clear, some groups of workers (such as nurses) have never had them applied, men's pay is affected by them more than that of women and basic pay continues to be of prime importance in determining take home pay even for those receiving bonus payments in the public services (Department of Employment, 1986, 1987).

Ninth, and by no means least important, the upsurge in public service union militancy in the 1970s not only changed the internal character of several unions, it also sharply revised their public profile. Within less than 10 years, public services unionism had moved to centre stage in British industrial relations and this was reflected both in the extensive (and often lurid and highly critical) attention paid to public service unionists and their leaders in the press and broadcasting media and, to some extent, in the decision of the TUC to establish in 1980-81 a Public Services Committee in addition to its already operating industry committees for local government and for the health services. The very breadth of trade union representation on that Committee demonstrated the wide-ranging interest of TUC affiliates in the fortunes of the public services. Whilst including the conventionally assumed public service unions already discussed, it

51

also embraces the two big general unions, electrical and engineering crafts, printers and builders. One matter the committee has preoccupied itself with has been the need to co-ordinate initiatives and responses from public service unions on such matters as pay, public expenditure, privatisation, pensions, redundancy and public or social ownership. The TUC Congress in 1981 required the committee to create a framework within which public service unions could unite on a common strategy and also called on the TUC 'to provide the organisational back-up to enable collective action to be mounted more effectively' (TUC, 1982: 280). But even such questions as a single pay settlement date for public services had proved contentious, for a variety of technical, procedural, organisational and political reasons, including a fear of driving a division between public and private sector workers. More modestly, the Committee has worked for some harmonisation on what it calls 'common core elements' of claims and campaigns. Special reports on such issues have been produced, liaison has been established with other TUC Committees (such as local government, Health and nationalised industries) and bulletins and leaflets produced for widespread distribution amongst membership. Just how difficult the matter of co-ordination and common approach can be is revealed not simply by such recent experiences as the differences between unions in the teachers' dispute, but more importantly by the overriding consideration of individual union autonomy, policy-making and accountability. After all, such issues constantly require attention on trade union sides of joint committees from workplace and employer level right through to national Whitley and other bargaining machinery, let alone such innovative bodies as COCSU and the TUC Public Services Committee.

As industrial action and strikes of one kind or another have increased across the public services, so too has there been a decline in the use of arbitration by the unions concerned. This is far more simply a matter of a change in method: its repercussions extend right through the _forms_ of organisation and representation of the unions involved. Mobilisation for industrial action, whether sponsored by and led nationally (or from 'above') or whether generated by local rank and file pressure (or from 'below'), constitutes an entirely different setting for bargaining and potential settlement than does presentation of a case for arbitration. Even when arbitration has been sought in an attempt to resolve disputes, the greater willingness of public service trade unions to take industrial action in support of their demands has quite altered the climate of arbitration in recent years.

The period of militancy and strike action did not cease with the Winter of Discontent nor has it manifested itself only in large, set-piece, nationally led and official stoppages. True, since Mrs. Thatcher's government was first elected in 1979, within a general downturn in strike activity growing over the 1980s, both public service and wider public sector workers' disputes have been prominent and large-scale. But local disputes have also persisted, especially in response to problems of redundancy, work reorganisation, cuts and privatisation and disciplinary action. Between 1980 and 1983 public sector workers were involved in almost 50 per cent of all redundancy disputes, by comparison with 15 per cent between 1976 and 1979 (IDS, 1987). This is also revealed quite clearly in the most recent Workplace Industrial Relations Survey (Millward and Stevens, 1986), as is the sharp contrast with the private sector. Amongst manual workers in the private manufacturing sector, strike action fell from 21 per cent of establishments reporting it in 1980 to 10 per cent in 1984: in public services the decline was only one per cent from 10 to nine per cent of establishments. Amongst non-manual workers, strike action in private manufacturing fell from three to one per cent of establishments: in contrast, in public services it hugely increased from nine to 38 per cent of establishments (ibid: 266). Amongst white collar workers:

> . . . much of the increase in strike action in the Education and Public Administration sectors reported . . . is accounted for by strike action among the white-collar workforce. In Public Administration, a half of workplaces with white-collar workers reported white-collar strike action in 1984 compared with only 13 per cent in 1980, and within the Education sector the proportion reporting strikes increased from seven per cent in 1980 to 45 per cent in 1984. (ibid: 267)

If anything, especially amongst public service manual workers, these figures understate the extent of strike action affecting establishments, because

of the importance for them of workplaces involving
less than 25 employees which were excluded from the
survey.
A similar picture emerges when non-strike
industrial action is analysed, with the public
services accounting for the bulk of the overall
increase, including bans on overtime, working to
rule, refusing to cover for absent colleagues and,
in teaching, not taking part in lunchtime
supervision. Selective action also continued to be
used by public service unions in the 1980s to great
effect, as in the non-collection of revenue in the
1981 Civil Service dispute, and the withdrawal of
labour from key installations, such as computer
centres and supply departments. Within the unions
themselves, there were often quite heated debates as
to the advantages and disadvantages of selective as
against 'all-out' action, but walkouts and one-day
demonstrations of support continued, as in the
action taken over the government's ban on trade
unionism at GCHQ and in support of the miners'
strike.
It has been in this area of disputes and
militancy that public service workers have
particularly attempted to distance themselves from
state policy, especially where reductions in
expenditure or the levels and quality of service
have been in question. Thus, teachers and civil
servants alike, have sought to explain to or even
enlist public and client support for their actions,
claiming that the workers' own self-interest has
been closely interwoven with the needs and wishes of
the community. Given the remarkable level of public
support for public services as expressed in
extensive opinion-polling undertaken for the TUC, it
might reasonably have been expected that the unions
would have been more able to mobilise support for
their campaigns and action. The NOP survey reported
that almost three-quarters (71 per cent) of those
asked thought that 'essential services like
electricity, gas and water' should be public and the
same proportion felt the same way about defence
establishments like dockyards and ordnance
factories. A majority favoured keeping buses public
(55 per cent) and 49 per cent supported the Airports
Authority remaining in public hands as against
private ownership, preferred by 34 per cent.
British Telecom also was thought better as a public
service (by 53 per cent as against 37 per cent for
privatisation (TUC, 1986)). Yet, despite this
generalised level of support it has proved extremely

difficult to mobilise public action in defence of
public service jobs and services and, not
infrequently strikes and other industrial action
have been seen as being more damaging to clients and
their loved ones than to the government.

Privatisation

Amongst the most difficult and threatening aspects
of Conservative government policy for the public
service unions and their members over the past eight
years has been that range of initiatives generally
embraced under the umbrella title of
'privatisation'. Privatisation includes, in its
various forms, complete sale of formerly publicly
owned bodies such as British Telecom, Britoil and
British Gas, the partial sale of companies such as
Jaguar cars from the Austin Rover Group, and the
whole or partial contracting-out of services
previously provided on an 'in-house' basis, such as
hospital laundry or catering services or office
cleaning in the Civil Service or refuse collection
in local government. Increasingly in the public
services, this last form of privatisation has, more
accurately speaking, been one possible consequence
of competitive tendering from 'in-house' groups as
well as from external companies. The pace and
location of the introduction of one or other form of
privatisation has varied not only between different
parts of the public services but also within given
services, such as local government. Some
departments have been subjected to privatisation
whilst others have not; some local councils have
looked favourably upon privatisation, whilst others
have not. By no means have all Conservative-
controlled councils approved of privatisation
measures: not all Labour-controlled authorities
have been equally hostile to the process.

At a largely ideological level, the
Conservative government's endorsement of
privatisation represents a clear enough expression
of its determination both to 'roll back' the
influence of state and public provision and to
reduce what it has seen as undue trade union
influence and restrictiveness in economic and
political life. According to this view, discussed
in more detail in the introduction to this book,
competition and the forces of the market need to be
allowed to come to bear upon the provision of
services, freed from the artificial limitations of
political preference and trade union power.

More practically, as expressed by Conservative

R. H. Fryer

MP, Michael Forsyth, in a pamphlet for the influential right-wing Adam Smith Institute, it is argued that private contractors will erase 'a long slate of restrictive labour practices and working agreements which work against the public' (Forsyth, 1983). Introducing the competition of private contractors into what has been represented as a domain of public service union monopoly is supposed to combine improvements in the quality of service with savings in cost, reductions in management time and, especially, increases in managerial control and accountability. These arguments were developed in the government's approach to privatisation of certain ancillary services in the NHS in a series of circulars and advisory notes culminating in HC(83)18 issued in September 1983 entitled <u>Competitive Tendering in the Provision of Domestic Catering and Laundry Services</u> (DHSS, 1983). In this, health authorities were instructed to test the costs of their laundry, domestic and catering services by putting them out to competitive tender. Although the exercise was subsequently criticised somewhat by a Parliamentary committee for imposing extra burdens on management, causing discontent and disruption and failing so far to 'bring home the bacon', by March 1986 competitive tendering in the NHS was reckoned to be achieving savings in the region of £52 million per year from the 670 tendering exercises reported to the DHSS. Interestingly enough, over three-quarters (76 per cent) of all tenders awarded by 1986 went to in-house tenders which contributed together some 59 per cent of savings. (See Chapter 4 for further discussion of the impact of competitive tendering in the NHS).

In the Civil Service, contracting-out has been encouraged in all departments and most have been implemented in the Property Services Agency (PSA) and in the Ministry of Defence. According to an IDS report, in the six years from April 1979, the PSA halved its labour force from 50,142 to 24,296 with commensurate savings in costs (IDS, 1986). Where services have operated across departments, very high levels of contracting-out have also been achieved. According to the chief secretary to the Treasury in 1986, 84 per cent of cleaning, 81 per cent of maintenance and 73 per cent of laundry services had been contracted out. In addition, of course, the Royal Navy Dockyards and the Royal Ordnance Factories have also been included in the wider policy.

Although some of the liveliest publicity has

been given to privatisation or attempted privatisation in local government, so far less has occurred there than in the NHS or Civil Service. In part, of course, this reflects the mixed complexion of local authority political control and in part the degree of local government autonomy from central government directives. The government has already declared its intention to introduce legislation obliging local councils to implement policies of competitive tendering, but already some of the bitterest confrontations have been associated with the imposition of private contractors, especially in cleansing and refuse collection. This has brought public service unions, especially on the manual worker side, into conflict not only with local authorities seeking to introduce private contractors but with the public services arm of the large and often international companies which typically operate in this field (Hastings and Levie, 1983; Whitfield, 1983; LRD, 1983; SCAT, 1985).

Already the government has begun the process of requiring local authorities to seek competitive tenders under rules laid down by statute (for further discussion of this, see Chapter 5). Thus, the Planning and Land Act of 1980 and the Transport Act of 1985 have each opened up major areas of public provision to private enterprise. A study by the University of York in 1984 and 1985 reported that, out of 75 authorities surveyed, 32 had contracted out building maintenance, 22 cleaning services, and nine refuse and waste disposal. Seven have also contracted out pest control. Elsewhere architecture, transport services, security, gardening, painting, car parks and horticulture have also gone to competitive tender.

What does all this mean for the trade unions in the public services? The reasons for union opposition to and fear of the imposition of privatisation are relatively easy to list and to understand, but it has proved far more difficult to combat. In short, the unions are concerned that private contractors and competitive tendering threaten reductions in staffing levels and wages, tighter managerial control and pressure for increased productivity, abolition of certain conditions of employment established through collective bargaining and on the basis of good employment practice, reductions in training and apprenticeships, cuts in bonus levels and holiday entitlement, fewer full-time and permanent jobs, changed rotas and duties and overall increases in flexibility at work. In large part their fears have been borne out where privatisation or competitive tendering have been introduced.

The two chief campaign strategies adopted by the unions to attack the process have been, first, their insistence (often with some evidence) that privatisation would herald lower standards of provision and, second, that the schemes were being introduced at the expense of some of the lowest paid and exploited public service workers who, nonetheless, had demonstrated their genuine commitment to their jobs and to the service of the general public. This has meant that the unions concerned have been obliged to initiate campaigns of information and education not only amongst the general public and for key decision-makers, but also amongst their own members. At the heart of these campaigns have been the twin and linked claims that carpet-bagging private contractors care as little for the standards of public service as they do for the grossly exploited labour they will seek to employ.

Despite the validity often associated with these claims, unfortunately they have not proved robust or popular enough to mobilise public or even sustained membership opposition to determined efforts to introduce privatisation and competitive tendering. There have been some notable victories (Williams, 1984). However, outright union opposition and even vigorous initial campaigns, including strike action and public meetings, have frequently had to come to terms with apparent membership acquiescence (however reluctant); the debilitating effects of long struggles of attrition, further weakened by the issue of redundancy payments; and an eventual unavoidable need to sit down and negotiate the best terms either of employment with a private contractor or of the conditions governing competitive tendering (Benlow and Scott, 1983; Williams, 1984). Quite bluntly, the issue has often come down to the matter of how best to save as many jobs as possible. A 'privatisation audit' by Services to Community Action and trade unions in 1985 estimated job losses ranging from 15 to 49 per cent in particular local authority contracting-out exercises. The report points out that such a scale of job losses can have widespread effects upon a local economy, both directly and indirectly, as well as increasing pressure upon welfare, social security and other support services. Yet, as Benlow and Scott so clearly put it, competitive in-house tendering offers little hope of countering these threats: 'It is foolish and naive for any union to have faith in the tendering process as a method of saving jobs. The multinational contractors they would be competing against have no commitment to the service and are able to stand temporary losses'. (op. cit., 34)

In circumstances where local councils are likely soon to be required to initiate competitive tendering, it is widely recognised that the unions most affected still have a long way to go in mobilising effective support from their members and the general public alike. Just what this implies for public service unions can be deduced from studies of the impact of privatisation already undertaken. Thus, Wendy Leedham's brief report on the privatisation of NHS ancillary services (1986) demonstrates that trade unionists in the NHS were clear that the policy of privatisation is part of a wider government strategy radically to restructure the nature and delivery of health care in Britain. In this, they saw the target being as much the whole established apparatus of the welfare state as the unions in particular. Even so, they expected the collective organisation of workers to be damaged, especially nationally, where they anticipated changes in collective bargaining and national negotiating arrangements, including the structure of the Whitley Council system itself. Most striking of all, it was the view of those local unionists studied by Leedham that 'the policy could not be overturned nationally without a change of government' (Leedham, 1986: 15) Faced with the threats of private contractors, most local union officials recognised the appalling dilemma of either seeking to resist the whole process (and probably failing) or of joining in the tendering process and having to make some concessions in order to minimise the damage to members' employment prospects. Even following this second strategy proved risky and complex, given the differences between unions, the hesitation expressed by professionals and those who sought to place patient care above all else and the extensive difficulties associated with orchestrating campaigns involving trades councils, politicians and the general public.

Not surprisingly in these circumstances, the whole question of privatisation is one which has preoccupied the TUC Public Services Committee as

R. H. Fryer

well as individual unions. Proposals are in hand
for a TUC conference on contracting-out, although
this was delayed by the general election. One of
the problems facing unions has been maintaining the
momentum of the campaign and the TUC committee has
expressed fears that, ironically, the Conservative
government's decision to delay the major
privatisation of local government until after the
election had led to some loss of motivation amongst
trade union members. Even so, individual and joint
unions' plans for campaign and anti-privatisation
publicity have continued. Thus, NUPE has detailed
plans for the expansion of its publication of
campaign and briefing materials, for joint education
workshops with NALGO, for further co-operation with
the Local Government Information Unit (to whom it
seconded a full-time officer for 12 months) with the
Association of Metropolitan Authorities and with the
Labour Party. The Labour Party itself has also
published an action-advice note from the Executive
entitled Measuring Up on improving the quality and
accountability of local services. In addition to
the information and publicity provided by the LGIU
and individual unions, the Joint Privatisation
Research Unit and the Labour Research Department
have continued to publish information about and
critiques of privatisation. Most recently the Joint
Unit has pointed to the alleged failure of one in
five private contracts in the NHS, despite the
general satisfaction expressed by the National Audit
Office in its own review of the same process (Joint
Privatisation Research Unit, 1987; Labour Research
Department, 1987; National Audit Office, 1987).

SOME CONCLUSIONS

As has been shown, the years leading up to Mrs.
Thatcher's first election victory in 1979 had
witnessed an enormous growth in public service
unionism, especially in the National Health Service
and local government. Unions which, in the 1950s
and 1960s, had scarcely been heard of beyond their
own immediate circle of members and employers, such
as NUPE, NALGO and COHSE, rapidly became household
names, more particularly as membership militancy and
disputes about pay and, later, collective bargaining
arrangements, figured in newspaper and television
reports. For many people, the most significant, or
at least most notorious, example of this sharply
increased militancy was the so-called 'Winter of

60

Discontent' immediately preceding the 1979 general election campaign, which still provided the Conservative Party in 1987 with a stick with which to beat all unions and especially those in the public services.

Just as in 1979 and 1983, the 1987 general election followed in the wake of major national public service disputes. On this occasion the disputes continued through and beyond the general election and concerned civil servants again and workers in the National Health Service. There can be little doubt that these disputes have proved something of an irritant to Conservative government ministers and, gradually since 1979, a range of policies has been advocated and, in part, introduced which are designed to reduce the significance and power of public service unionism. In some quarters, particularly those concerned with defence matters, trade unionism has been held to be incompatible with national security. Despite a dogged rearguard action by a handful of union stalwarts at GCHQ in Cheltenham, the Civil Service unions have so far been unable to reverse the government policy of banning trade union membership there (Council of Civil Service Unions, n.d.).

Elsewhere, the idea has more than once been floated of 'no strike' arrangements for the public services, particularly in the emergency or essential services. This notion has reappeared in 1987 as the long-running teachers' dispute has continued in respect of pay and collective bargaining arrangements. Changes in union recognition procedures and reductions in union facilities and collective bargaining have also been mooted in connection with government-initiated moves to privatise key areas of public service employment.

Despite undoubted setbacks during the years 1979 to 1987, both in terms of their fortunes and their expansion, the public service unions have fared better than their fellow unions in extractive and private and public manufacturing sectors. There must be every possibility, however, that the third successive general election victory for the Conservative Party in June 1987 will come to mark something of a watershed in the position of public service unions in Britain. The third term of Thatcher government will place the public services and public service trade unions at the centre of an ideological battleground. Municipal socialism and public service trade unionism, in particular those unions located in education and local government,

R. H. Fryer

will be seen as the two major obstacles to the
smooth implementation of radical Conservative
policies. Trade unionism in the public services
will be tested for its robustness and most
importantly its ability to mobilise public support.
As already noted, the trade unions in the public
services have not been successful in winning public
support in defence of public service jobs and
services. This support must be won if the unions in
the public services are to pass their most severe
test yet.

REFERENCES

Bain, G. S. and Price, R. (1980) Profiles of Union
    Growth, Blackwell, Oxford
Bain, G. S. and Price, R. (1983) 'Union Growth:
    Determinants and Destiny', in Bain, G. S. (ed.)
    Industrial Relations in Britain, Blackwell,
    Oxford
Barnard, K. and Harrison, S. (1986) 'Labour
    Relations in Health Services Management',
    Social Science in Medicine, 22(11), pp. 1213-28
Beechey, V. (1985) 'The Shape of the Workforce to
    Come', Marxism Today, August 1985, pp. 11-6
Benlow, D. and Scott, I. (1983) Fighting
    Privatisation: The Struggle for Wandsworth,
    NUPE/IWC, Nottingham
Beynon, H. (ed.) (1985) Digging Deeper: Issues in
    the Miners' Strike, Verso, London
Carpenter, M. (1977) 'The New Managerialism', in
    Stacey, M. (ed.) Health and the Division of
    Labour, Croom Helm, London
Carpenter, M. (1980) All For One: Campaigns and
    Pioneers in the Making of COHSE, COHSE, London
Carpenter, M. (1985a) They Still Go Marching On:
    A Celebration of COHSE's First 75 Years, COHSE,
    London
Carpenter, M. (1985b) Working for Health, COHSE,
    London
Clegg, H. A. (1979) The Changing System of
    Industrial Relations in Britain, Blackwell,
    Oxford
Clegg, H. A. (1982) 'How Public Pay Systems Have
    Gone Wrong Before', in Gretton, J. and
    Harrison, A. How Much Are Public Servants
    Worth?, Blackwell, Oxford

Coates, K. and Topham, A. J. (1986) Trade Unions and Politics, Blackwell, Oxford

Council of Civil Service Unions (n.d.) GCHQ: The Story of the Ban, COCSU, London

CPSA/IFF (1986) Membership Survey Report, IFF, London

CSO (1981, 1986) Social Trends, HMSO, London

CSU/SCPS (1985) GCHQ: The Campaign So Far, CSU/SCPS, London

Department of Employment (1986) 'The Labour Force in 1985', Employment Gazette, August

Department of Employment (1986, 1987) New Earnings Survey, HMSO, London

Dex, S. (1985) The Sexual Division of Work, Wheatsheaf, Brighton

Dex, S. and Perry, S. (1984) 'Women's Employment Changes in the 1970s', Employment Gazette, 92, pp. 151-64

DHSS (1983) Competitive Tendering in the Provision of Domestic, Catering and Laundry Services, DHSS, London

Drake, P., Fairbrother, P., Fryer, R. H. and Stratford, G. (1982a) Women in the SCPS, Warwick University, Coventry

Drake, P., Fairbrother, P., Fryer, R. H. and Stratford, G. (1982b) A Programme for Union Democracy, Warwick University, Coventry

Elliot, R. F. and Fallick, J. L. (1981) Pay in the Public Sector, Macmillan, London

Ellis, V. (1981) The Role of Trade Unions in the Promotion of Equal Opportunities, EOC/SSRC, London

Equal Opportunities Commission (1986) Women and Men in Britain: A Statistical Profile, HMSO, London

Fairbrother, P. (1982) 'Working for the State', Studies for Trade Unionists, 8, WEA, London

Foot, P. (n.d.) The Postal Workers and the Tory Offensive, S. W. Litho, London

Forsyth, M. (1983) The Myths of Privatisation, Adam Smith Institute, London

Fowler, A. (1975) Personnel Management in Local Government, IPM, London

Fryer, R. H. (1979) 'Trade Unions and the Cuts', Capital and Class, PAT, London

Fryer, R. H. (1983) An Epidemic of Industrial Troubles, Northern College, Barnsley

Fryer, R. H., Fairclough, A. and Manson, T. (1974)

R. H. Fryer

    Organisation and Change in the National Union
    of Public Employees, NUPE, London
Fryer, R. H., Fairclough, A. and Manson, T. (1975)
    Statistical Appendices, (three volumes),
    University of Warwick, Coventry
Fryer, R. H., Fairclough, A. and Manson, T. (1978)
    'Facilities for Female Shop Stewards', British
    Journal of Industrial Relations, 16(2), pp.
    160-74
Goodman, G. (1985) The Miners' Strike, Pluto,
    London
Hadjfotiou, N. (1983) Women and Harassment at
    Work, Pluto, London
Hall, D. (1983) The Cuts Machine, Pluto, London
Hastings, S. and Levie, H. (eds.) (1983)
    Privatisation?, Spokesman, Nottingham
Hayes, M., Joyce, P. and Williams, J. (1986) A
    Survey of NUPE Branches in Local Government in
    1982, PNL, London
Hobsbawm, E. (1984) 'The 1970s: Syndicalism
    Without the Syndicalists', in Hobsbawm, Worlds
    of Labour, Weidenfeld & Nicolson, London
Humphrey, P., Cund, M. and Hardinge, N. (1977)
    Structure Review of the Inland Revenue Staff
    Federation, (two volumes), IRSF/CSD, London
Humphrey, P., Cund, M. and Hardinge, N. (1977b)
    Which Way Now? A Review of Democracy and
    Participation in the IRSF, IRSF, London
Incomes Data Services (1986) Competitive Tendering
    in the Public Sector, IDS/IPM, London
Incomes Data Services (1987) Public Sector Trade
    Unions, IDS, London
Inland Revenue Staff Federation (1977) Report of
    the IRSF Structure Sub-committee, IRSF, London
IRSF/EPIC (1987) Best Practice and Realistic
    Expectations: The Role of Women in the IRSF,
    EPIC, London
Joint Privatisation Research Unit (1987)
    Contractors Failures, NUPE, London
Kessler, I. (1986) 'Shop Stewards in Local
    Government Revisited', British Journal of
    Industrial Relations, XXIV(3)
Kessler, I. and Winchester, D. (1982) 'Pay
    Negotiations in Local Government', Local
    Government Studies, 8(6), pp.19-31
Labour Research Department (1982) Public or
    Private? The Case Against Privatisation, LRD,
    London

Labour Research Department (1983) <u>Privatisation:</u>
    <u>Who Loses, Who Profits</u>, LRD, London
Labour Research Department (1985) <u>Privatisation:</u>
    <u>The Great Sell-Out</u>, LRD, London
Labour Research Department (1986) 'Women in
    Unions: a Long Way to Go', <u>Labour Research</u>, 75
    (4)
Labour Research Department (1987) 'Tell Sid the
    Tories have all the Shares', <u>Labour Research</u>,
    76 (6)
Lane, A. (1974) <u>The Union Makes Us Strong</u>, Arrow,
    London
Lane, A. (1982) 'The Unions: Caught on the Ebb
    Tide', <u>Marxism Today</u>, September
Leedham, W. (1986) 'The Privatisation of NHS
    Ancillary Services', <u>Studies for Trade</u>
    <u>Unionists</u>, 12, WEA, London
Liddle, R. and McCarthy, W. E. J. (1972) 'The
    Impact of the Prices and Incomes Board on the
    Role of Collective Bargaining', <u>British Journal</u>
    <u>of Industrial Relations</u>, 10(3)
Marchington, M. and Armstrong, R. (1982) 'A
    Comparison Between Steward Activity in Local
    Government and the Private Sector', <u>Local</u>
    <u>Government Studies</u>, 8(6)
Millward, N. and Stevens, M. (1986) <u>British</u>
    <u>Workplace Industrial Relations 1980-84</u>, Gower
    with DE/ESRC/PSI/ACAS, London
NALGO (1974) <u>Working Party on Organisation</u>, NALGO,
    London
NALGO (1975) <u>Equal Rights Working Party Report</u>,
    NALGO, London
NALGO (1981) <u>Equality?</u>, NALGO, London
National Audit Office (1987) <u>Competitive Tendering</u>
    <u>in the NHS</u>, HMSO, London
National Board for Prices and Incomes (1967) <u>The</u>
    <u>Pay of Manual Workers in Local Authorities, the</u>
    <u>National Health Service, Gas and Water Supply</u>,
    HMSO, London
National Union of Public Employees (1984) <u>The</u>
    <u>Report of the Women's Working Party</u>, NUPE,
    London
Newman, G. (1982) <u>Path to Maturity</u>, Coop Press,
    London
Price, R. and Bain, G. S. (1976) 'Union Growth
    Revisited: 1948-1974 in Perspective', <u>British</u>
    <u>Journal of Industrial Relations</u>, Vol. XIV (2)
Price, R. and Bain, G. S. (1983) 'Union Growth in

Britain: Retrospect and Prospect', British Journal of Industrial Relations, Vol. XXI (1)

Purcell, K. (1984) 'Militancy and Acquiescence Amongst Women Workers', in Siltanen, J. and Stanworth, M. (eds.) Women and the Public Sphere, Hutchinson, London

Rowbotham, S., Seagal, L. and Wainwright, H. (1979) Beyond the Fragments, Merlin Press, London

SCPS (1982a) Equality: The Next Step, SCPS, London

SCPS (1982b) Future Organisation and Structure, SCPS, London

SCPS (1983) Conference Papers

Services to Community Action and Trade Unions (1985) The Public Cost of Private Contractors, SCAT, London

Somerton, M. (1977) Trade Unions and Industrial Relations in Local Government, WEA, London

Spoor, A. (1967) White Collar Union: Sixty Years of NALGO, Heinemann, London

Steele, M., Miller, K. and Gennard, J. (1986) 'The Trade Union Act 1984: Political Fund Ballots', British Journal of Industrial Relations, XXIV(3)

Tavistock Institute of Human Relations (1973) An Exploratory Study of the RCN Membership Structure, Tavistock, London

Terry, M. (1982) 'Organising a Fragmented Workforce', British Journal of Industrial Relations, XX(1)

TUC (1974) Report, TUC, London
TUC (1976) Report, TUC, London
TUC (1976) Statistical Statements, TUC, London
TUC (1977) Report, TUC, London
TUC (1982) General Council Report, TUC, London
TUC (1983) Sexual Harassment at Work, TUC, London
TUC (1985) Statistical Statements, TUC, London
TUC (1986) Report, TUC, London
TUC (1986) Public Ownership, TUC, London

Whitfield, D. (1983) Making it Public, Pluto, London

Wigham, E. (1980) From Humble Petition to Militant Action, CPSA, London

Wilkinson, G., Elliot, B. and Travers, T. (1982) 'How Many Public Servants Do We Have and How Much Do They Cost?', in Gretton, J. and Harrison, A. How Much Are Public Servants

Worth?, Blackwell, Oxford

Williams, A. (1984) Fighting Privatisation: The Victory in Gloucester, NUPE/IWC, Nottingham

Winchester, D. (1983) 'Industrial Relations in the Public Sector', in Bain, G. S. (ed.) Industrial Relations in Great Britain, Blackwell, Oxford, pp. 155-78

Zeitlin, J. (1982) Trade Unions and Job Control: A Critique of Rank and Filism, King's College, Cambridge

Chapter 3

NEW MANAGERIALISM IN THE CIVIL SERVICE: INDUSTRIAL
RELATIONS UNDER THE THATCHER ADMINISTRATIONS 1979-86
(1)

R. Blackwell and P. Lloyd

INTRODUCTION

During the 1970s the Civil Service contributed
significantly to the public sector's growing
reputation as the major source of instability in
British industrial relations (Winchester, 1983).
1973 witnessed the first national strike by civil
servants followed some six years later by a wider
dispute involving more senior civil servants - the
mandarins of popular mythology. On each occasion
the issue was pay and government intervention in the
process of pay research (the system of comparability
established for the service in 1956) in an attempt
to maintain the integrity of incomes policy
(Capelli, 1983). However, in addition to the
problem of pay determination, proposed reductions in
levels of public expenditure and Civil Service
manpower emerged as major issues in the mid 1970s
when Labour introduced cash limits and manpower
targets. In practice, the primary impact of these
measures was on capital programmes, and manpower was
only modestly reduced to about 10 per cent of public
sector employment in 1979 (i.e. 732,000 persons, of
whom 566,000 were non industrial civil servants).
The prospect of redundancies alarmed unions and
staff wedded to notions of career service and job
security. In the period since 1979 concern with
these central issues of pay levels and machinery on
the one hand, and career opportunities and job
security on the other has, if anything, intensified.
The abolition of pay research in 1981; the
recommendations of a subsequent inquiry (Megaw,
1982); and the practice of collective bargaining
have to date failed to provide a stable, long term
solution to the apparently intractable problems of

reconciling comparability, ability to pay and market forces criteria in pay bargaining. Similarly, enthusiastic pursuit of manpower targets and efficiency savings - characteristics of the Thatcher years - may be seen as continuing and deepening policy trends established (albeit tentatively and reluctantly) by Labour from the mid-1970s. This chapter (which focuses primarily on non-industrial employees) argues however that, while important continuities exist, the Thatcher years do mark a significant turning point denoted by the emergency of 'new managerialism'; a coherent strategy for management which is intended to integrate and institutionalise key policy initiatives and operational priorities. However, before examining the new managerialism in any detail, it is necessary to say a little more about developments in the 1970s, especially in regard to the extent that they appeared to challenge central principles underpinning the long established Whitley system of industrial relations.

The first of these underpinning principles was that it was possible and practicable to distinguish between the state as state, in its general responsibilities towards society, and between the state as employer, in its duties towards its employees, a distinction implicit in the 1919 constitution of the national Whitley Council (Parris, 1973: 194). By the 1970s, commentators commonly referred to Whitleyism, the pervasive system of joint committees in the Service, as a system of collective bargaining (or joint regulation) (Loveridge, 1971; Parris, 1973). In fact, Whitleyism throughout its history embodied the whole range of rule-making methods, and it was necessarily accepted that ultimate authority lay outside the Whitley system in the Cabinet: '. . . and the government cannot be compelled to exercise its authority by way of Whitley procedure' (HM Treasury, 1965: para. 46). In fact, the development of collective bargaining was predicated upon the prosperity and political consensus of the post-war years which afforded management and unions considerable autonomy. Successive governments showed little interest in the detail of dealings with their staff. As one official in the Treasury commented, policy on the 'official' (i.e. management) side emerged:

. . . in the ordinary way by having talks amongst ourselves (in the Treasury), by writing

papers and briefing ourselves. In very large
degree we were self-governing in the sense that
the extent to which either the permanent
secretary or ministers concerned themselves
with these matters was pretty limited.
(Parris, 1973: 67)

In this context the National Whitley Council
fell into disuse and business was dealt with in a
number of forums, ranging from the relatively formal
meetings of standing committees, through working
parties, ad hoc meetings to informal off-the-record
discussion between the principal negotiators
(Parris, 1973: 55-6). A high degree of trust,
mutual respect and strong bargaining relationships
were established. The system was highly
centralised, focusing on dealings between the Civil
Service Department (CSD), established in 1968, and
senior officers of the individual unions and the
National Staff Side, the unions' federal, co-
ordinating body. The processes and structure of
industrial relations were thus similar to those
identified by Purcell, as crucial to establishing
'good industrial relations' (Purcell, 1981).
Incomes policies necessarily reduced the
autonomy of officials and unions in the area of pay.
Expenditure and manpower reductions not only reduced
the scope for integrative bargaining and management
concession but also necessitated more frequent and
systematic reference of proposed understandings and
agreements to ministers. Moreover, the process of
discussing resource reductions itself was highly
politically sensitive, involving decisions about the
relative merits of programmes and services as
resource savings and targets were pursued. Thus
ministers were inevitably more closely involved in
the running of the service from the mid-1970s.
The themes of economic policy in the 1970s also
affected the second central principle; namely, that
the government should act as a 'good employer',
reflecting best practice in the private sector. An
examination of government performance up to the late
1970s covering a wide range of issues from the
obligation to employ a quota of registered disabled
through to pay rates concluded that (with some
qualifications) the government had fulfilled its
commitments, particularly excelling in encouraging
union organisation and collective bargaining
arrangements (Beaumont, 1981). However, in a decade
of rising inflation, union officials and journals

record increasing disenchantment and cynicism with supposed government good practice, largely due to intervention in the process of pay determination, perceived by many employees to be at the core of the good employer commitment. The pay research system itself was designed to ensure that the remuneration of the bulk of civil servants (the higher Civil Service had separate arrangements from 1956) followed that attained by the employees of external 'good' employers doing comparable jobs. The parties were allowed considerbale input into the comparability process which was backed by an arbitration agreement allowing unilateral access to arbitration subject, in theory, to parliamentary approval and, in practice, to government's retention of the right to refuse access 'on grounds of policy' (HM Treasury, 1965; Parris, 1973; Capelli, 1983; Bulletin, Sept/Oct 1984, pp. 120-1).

This system of comparability inevitably conflicted with incomes policies involving phasing and staging of settlements and even suspension of the whole process by governments (Capelli, 1983). Nonetheless, the pay system continued in existence throughout the 1970s and the good employer commitment remained intact in many areas, including that of the encouragement of union membership.

The character of the unions changed markedly in the decade up to 1980. By then, all were affiliated to the TUC (the last to do so, the Association of First Division Civil Servants (FDA), affiliating after a ballot held in 1977) (Corby, 1984) and had endorsed the principle and practice of industrial action. Central co-ordination and representation was achieved through the 'National Staff Side' until it became discredited by divisions over strike action in 1979 and was replaced by the Council of Civil Service Unions (CCSU) in 1980, a federal body with an existence independent of the Whitley system. (The job territories of the main unions are outlined in Table 3.1).

During the 1970s pressure from both rising inflation and unemployment undermined political consensus over the role of the public sector. The Conservative party was much influenced by monetarist views, and particularly the crowding out hypothesis which argued that the growth of public expenditure and employment was a major cause of economic decline, 'crowding out' the wealth-creating sector (Bacon and Eltis, 1976; Jackson, 1980). Reducing the scale and scope of the public sector, and

Table 3.1 Grades represented by the Principal Civil Service
          Unions

UNION	TYPE OF MEMBERSHIP
Assoc of First Division Civil Servants (FDA)	Senior grades of the Home Civil Service. Its membership includes government economists, statisticians, museum keepers, lawyers and Inspectors of Schools. (Since 1975 the AIT, representing senior tax inspectors, has also worked in close collaboration with the FDA in order to formulate and pursue common policies on national issues).
Soc of Civil and Public Servants (SCPS)	Executive and directing grades of the Civil Service and comparable grades in other public bodies with Civil Service links. In the Civil Service, the Society is recognised for the middle grades of the Administration and related Groups.
Civil and Public Services Assoc (CPSA)	The recognised Union for clerical, typing and machine grades in the Civil Service and some other public bodies and fringe organisations (e.g. Forestry Commission).
Civil Service Union (CSU)	Represents mainly lower paid grades (e.g. cleaners and messengers), but also some senior grades, e.g. in the Forestry Commission and in the class of Instructional Officers.
Institute of Professional Civil Servants (IPCS)	Professional, technical, scientific and other specialists in the Civil Service or in independent organisations financed by central government.
Inland Revenue Staff Federation (IRSF)	A vertical departmental union representing filing and typing grades at one end to some of the senior posts in the Inland Revenue at the other.

Source: Industrial Relations in the Civil Service, Reference
         Document No. 1, Civil Service College, 1980

especially the non-market service sector, was therefore a major task of economic policy: a task which the leaked Ridley plan (Economist, 27.5.78) anticipated would inevitably involve conflict with public sector unions including those in the Civil Service. Since 1979 pay research has been abolished and ability to pay and market forces criteria dominated pay bargaining, and intensified pressure for resource reductions has been felt through a range of measures including cash limits, stringent manpower cuts, an incisive efficiency programme, significant load shedding and limited privatisation. Furthermore, the government has demonstrated a preparedness to bear industrial action unprecedented in scale and duration, and a willingness to use its new labour legislation to regulate the conduct of unions representing its own staff.

Although these developments clearly have profound implications for the principles and practice of industrial relations in the Service, the outline package itself might appear common to a number of public sector areas and a predictable application of general policy prescriptions, ideological commitments and political tenets. In some respects, however, the experience of the Civil Service has been special and different from that of other public sector areas. First, the relationship between the Civil Service and government is more direct than in other areas of the public sector where government influence is mediated by a number of factors, including separate sources of finance and alternative lines of political and managerial accountability, which both permit managers outside the Service greater room for manoeuvre and provide interest groups with independent resources upon which to contest policies and programmes. Changes in policy and practice have, therefore, been less diluted and felt more quickly and more sharply in the Civil Service than in some other areas. Second, the Service has to some extent served as a laboratory for testing and development of specific policy measures concerned with control and reduction of public sector resource commitments, notably manpower targetting, efficiency programming and decentralised management, for subsequent wider application (e.g. in the NHS). Third, the Civil Service appears to have been perceived and treated as a political adversary per se; an organisation run by centrist officials attached to consensus politics and pursuit of hidden departmental agendas and interests (Fry, 1984) - in short, a service dominated by mandarins in the mould of Sir Humphrey Appleby in 'Yes Minister'. Thus the familiar public sector package has been complicated by a particular determination to increase political control of the Service through the unification of the posts of Cabinet Secretary and Head of the Home Civil Service; through active intervention in senior appointments (interpreted by some as 'politicism', by others as mere activation of dormant formal powers (Johnson, 1985: 424-5; RIPA Report, 1985)); through a distancing of officials from the process of policy-making in favour of emphasis upon resource management responsibilities; and by direct political oversight of managerial performance. Concomitant demands for complete loyalty from civil servants, and hostility towards 'leakers', have produced some celebrated events including the trial of Clive Ponting under Section 2 of the Official Secrets Act. Ponting's acquittal, based on his contention that he acted 'in the interests of the State' (Ponting, 1985), has re-opened the whole question of the duties and responsibilities of civil servants and, in particular, whether there may be circumstances in which they have obligations beyond loyalty to the government of the day and its ministers. In 1986, controversy surrounding the sale of Westlands helicopters; the inquiries of several select committees (Defence Select Committee, 1986; Trade and Industry Select Committee, 1986); and active advocacy of a suggested new Code of Ethics by the FDA (FDA News, December 1984), have ensured that the question of civil servants' loyalties has remained a continuing constitutional, party political, and professional issue (Treasury and Civil Service Committee, 1986a).

Fourth, from the outset, the government viewed the Civil Service as uniquely privileged in its terms and conditions of employment, derived from the alleged insulation from market forces provided by pay and pension arrangements. 'Deprivileging' the Civil Service was, therefore, a specific short- to medium-term objective (Sunday Times, 18.11.79). However, this has involved not only abolition of comparability and (arguably) repudiation of other aspects of the 'good employer' commitment but also a determination to transform Civil Service management and its priorities. In consequence, numerous measures and initiatives have been launched (often initially in a rather piecemeal way); in part designed to introduce private sector techniques and proxies for market forces, and in part intended to reactivate previous proposals for management change (Fulton, 1968). But it is no longer adequate to regard this programme simply as an attempt to deprivilege or 'clout' the Civil Service (Fry, 1984). It is now clear that a distinctive feature of experience in the Civil Service as compared with both the recent past and concurrent developments in other public sector areas has been the emergence of the new managerialism: a strategy designed to integrate and institutionalise efficiency programming and political control. The landmarks in the development of this strategy have been the Financial Management Initiative (FMI) commenced in 1982 (Efficiency and Effectiveness in the Civil Service, 1982); a review of personnel work (Cassels, 1983); and the apparent introduction of greater flexibility in pay bargaining from 1985. The strategy involves a simultaneous centralisation of certain types of decisions and a decentralisation of operational decisions to line managers. Thus, ministerial control over key processes of policy-making and strategic departmental management has been tightened, while at the same time line manager discretion to manage resources has been increased although often within stringent budgetary constraints. Management information systems and central monitoring devices have been developed apace, managerial accountability has been stressed and a range of measures taken which are designed to encourage and reward the resource-efficient manager. This approach, which has similarities with that found in modern corporations (Purcell, 1983; Kinnie, 1985), is an attempt to create a 'new managerialism' in the Civil Service: that is, a management able to deploy optimally declining resource inputs within constraints acting as proxies for market forces. The strategy has profound implications for, amongst other things, the principles, structures and processes of industrial relations.

The following account details the emergence of this strategy; identifies some of the constraints and inconsistencies which may affect its longevity; and assesses its impact on industrial relations. Initially, the abolition of pay research in 1981 and subsequent variations and uncertainties in pay bargaining are examined, and prospects for the future reviewed. The early commitment to manpower targetting and reductions are analysed, and it is suggested that in future centrally imposed manpower targetting may be shelved in favour of the dominant strategy emphasising decentralisation and delegation. The important efficiency programme which, with personal backing from the Prime Minister, laid the basis for the emergence of the new managerialism, then receives attention before the core of the strategy itself – the FMI and its implications – are analysed in some detail. It is suggested that, in industrial relations terms, the primary impact of the FMI is likely to be felt at workplace level, precipitating further differentiation and fragmentation between and within departments and raising questions about the continuation of a truly national career Service. The impact of these developments on the Civil Service unions is considered explicitly in a separate section, in which it is argued that membership loss and declining influence within national Whitley structures may precipitate an increasing orientation towards extra Whitley activity (despite the appearance of growing rank and file militancy in some areas). Finally, some concluding remarks are offered in an attempt to summarise the analysis and tentatively assess the prospects for Civil Service industrial relations.

PENSION ARRANGEMENTS AND PAY BARGAINING

The desire to deprivilege the Civil Service always appeared most relevant to pensions and pay arrangements, which not only seemed to insulate the Civil Service from the market place, but also appeared to contain some features especially advantageous to staff. On the issue of pensions, the government moved swiftly. In 1980 the Prime Minister appointed an inquiry led by Sir Bernard Scott of Lloyds Bank into civil servants' apparently non-contributory and index-linked pension scheme. In fact, as the unions maintained, the pay research scheme contained procedures whereby the government actuary adjusted data collected on outside pay rates (downwards) to take account of differences in pension arrangements. The scheme was, therefore, only non-contributory in a formal sense. Moreover, the Scott inquiry surprisingly endorsed the principle of indexation as an ideal to be aimed at for all, merely recommending that the national deduction of the government actuary from salary be increased a little (Scott, 1981; Arthurs, 1985). Although, subsequently, management and unions did hold exploratory discussions on ways of making contributions more explicit, as suggested in the Scott report, official concern that an overtly contributory scheme might increase costs (and the Fowler review of the welfare state in 1984/85 delayed progress) ultimately proved fatal. In March 1986, the government announced in answer to a parliamentary question that it did not intend to alter the status quo. In contrast, pay bargaining arrangements have been subject to considerable change and uncertainty.

Renouncing incomes policy, the Conservatives entered office intending to make affordability a much more decisive influence on pay settlements in the Civil Service through more rigorous cash limits, implying an incomes/jobs trade off. The initial pattern reflected these priorities. The staged awards of 1979 were honoured and a recruitment freeze introduced, designed to reduce manpower by three per cent and contain spending within cash limits. Pay research was allowed to operate for 1980-81 within the context of a 14 per cent cash limit. The outcome - increases of just below 19 per cent - were reconciled with the cash limit by delaying the implementation of increases from 1st April to 7th May and by using further manpower savings to meet the balance; moves which met with considerable union protest including the calling of a full meeting of the National Whitley Council. However, for 1981 and indeed for subsequent years to 1986, the government announced and publicised at an early stage a specific pay 'factor' or 'assumption' contained within the overall cash limits. Apparently designed to foreclose some of the technically feasible ways of avoiding the full rigours of cash limits (used in 1980-81), and to reduce 'inflationary expectations', this system effectively established a pay norm (Bevan, 1981; Hackett and White, 1984). For 1986/87, however, the central pay assumption was replaced by decentralised departmental running cost budgets as the main control device. Departments' assumptions about pay were not publicly identified or known prior to negotiations commencing. A stated advantage of this new system is that, in line with the core of the new managerialism, it allows departmental managers more freedom to vary the mix of inputs within an overall cash allocation for administrative costs. Although facilitating greater flexibility, whether this development marks more than a mere formal abandonment of central pay assumptions in practice remains questionable (Treasury and Civil Service

Committee, 1986a). Below, we offer an account of the various pay rounds, focusing especially upon events surrounding the abolition of pay research and attempts to construct a new system of pay determination.

In June 1980, the government communicated to the unions its desire to review radically the pay research process, including examination of the possibility of a more flexible pay system both to accommodate regional variation and merit pay (Whitley Bulletin, August 1980: 19). Preliminary discussions were begun between the principal management and union negotiators, though reluctantly by the latter. Events were, however, overtaken by the inevitable clash over the current year's negotiations. At the end of October, the government informed the unions that, because of the overriding need to control inflation, pay research would shortly be suspended and would not operate for 1981-82. Access to data already collected by the Pay Research Unit (PRU) was refused, a decision upheld by the High Court and, as a result, a common CCSU claim for 15 per cent was submitted at the beginning of 1981 (a figure about or somewhat below that which the unions believed comparability data would justify). By the end of February the government's offer stood at seven per cent. Industrial action began on 9th March (access to arbitration being refused on grounds of policy) and lasted for a further 21 weeks. At the end of June the government announced the establishment of an inquiry under Sir John Megaw into Civil Service pay and, in July, revised its proposals, offering an additional £30 per head and guaranteeing genuine negotiations and access to arbitration for the following year, subject to the government's retention of the right to recommend rejection of arbitration awards to parliament (Bulletin, August 1981: 106-7). Later, in July 1981, with little prospect of a further new offer and the cost of the dispute to the unions rising, the CCSU's affiliates consulted members on acceptance or all-out strike action; only one union, the Inland Revenue Staff Federation (IRSF), voting in favour of the latter course (Bulletin, Sept/Oct 1981: 122).

Some features of the dispute revealed points of continuing importance and are worthy of further comment. Firstly, in contrast to previous campaigns of national industrial action which were organised and led by individual unions with limited National Staff Side involvement, the 1981 strike was led and co-ordinated centrally by the CCSU. All the unions were involved in planning and decision-making at the centre. Previous inter-union rivalries and sectional conflicts (Painter, 1982: 25-26) were set aside and an unprecedented degree of unity was displayed. Secondly, the conduct of the dispute by the unions demonstrates the underlying philosophy behind national industrial action in the Service, enunciated in the Civil Service Clerical Association (the forerunner of CPSA) strike policy document of 1969 (CSCA, 1969) and only recently repudiated. The campaign involved limited all-out national strikes of one day's duration, more widespread industrial action short of strikes (e.g. overtime bans), and carefully targeted selective all-out action. The latter formed the main element of the campaign and the 1969 document. It was based on the premise that all-out national action would be both undesirable and imprudent, as it would be seen to present a major constitutional challenge to the government of the day: a challenge the government would be bound to take up and, with all the resources of the state at its disposal, bound to win. Instead, selective action should be targeted to cause maximum disruption to the government machine and to mobilise powerful interest groups in favour of settlement (e.g. farmers by cutting off their supply of grants), but should avoid causing the general public undue inconvenience. Thus, in 1981, the tax collection service and computer installations processing internal business and the work of powerful clients were major targets of action, while DHSS local offices were not. The strategy is, of course, predicated upon the assumption that the government will not be able, or will not choose, to bear the political, social and economic costs of such action, an assumption largely accurate in the 1960s and 1970s but not in the 1980s. In addition, this strategy can create some tensions within and between unions on the advisability of selecting particular areas (e.g. in the Ministry of Defence), and some frustration from members over their involvement or non-involvement since selection is not primarily based on the degree of organisation and militancy (hence disenchantment amongst CPSA members in DHSS local offices, perhaps one of the most militant areas of membership, at their non-involvement). One consequence of the 1981 defeat, buttressed by the contrasting outcomes of selective action in 1982 in the NHS, and all-out action in 1983 in the water industry, has been to push CPSA and the Society of Civil and Public Servants (SCPS) policy towards favouring all-out action. Paradoxically, the outcome of the 1981 dispute appears to have altered members' willingness to take national industrial action over pay, although the close voting figures for 1985-86 (Bulletin, May 1985: 1) warn against assuming a permanent change of mood. Finally, and most obviously, the dispute demonstrated the strength of the government's commitment to 'affordability' which, in 1981, involved ending the pay agreement without giving the required six months' notice.

Since 1981 the history of pay bargaining has been characterised by faltering attempts to move towards a long-term system of pay determination based on the Megaw report; the continued prominence of affordability and market forces criteria; and continuing union disenchantment. From 1980 to 1985 (prior to the 1985 increases) the CCSU estimates that the real pay of civil servants fell by 15 per cent and that, relative to outside earnings, pay fell by 29 per cent. The Treasury, using a different statistical base for roughly the same period, estimates that Civil Service pay rose 2.2 per cent more than retail prices and fell short of outside pay by only 3.4 per cent (Financial Times, 13.8.85). Whatever the truth about changes in real and relative pay, and despite the lack of industrial action, there is some evidence of discontent. A survey of pay dissatisfaction amongst full-time men, focusing upon 1983 pay rises, found that 52 per cent of public service males were dissatisfied with their 1983 increases, and that 78 per cent felt they were worse off compared with other groups - the highest level of felt relative pay deprivation for those in work (Daniel, 1984: 9-10). Table 3.2 outlines the developments in each pay round.

The salient features of the various outcomes can be briefly summarised as follows: the 1982-83 settlement derives from an arbitration award in response to the union claim for 13 per cent (with an underpinning minimum weekly rise) and a government offer of four per cent; all the other outturns were based on the government's final offer. In no year did all the individual unions accept an offer but in only one year did all the unions reject an offer (1984-85). Access to arbitration was requested by the unions but refused in 1984-85 and 1985-86. The 1985/86 outcome followed legal action against CPSA to enforce a secret ballot under the 1984 Trades Union Act, which produced a small majority against

strike action (Red Tape, March (2) 1985 and April
(2) 1985). The government's final offer was
marginally raised during the ballot. The 1986/87
outcome refers to a claim submitted by the CCSU on
behalf of CPSA, SCPS, IRSF and the Civil Service
Union (CSU) only. The final offer fell within the
interquartile range identified by an Office of
Manpower Economics survey of pay movements. It was
accompanied by considerable grade restructuring and
some scale shortening (primarily benefitting the
lower paid) as a result of a separate and additional
exercise (Red Tape, April (1) 1986, May (2) 1986,
June (1) 1986; Opinion, May 1986). However,
perhaps the most important developments have been
those associated with attempts to move towards a
long-term system of pay determination based on the
Megaw report.

Table 3.2 Civil Service Pay 1980-86

FINANCIAL YEAR	PAY FACTOR	VALUE OF PAY INCREASE
1980-81	14%	16.8%
1981-82	6%	7.5%
1982-83	4%	5.9%
1983-84	3.5%	4.86%
1984-85	3%	4.55%
1985-86	3%	4.9%
1986-87	None	6%

Source: CCSU: Bulletin, August 1984, January 1985,
         June 1985

The Megaw report attempted to reconcile market
forces, affordability and comparability. It
recommended a revised system of comparability based
on the collection and analysis of data by a new
independent body (the Civil Service Pay Information
Board), comparing 'benchmark' jobs in each of 15 to

R. Blackwell and P. Lloyd

20 new pay bands with external analogues drawn exclusively from the private sector and including more small firms than previously. Comparison should be made by 'factor' analysis job evaluation rather than whole job comparison as under pay research. Total remuneration studies should occur only every four years, intervening exercises limiting themselves to movements in outside pay and only analogues with settlement dates in common with the Service should be used (to avoid problems of 'uprating' data). Settlement should occur in the interquartile range indicated by the data, for both total remuneration studies and pay movement exercises (necessary adjustments indicated by the former being made over an unspecified period of years). At this stage other factors, such as internal relativities, market forces (recruitment and retention needs), possible decentralisation of pay (departmentally and geographically), and the encouragement of efficiency should be considered. Disputes should be resolved by arbitration on agreed application and mediation. Industrial action should be subject to an agreed 'cooling off' period. Cash limits should be set prior to negotiations commencing (Megaw, 1982; Capelli, 1983; Gretton and Harrison, 1983).

Neither side unreservedly welcomed the report. Despite the Chancellor's statement to the Megaw inquiry that 'the Government as an employer did not believe it should seek year after year to pitch Civil Service pay settlements below market rates in the private sector' - a statement from which his successor assured the unions he 'did not resile' in 1984 (FDA News, Jul/Aug 1985) - the prominence given to comparability and, in particular, the proposed four-yearly total remuneration studies, does not appear necessarily compatible with the desire of the government to hold down pay, justified on market forces and affordability criteria. For the unions, the recognition of comparability criteria, and in particular the proposed total remuneration studies, are regarded as some of the report's more encouraging features and essential elements in a new pay system. The recommendations on conflict resolution were more welcome to the Treasury, reflecting government views, than to the CCSU which regards unilateral access to arbitration as essential (Bulletin, July 1983: 102). A number of unions (notably CPSA) also regard low pay as a specific issue that requires attention. On these central concerns there is, therefore, sharp disagreement.

82

Following the 1983 settlement there was a desire by both parties to see whether a new system could be gradually constructed using Megaw as a starting point only. As a first step, and following a number of meetings in the autumn, a report on pay movements was commissioned from the Office of Manpower Economics. It was understood by the official side (and thence ministers) that failure to settle within the interquartile range would seriously damage if not destroy the chances of union agreement to a new long-term system. If settlement was achieved within that range, on the other hand, the unions would be able and obliged to continue talking. In this context, the government indicated that the report would 'inform but not constrain' negotiations. The report itself showed an interquartile range of 5-6.9 per cent increases in basic pay (5-7 per cent in total pay) (FDA News, April 1984); the CCSU lodging an upper quartile claim of seven per cent (plus £7 underpinning minimum), which is justified by evidence of decline in real and relative pay since 1980. However, negotiations on this claim (and relations generally between the parties) were disrupted by the General Communications Headquarters (GCHQ) union ban announced in January 1984. In April the official side offered three per cent raised to 3.7 per cent in early May and again to an average 4.55 per cent overall later that month. No further offer was made, access to arbitration was refused (Bulletin, August 1984: 106; Sept/Oct 1984: 118-9) and the pay increases implemented in October, the CCSU making it 'absolutely clear that the offer in no way discharges either the 1984 pay claim or the findings of the Office of Manpower Economics report and as such remains unacceptable to us' (Bulletin, November 1984: 134).

At first sight, events in 1983 and 1984 seemed to signal an end to the prospects of establishing new pay machinery. The apparently decisive influence of ability to pay criteria only served to deepen existing union scepticism (e.g. in SCPS) about the possibility of reaching a 'useful' agreement and raised questions about whether the government was really convinced of the desirability of a new system. In fact, despite the bitterness surrounding these events, within one year the official side approached the unions both individually and collectively with new proposals. Briefly, it was proposed that the parties would negotiate pay increases within the context of the

interquartile range of settlements in the private
sector. Arbitration would be available on joint
application but would be obliged to operate within
the interquartile range. The government would
retain the right to suspend the agreement
'temporarily and exceptionally to safeguard the
public purse or public policy' (Bulletin, November
1985: 2). Initially, only the Institution of
Professional Civil Servants (IPCS) and the Prison
Officers' Association (POA) found these proposals
worth pursuing.

During 1985 significant steps were taken to
introduce greater flexibility into the pay system.
In April a merit pay scheme was introduced for
senior officials, despite union opposition, enabling
pay and performance to be linked more closely. The
development of running cost budgets for departments
and abandonment of central pay assumptions was
accompanied by the introduction of Special Pay
Additions (SPA) (temporary cash additions to pay for
a specified period, usually of two to three years)
to meet acute recruitment and retention difficulties
in respect of particular skills and/or localities.
A number of such payments have been made, mainly but
not solely to small groups of staff (an SPA was
awarded to 5,000 staff in the secretarial category
during 1985). It will be noted that the
introduction of greater flexibility into pay
arrangements undoubtedly reflects long-standing and
genuine government concerns and may mark the
beginning of the end of national pay bargaining in
favour of differentiation on the basis of merit,
skill, department and geography (Guardian, 21.8.86
and 30.8.86).

It remains the case, however, that both sides
broadly favour the establishment of new machinery
for pay determination. Although the cumulative
effect of the sequence of events outlined, and the
distance remaining between the parties (e.g. on the
'get out' clauses) makes service-wide agreement
unlikely, pressures for a new deal do exist. On the
union side, the experience of free collective
bargaining has not been a happy one, and there are
groups with sectional interests that might stand to
gain from a Megaw-conditioned agreement, at least in
the short term (e.g. specialists represented by
IPCS). For ministers, as one official commented,
there are attractions to putting pay 'on automatic
pilot' in so far as this is practicable, in terms of
removing a time-consuming and irksome issue from the
political agenda; reducing the prospects of

conflict (with potential economic and political costs); and establishing a basis for stable staff relations. It remains to be seen whether sufficient common ground exists for an agreement (or agreements) to be reached.

In contrast, the higher Civil Service has enjoyed a settled system of pay determination for a number of years. Since 1971 the pay of senior civil servants (grades above assistant secretary) has been determined by the government on advice from the Review Body on Top Salaries (TSRB), an independent body responsible for providing advice on the salaries of a wide range of groups (including ministers and MPs). For senior grades within the Civil Service, the TSRB has tended to use whole job comparisons with external analogues complemented by an element of subjective judgement to take into account unquantifiable dissimilarities between jobs (e.g. differing standards of accountability and levels of fringe benefits). Although successive governments have committed themselves to accepting TSRB recommendations unless there are 'clear and compelling reasons to the contrary', the high visibility and sensitivity of increases in remuneration for the occupations covered has meant that in practice its recommendations have had a chequered history (Expenditure Committee, 1977). Between 1971 and 1982 the TSRB issued six reports on the higher Civil Service, none of which was implemented in full, and the first three sets of recommendations under the Thatcher administrations were either reduced or set aside in toto. Over the years, these decisions disrupted internal relativities, especially at the interface between the differing pay systems, and brought forth complaints from the FDA that top posts had become unattractive to the most able, with potentially damaging effects on the quality of advice and service to the government (Corby, 1982). More recently, the government has fully implemented TSRB recommendations in stages, notably in 1985, when increases ranging from five to 46 per cent were approved (FDA News, Jul/Aug 1985; Opinion, August 1985). Howver, the TSRB's recommended increases for 1986/87 were once again reduced apparently without explanation. Discretionary increments related to performance are, however, to be introduced for deputy secretaries and under secretaries (FDA News, June 1986).

In a brief chapter on the higher Civil Service, the Megaw report recommended the maintenance of the

TSRB but much greater co-ordination (including a common timetable and common data collection and processing methods) between it and the system recommended for the bulk of the Civil Service in order to attain a coherent pay structure and reduce the visibility of the higher Civil Service's awards (Megaw, 1982)). Whether these measures would achieve the desired ends is difficult to judge at present. In the meantime, the fate of past recommendations by the TSRB suggests unpredictable future changes in higher Civil Service remuneration.

THE DEVELOPMENT OF NEW MANAGERIALISM

None of the uncertainties surrounding policy on pay has afflicted the government's approach to running the Service. From the outset, reducing the level of resources consumed by the Service has been a major management priority, subject to a high degree of ministerial oversight and involvement.

The resource reduction policy has a number of separate, but in practice interacting, elements which in 1982 produced the core of a firm, long-term strategy in the form of the Financial Management Initiative (FMI). Before considering the FMI and its implications in more detail, we examine two important elements of the overall approach – manpower reductions and efficiency reviews – which contributed key themes in the development of strategy.

Manpower economies

In May 1980 the Prime Minister announced her decision to reduce Civil Service manpower by some 100,000 posts (or 14 per cent on levels at 1st April 1979) by 1st April 1984. Finding cuts of this magnitude was inevitably a highly politically sensitive activity, requiring policy commitments to be weighed against each other, which in part accounts for variation in the departmental sub-targets established following negotiations between CSD and departmental ministers. Similarly, within departments, ministers were inevitably closely involved in decisions about which functions could be acceptably curtailed or dropped (sometimes involving legal considerations) to achieve manpower savings. Although the performance of departments varied, both absolutely and in relation to their sub-targets, the overall target reduction was in fact exceeded. In November 1983 a further target reduction of six per cent by 1st April 1988 was announced (Lloyd and Blackwell, 1985: 26-8, 32). Table 3.3 outlines the details of performance to 1984 and targets for 1988.

According to the Treasury, 'increased efficiency after changes in work practices' accounts for 55 per cent of the 1979-84 reduction, 'cutting or dropping functions' 20 per cent, and privatisation, contracting out and hiving off 12 per cent (HM Treasury, 1984: 3). However, despite the size of the reduction, apparently involving widespread changes in working practices, the unions were unable to launch any substantial service-wide campaign of industrial action (although significant sectional campaigns have been undertaken in at least DHSS). There are a number of reasons for this. While rights of consultation over staff inspection reports were progressively acquired from the early 1970s, and national consultative rights confirmed in 1982, manpower levels have never been regarded as a negotiable item but rather a matter of government policy subject to parliamentary vote. Instead of opposition through industrial action, at national level the unions have sought to affect policy decisions on manpower levels mainly by political lobbying and campaigning. (In this context the findings of the 1980 workplace industrial relations survey, in which 23 per cent of central government establishments reported 'negotiations' over manning levels for non-manual workers at workplace level and 69 per cent reported central negotiations, are probably somewhat misleading (Public Money, 1984B)). Secondly, the variable impact of the reductions, both across and within departments, has made the task of attaining units, either between workplaces in departments or on a service-wide basis, very difficult indeed. Finally, and perhaps decisively, there has been no major programme of compulsory redundancies, other measures on the whole sufficing (Lloyd and Blackwell, 1985).

There have, however, been instances of local disputes related to staffing levels. An example of substantial industrial action occurred in DHSS local offices in Birmingham and Oxford, involving CPSA and SCPS members, from September 1982 to January 1983. The strikes arose separately and spontaneously from the Erdington office in Birmingham (subsequently spread to all 11 Birmingham offices) and the Oxford area office; in both cases staff claiming they were unable to cope with workloads, especially in the supplementary benefit sections. On 24th September a one-day Midlands-wide strike was organised in DHSS

Table 3.3 Civil Service Manpower 1979-88

DEPARTMENTS	NUMBERS AT 1ST APRIL NOS. 1979	1984	% CHANGE 1979-84	TARGETS FOR 1ST APRIL 1988 STAFF NOS.	% CHANGE
All	732,300	624,000	-15	592,700	-6
Agriculture	14,000	11,500	-18	11,300	-2
Treasury	126,900	113,000	-11	104,200	-8
Defence	247,700	200,000	-19	170,000	-15
Education	2,600	2,400	-8	2,400	0
Employment	53,700	57,700	+7	54,000	-6
Energy	1,300	1,100	-15	1,000	-9
Environment	56,000	37,000	-34	34,600	-6
Foreign Office	12,000	11,200	-7	10,500	-6
Health and Social Security	98,400	90,700	-8	87,900	-3
Home Office	33,500	35,800	+7	41,100	+15
Industry	19,500	14,900	-24	14,900	0
Lord Chancellor's departments	16,500	17,300	+5	17,400	+1
Scottish Office	10,900	9,800	-10	9,500	-3
Transport	13,900	14,200	+2	14,200	0
Welsh Office	2,600	2,200	-15	2,200	0

Source: David Thomas, 'How Much are Public Servants Worth?', Public Money, March 1985

offices in support of the Birmingham strikers and on 3rd December the unions called a one-day strike throughout DHSS offices, which is reported to have closed at least 369 of the 514 local offices (The Times, 4.12.82). The strikes became the subject of departmental negotiations and were finally settled (at the third attempt) on terms which included a joint review of the department's complementing system and assurances on future staffing levels in Birmingham and Oxford. Since these disputes, there have been reports on significant local industrial action in the DHSS arising from the CPSA's long standing ban on overtime and use of casual workers, e.g. at the Leicester offices (Red Tape, August (2) 1985). However, as a result of initiatives announced in the 1986 budget, including the 'Restart' programme, an increase of 5,000 was announced in the DHSS complement (involving about 2,800 new staff) and a further 3,000 additional permanent posts allocated to the Manpower Services Commission. In respect of DHSS, these new posts were welcomed by the unions but criticised as inadequate (Red Tape, April (2) 1986). Whether these increases in staff derive from concern at the incidence of industrial action is not known. Equally, their likely impact on workloads and conflict levels remains a matter of speculation at present.

The pursuit of manpower reductions between 1979 and 1984 may be seen as something of a success from the government's viewpoint. The size of the Service has been reduced beyond the target set and overt industrial conflict has been limited. Nonetheless, there is good reason to believe that beyond 1988 the prominence given to manpower targeting may be reduced. Not only will spectacular cuts be more difficult to achieve but, more importantly, manpower targets are in a number of instances incompatible with the emerging strategy for a cost-based management system including the provision of running cost budgets for departments. For example, it can be argued that increasing the number of VAT collectors investigating under-declaration would yield substantial net savings, while 'civilianising' some back-up posts held by military personnel might reduce overall costs while increasing civilian manpower in the Civil Service (Lloyd and Blackwell, 1985: 32-3; Thomas, 1985).

Reducing the scope of the public sector through privatisation has been a major government priority. Evidence from our interviews suggests that up to

R. Blackwell and P. Lloyd

1984 it was pursued by some departments primarily as a way of achieving manpower targets. Unlike other areas of the public sector, denationalisation and contracting out have had limited impact, and load shedding (curtailing or dropping non-market functions) has been rather more important (Steel and Heald, 1984) as the figures quoted earlier indicate. In achieving the 1988 target reductions, however, privatisation appears more prominent, with the planned privatisation of the Royal Ordnance factories yielding 18,000 posts out of the Ministry of Defence's target reduction of 30,000. Moreover, the government has signalled its intention to require departments to examine the scope for competitive tendering and contracting out of their activities, but with the specific objective of achieving greater value for money rather than simply finding manpower cuts (Guardian, 15.10.86). Because ideological differences between government and unions are greatest on privatisation, and the CCSU has been most persistent in its campaigning on this issue, with some claimed successes (see for example IPCS Bulletin, 14.5.84 and 30.7.84), this change of emphasis is unlikely to bring greater co-operation. Indeed, for some unions (e.g. CSU) this shift in priorities raises the prospect of further membership loss. In future, 'privatisation' may thus replace manpower targets as the major issue after pay.

Efficiency initiatives
One of the central criticisms made of the CSD from the mid 1970s was its alleged failure to control manpower and promote efficiency. In 1981 Mrs. Thatcher announced the winding up of the CSD, its pay and manpower functions being transferred to the Treasury and the remainder, entitled the Management and Personnel Office (MPO), attached to the Cabinet Office. An intended consequence of this reorganisation was that the Prime Minister retained ministerial responsibility for efficiency, in which she has taken particular interest (Fry, 1984: 330-1). In May 1979, Sir Derek (now Lord) Rayner was appointed to advise the Prime Minister on efficiency. He established a small Efficiency Unit which, following his departure in 1983, has been led by Sir Robin Ibbs. Based in the MPO, it reports direct to Mrs. Thatcher. The declared aim of the unit's studies or scrutinies has been to promote long-term change, notably greater responsibility and accountability in management systems. Attention has particularly focused on the specification and

90

achievement of clear objectives by managers and the need for managers to give much greater weight to value for money and cost considerations in reviewing working practices and establishing administrative routine (Allen, 1981; Beasley, 1983; Gray and Jenkins, 1984). By the close of 1984, there had been 176 departmental scrutinies and 90 scrutinies as part of multi-department reviews. These scrutinies identified £67m of once-and-for-all savings, and savings and extra income worth £600m per annum (Efficiency Unit, 1985: 9). One factor reducing managerial resistance to changes in cherished procedures and programmes was the perceived contribution that the scrutinies could make to achieving manpower targets (a political priority) up to 1984. In the period since 1984, with reduced emphasis on manpower reductions and hence pressure on departments from that source, it is noticeable that attention has re-focused on the process and timescale of implementation of scrutinies (Efficiency Unit, 1985) and upon the potential for expenditure savings from contracting out (Guardian, 15.10.86). From the outset, however, unions have viewed these studies primarily as exercises based on ideological antipathy to public services in which cost and job cutting become goals per se at the expense of effectiveness (that is, concern with the volume, quality and consistency of outputs - services to the public) (Christie, 1982; CCSU, 1982). In practice, unions have had little impact upon the programme or process of reviews because of their high political priority and the personal involvement of the Prime Minister. Moreover, although there has been no empirical research on the impact of the efficiency programme on effort standards and job controls, it seems likely that the frontier of control has shifted to management's advantage.

The efficiency programme undoubtedly provided a major impetus to the development of the new managerialism, in particular by emphasising the role of line managers and demonstrating how responsibilities could be delegated and decentralised both 'from the centre' and from departmental headquarters to line managers (Peat, Marwick & Mitchell, 1984: 16-7, 29-30). Indeed, at a technical level, the FMI can be regarded as an attempt to 'universalise MINIS (the management information system developed by Michael Heseltine at the Department of the Environment) and institutionalise Raynerism' (Fry, 1984). Whatever

R. Blackwell and P. Lloyd

the fate of the Efficiency Unit and particular
scrutinies, this contribution to strategy represents
a lasting achievement.

**The Financial Management Initiative (FMI) and new
managerialism**
The FMI constitutes the core of a strategy in the
sense that it seeks to develop 'a consistent
approach over time which is intended to yield
results in the medium- to long-term for a specific
problem' (Thurley and Wood, 1982: 197). The
specific problem (or perhaps more appropriately in
this case, set of related problems) identified has
been reducing resource commitments and consequently
the need to promote and instill the most efficient
and cost-conscious management practice possible at
all levels of the service. The specific approach
adopted has been to devolve and delegate managerial
responsibilities wherever possible to the lowest
level of line management practicable, allowing
greater discretion and autonomy within clear and
absolute budgetary limits. Central control and
direction is retained through budgetary mechanisms;
development of sophisticated monitoring systems at
central and departmental levels allowing scrutiny of
line manager cost effectiveness; and the
development and transmission of management skills,
beliefs and values appropriate to the strategy
(through training, publications, management seminars
and gatherings) (Fry, 1984; Gray and Jenkins, 1984;
Peat, Marwick & Mitchell, 1984; Financial
Management, 1983; Progress in Financial Management,
1984; MPO, 1983).
    The importance attached to the FMI approach is
clearly demonstrated by the ways in which other key
areas of central authority have been forced to adapt
to its themes. In the field of personnel
management, central control has been relaxed, some
responsibilities devolved to departments, and within
departments delegated to line management (Cassells,
1983). Although manpower targets exist for 1988 and
pay remains a central Treasury responsibility, as
discussed previously running cost budgets have been
introduced for departments, and there is evidence of
growing departmental influence and flexibility in
both areas.
    Despite substantial obstacles to
decentralisation of authority (Plowden, 1985: 399-
402), and doubts about the practicality of a cost
centre approach (RIPA, 1983: 49-51), the FMI marks a
significant departure in industrial relations,

traditionally characterised by centralised structures and processes, increasing the scope and significance of dealings below national level. Although the impact of the FMI and new managerialism is only beginning to be felt within workplaces, a number of general scenarios may be envisaged: simple union and staff acquiescence in the face of more assertive local management; the development of a consensual management and union reaction to pressures perceived as external to the workplace (encouraging the type of establishment unionism identified by Brown (1983) in the private sector) or a growing rift between local management and unions, perhaps manifest in increased local conflict. An apparent example of the latter scenario, and an indication of political commitment to FMI, occurred in the DHSS Newcastle central office from May to December 1984 when management and ministers were prepared to bear a long dispute to acquire a modest saving by shift reorganisation, involving reductions in allowances for computer operators (Red Tape, May (2) 1984; January (1) 1985) apparently at very considerable net cost (Guardian, 14.11.85).

Some 18 months later, the first and possibly last national dispute over the FMI briefly flared. In April 1986 devolved budgets were introduced within the prison service, precipitating a national overtime ban by the POA. However, following extensive rioting on 30th April, the overtime ban was lifted and negotiations commenced on a disputes procedure to regulate local disagreements arising from application of the FMI. Since then, there has been a wider public debate on the issues at the heart of the dispute, including the Home Office's determination to reduce the substantial overtime levels in the prison service and to change what it regards as outmoded working practices and, on the other hand, the POA's determination to defend pay and conditions, including staffing levels (Guardian, 22.7.86).

Table 3.4 gives a broad picture of the state of workplace industrial relations prior to the FMI, permitting more detailed comment about the challenges presented to management and unions by decentralisation.

The table suggests that, while unions are relatively well represented and engaged in joint institutions and discussions, establishment (i.e. workplace) level negotiations over important matters are less common (excepting redeployment). Indeed, although not included (as no distinction is made

Table 3.4   Dimensions of Industrial Relations in Central Government Establishments in 1980
(Non-manual workers only unless otherwise indicated)

% of establishments employing non-manual workers	Recognising Trade Union Staff Assoc (1)	Average union density	Someone who spends major part of time on personnel/ industrial relations (1	Someone called personnel or industrial relations manager (1)	Proportion with union represent-atives (2)	Proportion with training for union represent-atives (2)	Proportion with consult-ative committee (1)	Negotiations at establishment level over		
								Manning levels (1)	Recruit-ment (2)	Redeploy-ment
Central govern-ment	93	60	50	14	90	31	52	23	28	62
Public sector	92	61	46	23	70	23	46	28	29	55
Private sector	30	31	40	24	63	22	33	44	42	58

Source: Public Money, 'Public Sector as Employer I and II', March 1984 and June 1984;   tables 5, 190, 12, 13, 15, 18, 19
(Weighted samples vary)

Notes: (1) all establishments (includes manual workers)
        (2) % of establishments recognising non-manual trade unions

between establishment and national level negotiations), central government establishments, recognising non-manual trade unions, reported substantially less negotiations over production methods and capital investment than any other area of the public sector (Public Money, 1984a, 1984b). These findings tend to suggest a need for greater training and specialist advice for negotiators (on both sides) as a consequence of the FMI. One union (SCPS) has already moved to revamp its structure and to establish a system of trained shop stewards (Drake, 1982; SCPS, 1983). Moreover, merger discussions between SCPS, CPSA and CSU have been partly motivated by the desire to achieve economies of scale enabling the setting up of a dispersed network of offices and full-time officials, which currently all unions lack. In some departments, there is evidence of conscious union attempts at co-ordination across workplaces and regions in order to spread lessons and precedents (e.g. in the cuts and new technology campaigns run jointly by CPSA and SCPS in DHSS). For the future, then, there is the prospect of workplace industrial relations becoming increasingly important and variegated in the Service.

TRADE UNIONS SINCE 1979

Events since 1979 have had considerable impact upon the principal Civil Service unions. Manpower cuts, the union ban at GCHQ, and the agreed transfer of members in British Telecom from CPSA (40,000 approximately) and SCPS (10,000 approximately) to other unions have reduced aggregate union membership (see Table 3.5).

Although the 1984 workplace industrial relations survey reported comparatively high union density in public administration – an average of 73 per cent for manual workers and 80 per cent for non-manual employees (Millward and Stevens, 1986: 53-6) – there is some evidence that these figures may mask declining density in the Civil Service. Thus, it appears that membership of SCPS fell from 85 per cent of potential in 1980 to 76 per cent of potential by 1984 (Opinion, August 1985). The combined effect of these developments has been to reduce the income base of the unions, giving impetus to merger discussions between them. One merger has been effected (between IPCS and the Association of Government Supervisors and Radio Officers (AGSRO)).

R. Blackwell and P. Lloyd

Table 3.5   Total Membership of the Principal Civil
            Service Unions (1)

UNION	1980	1985
Civil and Public Services Association (CPSA)	223,884	149,782
Society of Civil and Public Servants (SCPS)	108,697	85,597
Institute of Professional Civil Servants (IPCS)	98,753)	
Association of Government Supervisors and Radio Officers (AGSRO) (2)	12,026)	90,242
Inland Revenue Staff Federation (IRSF)	65,257	55,048
Civil Service Union (CSU)	46,928	35,037
Prison Officers' Association (POA)	20,469	23,395
Association of First Division Civil Servants/ Association of HM Inspectors of Taxes (FDA/AIT)	8,368	7,703

Source: TUC Annual Congress Reports, 1980 and 1985

Notes: (1) Table includes membership outside Civil
             Service proper
         (2) AGSRO transferred engagements to IPCS
             in 1984

However, the proposed merger between CPSA and SCPS was aborted at the last minute in 1985 when CPSA's conference rejected plans which had been worked out over a number of years as a consequence of a split in the CPSA 'Broad Left', which resulted in 'Militant Tendency' combining with 'Daylight' (the moderate group) to vote down the proposal (Red Tape, June (1) 1985; Opinion, June 1985).

In 1986 SCPS and CSU, the latter particularly affected by the GCHQ union ban, announced their intention to amalgamate in 1987 (Opinion, April 1986). The logic of combining resources to gain economies of scale would appear to be indisputable. The privatisation undertaken and planned involves increased costs in establishing and servicing new negotiating mechinery; campaigning and political lobbying requires a considerable and expensive research, publishing and co-ordination effort; the FMI and the incidence of local disputes makes a dispersed regional network of officials highly desirable; and, finally, the cost of dispute pay during official selective strikes appears increasingly burdensome (CPSA/SCPS, 1983, 1984). To date, factional infighting in CPSA, the largest and pivotal union, has been the main obstacle to restructuring, but there are no indications of new divisions emerging within union ranks.

A feature of the Thatcher years has been the unprecedented degree of unity displayed by the Civil Service unions, not only during the 1981 dispute but in general dealings with the government. In large part, this has been born of necessity, arguably a defensive reaction to a radical assault upon the public sector and its established pattern of industrial relations (Heald and Morris, 1984). Ironically, the abolition of pay research, within which individual unions were able to pursue the interests of their particular members, may have contributed to the new-found unity. One effect has been to create a bargaining role for the CCSU, both in the various pay rounds and in pursuit of a new pay system for the service as a whole. Despite some sectional and political differences, a common public position has generally been maintained. But the recent decision of two unions (IPCS and POA) to enter discussions upon government proposals for a new system of pay determination may yet prove to be a watershed, especially as the official side have indicated a willingness to reach separate agreements with individual unions (something not favoured in the earlier discussions upon Megaw). If an agreement or agreements were to be reached with a union or unions, sectional differences (e.g. between specialists and administrators, between low paid and higher paid) between and within unions might resurface. This could potentially have a number of consequences including a weakening of the role of the CCSU, a loss of bargaining power (as the prospect of co-ordinated industrial action receded), and the creation of further barriers to restructuring and mergers. Although important points of unity would remain (for example, on GCHQ and opposition to privatisation), the prospect of increasing division and ineffectiveness could face the Civil Service unions, with all the implications that this might have for recruiting and retaining members in the late 1980s.

Whether the experience of the Thatcher administrations has precipitated or enhanced discontent and industrial militancy in the Civil Service is a controversial question open to debate. Evidence of high relative felt pay deprivation (Daniel, 1984), low morale (TSRB, 1985: 411-2), the incidence of 'leaks' and interest in redefining the obligations of civil servants (Plowden, 1985: 411-2) may be taken as symptoms of general discontent amongst civil servants. The 1981 pay dispute and other prominent instances of industrial action, for example in DHSS and the prison service, have been taken as evidence of rising industrial militancy in the media and by some commentators (Painter, 1982). However, both arguments must be placed in the context of research and analysis, which suggests that longer-run trends may be at work. This evidence of recent discontent must be seen in the context of survey evidence of rising overall job dissatisfaction in public administration from 1974 to 1978 (Beaumont and Partridge, 1983) and arguments about rising militancy in the 1980s set against earlier evidence of increased resort to industrial action in the 1970s, in national government and other public services, related to incomes policies (Beaumont, 1982; Winchester, 1983). Furthermore, if growing discontent is feeding into rising union militancy in some circumstances, there is also reason to believe a contrary trend towards non-unionism may be developing in some areas, as indicated by the formation of two minor breakaway unions in the Ministry of Defence and Immigration Service, and the (admittedly limited) evidence of declining union density.

Detailed examination of the record of

industrial action over the relevant period is not assisted by the tendency to combine local and national government in the category of 'public administration' and by the fact that separate data on industrial action in the Service was not compiled prior to 1979. However, preliminary analysis of union records indicates a slowly rising tide of requests for authority to take industrial action (on working conditions, local allowances and the like) from the mid 1970s. Official concern at this trend was indicated prior to the 1979 general election by the establishment of an industrial relations division in the CSD, the provision of detailed written advice to departments on handling local industrial action in April 1978, and the decision to collect data on disputes for 1979 onwards. This suggests that sectional and local action are not new phenomena. In this regard, the most plausible interpretation of the rising militancy hypothesis, suggested by union accounts of growing sectional and localised industrial action in the 1980s (in journals and interviews), is that an existing trend has been significantly enhanced and reinforced under the Conservatives. At first sight, recent survey evidence appears to support this proposition. Between 1980 and 1984 the proportion of workplaces in public administration experiencing strike action amongst white collar employees rose markedly from 13 to 50 per cent. However, a major part of this increase in strike action appears to be accounted for by protest strikes over the GCHQ union ban in 1984, rather than by a growth of local or sectional action. Moreover, comparison between the two survey years indicates that the proportion of workplaces experiencing limited action short of strikes in the previous year amongst non-manual staff in public administration actually fell from 41 to 30 per cent (Millward and Stevens, 1986: 267-73). In addition, although interesting, these figures may reflect developments outside the service and the peculiarities of the sample years, and they tell us little about the number as opposed to the extensiveness of industrial action. Overall, therefore, the survey data must be interpreted with caution and appears to be rather inconclusive. The main evidence of an increase in local action must at present rest on the comments of some union officials (in interview) who believed that there had been an intensification of local conflict and noted a change of issues on which members wished to take official action (towards ones relating to the effects of

R. Blackwell and P. Lloyd

government policy).

Increased political radicalism and factional conflict within the Civil Service unions are occasionally quoted as indicators of growing militancy and are worthy of comment. The long established factionalism within CPSA has continued unabated in the 1980s and, despite a change from bloc voting at conference to individual workplace ballots (Undy and Martin, 1984: 98-100), the 'Broad Left' achieved two notable victories in executive elections in 1982 and 1984 prior to the emergence of a split between Militant Tendency and non-militant supporters. Subsequent elections have produced 'moderate' executives despite the emergence of a minor rift in the ranks of the Daylight group. However in 1986 Alistair Graham, the moderate general secretary of the CPSA who played a leading role in the development of 'New Realism', resigned to become director of the Industrial Society (Red Tape, April (1) 1986). In the election for his successor, the Militant Tendency scored a major and unexpected victory in the first ballot when their candidate, John Macreadie, narrowly defeated the sitting moderate, deputy general secretary John Ellis. In an accompanying election, a non-militant leftist defeated the incumbent moderate treasurer (Guardian, 2.7.86). But following an inquiry into alleged voting irregularities the elections were re-run and, although the outcome of the election for treasurer was unchanged, Ellis emerged victorious (on a minority of the vote) in the key election. Nonetheless, the ballots demonstrated once again that the left is well entrenched in CPSA, enjoying general dominance in a number of departments (notably DHSS, Department of National Savings and Land Registry) and particularly important localities (e.g. the DHSS Computer Centre in Newcastle and the Vehicle Licensing Centre in Swansea). Although factionalism and left wing radicalism are hardly new amongst CPSA activists (see Wigham, 1980: 104-14, 186-200), it is clear that there is now a bedrock of rank and file support for left wing groupings, including Militant, that may not have existed in the 1970s.

Factional conflict has generally been less pronounced in the other unions. Since the early 1970s the SCPS has adopted a generally radical stance that has not come under serious challenge, although the introduction of individual balloting for the Executive from 1986 (in the wake of the Trade Union Act 1984) may stimulate greater overt political organisation and competition. Following the 1981 pay dispute, a significant Broad Left challenge to the traditional IRSF leadership emerged, but appears to have subsequently receded. A small Broad Left apparently based upon specialists with a social science background has operated intermittently in IPCS in the 1980s. In the longer term, the lack of a settled system of pay determination, continued pressure on resources, and the pace of technological change clearly raise important issues and require controversial decisions. The decentralisation undertaken and envisaged by government strategy increases the prospect of local-national conflict in unions. In short, factional organisation is unlikely to decline significantly in the Civil Service unions.

But it is difficult to know how much importance to attach to the apparent emergence in the 1980s of left wing groups as a measure of rank and file militancy. Recessions are generally thought to favour a reassertion of cautious national officials and bodies to protect organisational capacity and financial well-being, controversial steps which may encourage factionalism, focusing as much on questions of internal control and autonomy as employer policy. The rising militancy hypothesis can plausibly be countered by the possibility that the unions will be increasingly caught between the devil (of government policy) and the deep blue sea (of general membership weariness and apathy).

Relations between unions and management are, however, likely to be profoundly affected by any change in government policy towards union membership. While this aspect of the 'good employer' commitment remains formally intact, reports that the Civil Service handbook had been redrafted to remove the previous positive encouragement to union membership (Guardian, 8.7.85) have brought its continuation into question. Moreover, union officials claim it has been frequently 'chipped away at' since 1979, the most noted example being at GCHQ when, in January 1984, the government announced that, on grounds of national security, its 8,000 staff would no longer be eligible for union membership (Arthurs, 1985). The strength of the reaction to this issue, including a national half-day strike and protest action in which even the FDA participated, is partly explained by its implications for the encouragement of union membership and the fear of extension into other areas. Staff continuing in union membership after the ban have been penalised in regard to pay and promotion, and some who left but rejoined their unions have been threatened with dismissal, were subject to disciplinary action and fined during 1986 for being in breach of their conditions of service. Subsequently, Sir Robert Armstrong, Cabinet Secretary and Head of Home Civil Service, signalled to the unions that the threat of dismissal was effectively lifted from the union members until after the next general election (Guardian, 16.3.86, 20.3.86; Bulletin, Sept/Oct 1986: 133-7). Some union officials believe that the robust support received from other union colleagues (notably 'the moderates' with members in electricity supply such as Eric Hammond of the EETPU) accounts for the unwillingness of the government to attempt to settle the matter by force majeure. However, those who remained in membership were subsequently dismissed from GCHQ shortly after the EETPU was expelled from the TUC at its 1988 Congress. Events at GCHQ are not the only example of what the unions regard as a changed attitude towards the desirability of union membership.

Following the 1981 dispute, the official side informed the unions that in the event of national action in future the continuation of check-off arrangements for union subscriptions could not be guaranteed for the duration of the action. In 1982 the Facilities Agreement, which establishes the basis and modus operandi of the representative system in the Service (first agreed in 1974), was revised, partly as a result of backbench pressure from Conservative MPs, and the distinction between industrial relations activity and trade union activity (the latter partly funded by the unions themselves) tightened (Bulletin, July 1982: 131, 138-41). In addition, more rigorous monitoring procedures were established and the unions were informed of the official side's intention to reduce the overall cost of facilities from 0.225 per cent of the non-industrial wages bill in 1984 to 0.2 per cent by 1986 with further subsequent reductions (Bulletin, August 1985: 122-3). Facility time thus remains a matter of general political interest, controversy and central control).

Although not bearing directly on encouragement to union membership, two other developments have given rise to union disquiet. In correspondence during 1982 with the general secretary of SCPS, the principal establishment officer of DHSS warned that participation in industrial action remained a factor in assessing fitness for promotion to managerial posts. Subsequently the head of the House Civil Service assured the FDA that there was no promotion ban as a result of participation in industrial action in 1982 and over GCHQ, but said that he could give the union no binding assurance that it would not be a factor in future promotions to managerial posts (FDA News, May 1984). Secondly, in 1985 the government announced new expanded and more general rules governing the grounds under which a civil servant can be regarded as justifiably removed from employment held to be vital to national security (FDA News, January 1985). In both cases unions claim to detect an intention to deter participation in union activity.

More generally, the unions have complained of reduced consultation prior to important decisions affecting employment conditions, e.g. on merit pay (FDA News, May 1985), and have viewed with suspicion the development of active communications policies in departments in place of the previous passive policy which relied upon unions to communicate much information, for example on new pay rates. In the context of the stated desire of the government to reduce the power of unions in society, and especially in the public sector, these developments appear to the CCSU designed to marginalise union influence and to discourage union membership and participation. Unable to gain satisfaction within Whitley procedures, unions have increasingly turned towards political campaigning and lobbying, highlighting the impact of government policy in an attempt to galvanise membership resolve and build public support for changes in government policy. In 1986, IRSF members voted by a large majority to establish a political fund (Guardian, 10.3.86) and other unions (including CPSA and IPCS) are committed to holding ballots on the same issue. In addition, the FDA has decided to hold a ballot on whether to establish a political fund. In all cases, unions have been motivated in part by a desire to protect themselves from possible interpretations of what constitutes expenditure on 'political objects' under the 1984 Trade Union Act (Blackwell and Terry, 1987).

At the same time, the unions have shown increased interest in extending the employment rights of civil servants, currently less than those of the general population (Corby, 1984: 19) and in using the law to restrain ministers and management. One of the unintended consequences of legal action over the GCHQ union ban may have been to establish a 'legitimate expectation' of consultation for unions, open to judicial review, outside the area of national security (New Law Journal, 1984: 1049-50). In this respect the Law Lords' decision may be of enduring significance, perhaps pushing issues permanently into the legal arena. Furthermore, doubts about the lawfulness of industrial action bearing on government policies, which courts might judge to be primarily political following the redefinition of a trade dispute in the Employment Act 1982 (Morris, 1984), together with continued political interest in legislating on industrial action in 'essential services', suggest an expanded role for the legal profession in Civil Service industrial relations. In these circumstances, the trend towards political lobbying and campaigning by unions is unlikely to diminish. The establishment of a joint review of longer-term industrial relations issues (at union request following events at GCHQ) has provided an internal forum for discussion of the unions' major concerns with the most senior civil servants. But, while the review may enable less conflictual channels of communication, it is clear that officials do not at present possess the authority to resolve matters perceived as central to 'good industrial relations' by the unions.

SUMMARY AND CONCLUSION

Anthony Ferner has postulated the existence of:

> . . . a continuum of State influence. At one extreme the State merely provides the rules within which private enterprise operates. At the other, the goals, objectives and rules of operation of some enterprises may be almost entirely determined by the State. (Ferner, 1985: 48)

By definition, the Civil Service is an example par excellence of the latter type of organisation and may be regarded as a key arm of the state in determining the constraints placed on enterprises generally. However, the internal governance of the Service, including the substance and methods of regulating employment, may be in practice more or less subject to political determination by ministers and the Cabinet, or less directly Parliament, depending upon historical circumstances and context. During economic prosperity, public spending needs may be comfortably accommodated and policy-makers may become preoccupied with external regulation, allowing considerable autonomy to officials to pursue favoured labour relations strategies and so on. Economic decline, continuing significant resource commitments to the public sector and policy preoccupied with reducing the perceived burden of government, inevitably diminishes the scope of official autonomy. Accompanied by suspicion of the ancien regime, its apparent influences, privileges and habits of mind, as these changed circumstances have been since 1979, the necessity of ministerial intervention in the detailed running of the service has been enhanced and stressed at the highest levels. In the process, the largely dormant potentialities of the constitutional position of the Cabinet, in reality accepted within Whitleyism (notwithstanding the assumption of role separation by the state), has become evident, indicating that amongst other things the formal position of the Civil Service on Ferner's continuum, abstracted from historical context, tells us little about the role and involvement of government ministers, in particular in the conduct of employee relations.

Since 1979 the traditional principles and processes of industrial relations have looked increasingly anachronistic and untenable. Even ministers reluctant to engage in 'management' are inevitably drawn in by central policy commitments requiring careful scrutiny and politically sensitive decisions on the level of pay increases, departmental running costs and reductions in manpower. In this regard the separation of the roles of the state as employer and as government may appear impractical to maintain and undesirable in conception; the 'good employer' commitment (in its traditional sense) may be perceived as burdensome and unfair in comparison with private sector recession-induced 'rough justice'. It could no doubt be argued that 'good' employers in the public sector in the 1980s reduce non-market function to a minimum and ensure that they are undertaken at minimum cost. In the circumstances there has been little scope for national collective bargaining (that is, joint regulation of employment) and other forms of rule-making, notably joint consultation, but including unilateral government-employer

R. Blackwell and P. Lloyd

regulation and statutory regulation, have become
more important. Indeed, the unions have complained
that the scope and significance of joint
consultation has been reduced, with the
opportunities for discussion of options early in the
decision-making process being largely replaced by
consultation on the details of implementation after
final decisions have been taken. Whereas in the
1960s and 1970s consultation tended to shade into
collective bargaining, to the extent that it is
often difficult to tell which of the two rule-making
methods predominated in specific instances (both
sides referring simultaneously to 'consultation and
negotiation' resulting in 'agreements'), the content
of consultation has shifted nearer to the other end
of the spectrum, unilateral regulation. Thus on
occasion union officials commented that they felt
they had only been invited to particular meetings in
order that subsequently it could be said that the
unions had been consulted.
    In the main, this development would appear to
be a natural consequence of areas of employment
becoming matters of high policy and great
ministerial interest. It has not, however, been an
unintended consequence as, on the one hand,
ministers have consciously sought to protect the
policy-making process from what is often regarded as
improper influence, while on the other stressing to
officials the need to assert 'the right to manage'.
One senior ex-CSD official commented, for example,
on the 'terrible trouble' the official side had got
into over 'the sloppy language' of 'negotiations'
and 'agreements' used in the 1970s. Another manager
felt that greater caution by officials might have
contributed to reduced opportunities for union
comment. Faced with a radical government, whose
choice among politically sensitive policy options
could not always be predicted, and conscious of the
possibility of 'leaks', he said officials tended to
proceed with greater caution than previously. The
result was that unions were only brought in when it
was felt safe to do so - which sometimes meant after
firm decisions had been made.
    In this changed context, it is not surprising
to hear complaints that, on the one hand, the Civil
Service is becoming 'politicised' (e.g. in relation
to appointments) and, on the other, that unions'
activities and policies are 'too political'; and
even that proposed union industrial action poses a
constitutional threat (Prentice, 1982). Unable to
bargain, unions have inevitably looked outside the

106

industrial relations sphere to achieve influence through political campaigning, lobbying and legal action.

The processes of industrial relations have been necessarily affected. Although the various formal and informal contacts remain, suspicion is more pervasive. Power centralisation in the hands of negotiators had been reduced by government and ministerial over-determination and by increasingly assertive union executives and restive activists, and, more generally, by policies designed to decentralise authority and responsibility. Normative consensus between the principal negotiators has diminished and ideological conflict become more common at all levels. Thus, in contrast to the past, high levels of trust and strong bargaining relationships have become difficult to establish and maintain.

These themes and trends have coalesced in the new managerialism developed over the Thatcher years. The longevity of this strategy will depend upon a number of factors, including the willingness of ministers to adopt a 'hands off' approach to line managers' conduct, requiring redefinition of ministerial responsibility and parliamentary accountability, and a preparedness by ministries and the Treasury to view decentralised budgetary mechanisms as more than an opportunity for continuous resource cutting (Plowden, 1985). The result of the 1987 general election has undoubtedly been important in affecting the climate in industrial relations, but there are good reasons for believing that elements of the strategy may have been of enduring significance, whatever the outcome. In the late 1980s and 1990s, governments are likely to attach greater importance to maximising efficiency in the use of limited resources to achieve identifiable results rather than to the procedural values of precedent, consistency and so on previously dominant (Johnston, 1985: 428). New managerialism institutionalises these concerns without sacrificing ministerial oversight and central control. Delegation to line managers of personnel management removes issues and activities which, according to officials, ministers often find trivial and tiresome. Although attitudes towards union membership may change, flexibility in pay bargaining is likely to be a future requirement at least on grounds of cost and political expediency. In short, aspects of the new managerialism are likely to become well entrenched even if attitudes

R. Blackwell and P. Lloyd

to union membership and the role of the Civil
Service per se change. In the process, the concept
of a career Civil Service in which life-long
commitments are made by employer and employee
towards each other, may disappear in favour of
differentiation between a core of senior, permanent
policy advisers and managers on the one hand and, on
the other, layers of more or less peripheral junior
employees working in dispersed office networks
enjoying a primarily instrumental relationship with
their employer.
   In an era of constrained resources and
continuing pressure on public expenditure, a return
to the status quo ante seems unlikely. Change is
already sufficiently advanced to render traditional
principles and assumptions untenable. The adoption
and extension of the new managerialism suggests
greater decentralisation, increased differentiation
between and within departments, and greater concern
with sectional and local issues in industrial
relations. But, whether this emergent system, which
is based upon no explicitly articulated or agreed
assumptions about the relationship between
government and its employees, can ensure the type of
stability characteristic of the traditional system
for the bulk of its existence remains highly
questionable.

NOTES

   1.   This paper arises from research on 'Staff
Relations in the Civil Service Since 1973', funded
by the Economic and Social Research Council and
based at the Royal Institute of Public
Administration. We are grateful to HM Treasury and
the Council of Civil Service Unions for their co-
operation during research fieldwork and for the
advice of the project's research panel.
Responsibility for the paper rests solely with the
authors.

REFERENCES

Allen, D. (1981) 'Raynerism: Strengthening Civil
     Service Management', RIPA Report, 2(4) Winter
Arthurs, A. (1985) 'Industrial Relations in the
     Civil Service: Beyond GCHQ', Industrial
     Relations Journal, 16(2), Summer

Bacon, R. and Eltis, W. (1976) Britain's Economic Problem: Too Few Producers, Macmillan, London

Beasley, I. (1983) 'The Rayner Scrutinies', in Gray, A. and Jenkins, B. (eds.) (1983) Policy Analysis and Evaluation in British Government, RIPA, London

Beaumont, P. B. (1981) Government as Employer - Setting an Example?, RIPA, London

Beaumont, P. B. (1982) 'Strikes and the Public Sector: The Position in Britain', Employee Relations, 4(2)

Beaumont, P. B. and Partridge, M. (1983) Job Satisfaction in Public Administration, RIPA, London

Bevan, G. (1981) 'Cash Limits and Public Sector Pay', Public Administration, 59(4), Winter

Blackwell, R. and Terry, M. (1987) 'Analysing the Political Fund Ballots: A Remarkable Triumph or the Victory of the Status Quo?', Political Studies, forthcoming

Brown, W. (1983) 'Britain's Unions: New Pressures and Shifting Loyalties', Personnel Management, 15(10), October

Bulletin, The (Journal of the Council of Civil Service Unions)

Capelli, P. (1983) 'Comparability in the British Civil Service', British Journal of Industrial Relations, XXI(1), March

Cassells, J. S. (1983) Review of Personnel Work in the Civil Service, HMSO, London

Christie, C. (1982) 'The Real Rayner Targets', RIPA Report, 3(1), Spring

Corby, S. (1982) 'Civil Service Pay: Megaw in Context', Public Money, 2(3), December

Corby, S. (1984) 'Civil Servant and Trade Union Member: A Conflict of Loyalties?', Industrial Relations Journal, 15(2), Summer

Council of Civil Service Unions (CCSU) (1982) 'Memorandum', in Treasury and Civil Service Committee, Third Report Session 1981-82: Efficiency in the Civil Service, Vol. II, HC.236.II, HMSO, London

CPSA/SCPS (1983) Going Forward Together, CPSA/SCPS, London

CPSA/SCPS (1984) Going Forward Together: A Progress Report, CPSA/SCPS, London

Civil Service Clerical Association (CSCA, now CPSA) (1969) CSCA Strike Policy, CSCA, London

Daniel, W. (1984) 'Deprivation', Public Money, 4(2), September

R. Blackwell and P. Lloyd

Defence Committee (1986) <u>Fourth Report, Session</u>
    <u>1985/86: Westland plc - The Government's</u>
    <u>Decision Making</u>, HC.519, HMSO, London
Drake, P. (1982) <u>A Programme for Union Democracy,</u>
    SCPS, London
Efficiency and Effectiveness in the Civil Service
    (1982) <u>Efficiency and Effectiveness in the</u>
    <u>Civil Service: Government Observations on the</u>
    <u>Third Report from the Treasury and Civil</u>
    <u>Service Committee</u>, Cmnd. 8616, HMSO, London
Efficiency Unit (1985) <u>Making Things Happen: A</u>
    <u>Report on the Implementation of Government</u>
    <u>Efficiency Scrutinies</u>, HMSO, London
Expenditure Committee (1977) <u>Eleventh Report,</u>
    <u>Session 1976-77: The Civil Service</u>, HC.535,
    Vol. II, Part II, HMSO, London
<u>FDA News</u> (Journal of the FDA)
Ferner, A. (1985) 'Political Constraints and
    Management Strategies: The Case of Working
    Practices in British Rail', <u>British Journal of</u>
    <u>Industrial Relations</u>, XXIII(1), March
Financial Management (1983) <u>Financial Management</u>
    <u>in Government Departments</u>, Cmnd. 9058, HMSO,
    London
Fry, G. K. (1984) 'The Development of the Thatcher
    Government's Grand Strategy for the Civil
    Service: A Public Policy Perspective', <u>Public</u>
    <u>Administration</u>, 62(3), Autumn
Fulton, Lord (1968) <u>The Civil Service</u>, Vol. I,
    Cmnd. 3638, HMSO, London
Gray, A. and Jenkins, B. (eds.) (1983) <u>Policy</u>
    <u>Analysis and Evaluation in British Government</u>,
    Royal Institute, London
Gray, A. and Jenkins, B. (1984) 'Lasting Reforms
    in Civil Service Management?', <u>Political</u>
    <u>Quarterly</u>, October
Gretton, J. and Harrison, H. (eds.) (1983) <u>How</u>
    <u>Much Are Public Servants Worth?</u>, Blackwell,
    Oxford
Hackett, H. and White, G. (1984) 'Public Sector
    Pay: An Impending Crisis', <u>Public Money</u>, 4(1),
    June
Heald, D. and Morris, G. (1984) 'Why Public Sector
    Unions are on the Defensive', <u>Personnel</u>
    <u>Management</u>, 16(5), May
<u>IPCS Bulletin</u> (Journal of IPCS)
Jackson, P. (1980) 'Public Expenditure Cuts:
    Rationale and Consequence', <u>Fiscal Studies</u>,
    1(2), March
Johnston, N. (1985) 'Change in the Civil Service:

Retrospect and Prospects', _Public Administration_, 63(4), Winter

Kinnie, N. (1985) 'Changing Management Strategies in Industrial Relations', _Industrial Relations Journal_, 16(4), Winter

Lloyd, P. and Blackwell, R. (1985) 'Manpower Economies, Management and Industrial Relations in the Civil Service', _Industrial Relations Journal_, 16(4), Winter

Loveridge, R. (1971) _Collective Bargaining by National Employees in the United Kingdom_, Ann Arbor, Michigan

Management and Personnel Office (MPO) (1983) _Civil Service Management Development in the 1980s_, MPO, London

Megaw, Sir John (1982) _Report of an Inquiry into Civil Service Pay_, two volumes, Cmnd. 8590, HMSO, London

Millward, N. and Stevens, M. (1986) _British Workplace Industrial Relations 1980-84_, Gower, Aldershot

Morris, G. (1984) 'Industrial Action in Public Enterprises: The Legal Issues', _Public Administration_, 63(2), Summer

New Law Journal (1984) 'Editorial', 30th November, _New Law Journal_, 134(6180)

Opinion (Journal of SCPS)

Painter, C. (1982) 'Civil Service Staff Militancy: Joining the Mainstream of Trade Unionism', _Public Administration Bulletin_, 40, December

Parris, H. (1973) _Staff Relations in the Civil Service_, George Allen & Unwin, London

Peat, Marwick & Mitchell (1984) _Financial Management in the Public Sector: A Review 1979-84_, Peat, Marwick & Mitchell, London

Plowden, W. (1985) 'What Prospects for the Civil Service?', _Public Administration_, 63(4), Winter

Ponting, C. (1985) _The Right to Know: The Inside Story of the Belgrano Affair_, Sphere Books, London

Prentice, R. (1982) 'Civil Service Militancy: A Constitutional Threat', _Public Money_, 2(1), June

Progress in Financial Management (1984) _Progress in Financial Management in Government Departments_, Cmnd. 9297, HMSO, London

Public Money (1984a) 'Public Sector as Employer: How Industrial Relations Compare with the Private Sector - I', _Public Money_, 3(4), March

Public Money (1984b) 'Public Sector as Employer:

R. Blackwell and P. Lloyd

How Industrial Relations Compare with the
Private Sector - II', Public Money, 4(1), June
Purcell, J. (1981) Good Industrial Relations:
Theory and Practice, Macmillan, London
Purcell, J. (1983) 'The Management of Industrial
Relations in the Modern Corporation: Agenda
for Research', British Journal of Industrial
Relations, XXI(1), March
Red Tape (Journal of CPSA)
Review Body on Top Salaries (1985) Eighth Report,
Cmnd. 9525-I, HMSO, London
RIPA (ed.) (1983) Management Information and
Control in Whitehall, RIPA, London
RIPA Report (1985) 'Is the Civil Service Becoming
More Politicised?', RIPA Report, 6(2), Summer
Scott, Sir Bernard (1981) Inquiry into the Value
of Pensions, Cmnd. 8147, HMSO, London
Society of Civil and Public Servants (SCPS) (1983)
Future, Organisation and Structure, SCPS,
London
Steel, D. and Heald, D. (eds.) (1984) Privatising
Public Enterprises, RIPA, London
Thomas, D. (1985) 'How Much are Public Servants
Worth?', Public Money, 4(4), March
Thurley, K. and Wood, S. (eds.) (1982) Industrial
Relations and Management Strategy, Cambridge
University Press, Cambridge
Trade and Industry Committee (1986) Second Report,
Session 1985/86: The Tin Crisis, HC.305-I and
II, HMSO, London
Treasury and Civil Service Committee (1986a) Third
Report, Session 1985/86: The Government's
Expenditure Plans 1986-87 to 1988-89, HC.192,
HMSO, London
Treasury and Civil Service Committee (1986b)
Seventh Report, Session 1985/86: Civil
Servants and Ministers: Duties and
Responsibilities, two volumes, HC.92-I and II,
HMSO, London
Treasury, HM (1965) Staff Relations in the Civil
Service, HMSO, London
Treasury, HM (1984) Economic Progress Report, 168,
June
Undy, R. and Martin, R. (1984) Ballots and Trade
Union Democracy, Blackwell, Oxford
Whitley Bulletin (Journal of the National Staff
Side)
Wigham, E. (1980) From Humble Petition to Militant
Action, CPSA, London

Winchester, D. (1983) 'Industrial Relations in the
Public Sector', in Bain, G. S. (ed.)
Industrial Relations in Britain, Blackwell,
Oxford

Chapter 4

INDUSTRIAL RELATIONS IN THE NATIONAL HEALTH SERVICE
SINCE 1979

R. Mailly, S. J. Dimmock and A. S. Sethi

INTRODUCTION

Industrial relations in the National Health Service
(NHS) have undergone dramatic changes since the
early 1970s. This chapter will concentrate on
changes since 1979, although it is necessary to
consider briefly the circumstances in the preceding
years.
    The NHS was established in 1948 following the
National Health Service Act of 1946. It has become
one of the largest organisations in Western Europe,
employing in 1984 1.2 million people (1). The NHS
is funded by central government out of sums
allocated annually (2). The government does not
employ staff in the NHS, although the Secretary of
State is accountable to Parliament for the provision
of health services. Regional and district health
authorities are the employers, having effective
responsibility for the day-to-day management of
services.
    The Whitley Councils system for determining pay
and conditions was introduced at the NHS's
inception. National bargaining over terms and
conditions of employment applicable to all staff is
conducted by the General Whitley Council, whilst
various functional Whitley Councils serve as
negotiating fora on conditions applicable to
individual groups of staff (3). Industrial action
over pay was virtually unknown during the 1950s and
1960s: disputes tended to be referred to
arbitration. As Clegg and Chester (1957: 142) point
out, this was largely due to the weakness of the
trade union side. Trade union membership was low in
comparison with other areas of the public sector,
and a sizeable proportion of staff were members of

114

professional associations: notably, the British Medical Association (BMA) and the Royal College of Nursing (RCN) (see Table 4.1).

The centralisation of negotiations left little scope for the development of local bargaining (4). Although in 1950 the General Whitley Council agreed a national model constitution for Joint Staff Consultative Committees (JSCCs) at hospital level, their introduction was sporadic. In hospitals in which they were introduced, the subject matter of agendas dealt with minor issues. In 1966, Miles and Smith undertook a survey of 197 hospital JSCCs and concluded that 'consultation in the hospital service must, with few exceptions, be pronounced a failure' (Miles and Smith, 1969: 41).

The underlying reasons for, and the nature of, the transformation in industrial relations between the late 1960s and the mid-1970s have been well documented (Dimmock and Farnham, 1975; Manson, 1977; Bosanquet, 1979; Carpenter, 1982; Barnard and Harrison, 1986). An indication of the main arguments will suffice here. The introduction of bonus schemes for ancillary staff following the reports of the National Board for Prices and Incomes in 1967 and 1971 (Reports 29 and 166) is given weight by many commentators as underlying the development of trade union organisation at local level in the NHS. There seems no doubt that in those health authorities in which the schemes were introduced, the explicit emphasis on the 'cash nexus' and the use of work study assisted the development of a trade union consciousness amongst ancillary workers. However, the coverage of schemes was patchy - by the early 1980s extending to only 50 per cent of ancillary staff (IDS, 1984). The impact of incomes policies on NHS employees is given particular emphasis by Bosanquet (1982a). The initial cause of the ancillary staffs' first national dispute in 1972 was the separation of the pay link with local government workers due to the introduction of a new incomes policy by the Heath government. The action spread from a local dispute in Bristol and could therefore be seen as rank-and-file led. The dispute marked a watershed in NHS industrial relations.

Recruitment by trade unions, particularly NUPE and COHSE, increased significantly. The previous 20 years of industrial peace was shattered as, in the years up to 1979, virtually every occupational group took some form of industrial action.

Table 4.1 Trade Union Membership Density in the NHS 1948–78 (UK)

	1948			1966			1974			1978		
	Labour force '000s	TU members	Density %	Labour force '000s	TU members	Density %	Labour force '000s	TU members	Density %	Labour force '000s	TU members	Density %
All industries	20,270	9,118	45.0	23,048	9,680	42.0	22,820	11,226	49.2	23,544	12,602	53.5
Public sector (ex steel)	4,637	3,278	70.7	5,386	3,591	66.7	5,899	4,403	74.6	---- NOT AVAILABLE ----		
Health	522	222	42.6	934	301	32.2	1,137	627	55.1	1,250	950	76.0

Source: 1948–74: Bain, G. S. and Price, R. J. Profiles of Union Growth, Blackwell, Oxford, 1980.

Notes: Public sector figures use the definition of Bain and Price, and the 1948 figures include industries nationalised after that date in order to give a base for comparison. Steel is excluded. Some figures are rounded.

Source: 1948: All industries' figures calculated from report of the Certification Officer, 1979, and Gennard, J. et al., 'The Extent of Closed Shop Agreements in British Industry', Employment Gazette, January 1980. Health figures are unpublished estimates. Labour force figures from Department of Employment Gazette, 86:7, 1978.

Source: Barnard and Harrison (1986). Accurate figures beyond 1978 are not available, but see Table 4.3 on membership of major trade unions.

A further possible encouragement to union growth and the changed industrial relations climate was the extended managerial hierarchies introduced by the NHS reorganisation of 1974 and the increasing concentration of employees in large district general hospitals (5). The series of employment statutes (commencing with the 1971 Industrial Relations Act) passed by governments during the 1970s were particularly influential. Their emphasis on the formalisation of workplace industrial relations, as a means to strengthen collective bargaining, led to the development of industrial relations machinery at local levels in the NHS. In addition, the legislation encouraged many professional associations (examples include the BMA, the RCN, the Royal College of Midwives, the Chartered Society of Physiotherapy, and the Society of Radiographers) to seek legal certificates as trade unions (6). Not only did these organisations receive certificates as trade unions, they also began to adopt some of their organisational features: increasing the number of their full-time officers and, by the late 1970s, developing a local 'steward' system of representation (Dyson and Spary, 1979). Simultaneously, unions such as NUPE and the TGWU were taking cautious decisions to devolve power within their own organisations (Fryer et al., 1974; Undy, 1978).

By 1978, the character of industrial relations in the NHS was substantially different from that of 1970. However, it is important to recognise that four fundamental elements survived the industrial relations turbulence of the 1970s. First, the notion of vocational commitment still exercised a deep influence on the attitudes of trade unions' leaders and their membership. This is well illustrated by Neale:

> This is part of what makes hospital workers different from factory workers. The theatre has a more rigid hierarchy than any factory. But the hierarchy seems more justifiable to the workers. The surgeon isn't just using class power when he behaves like a pig to the technician. He's also nervous. The team isn't just a pyramid of privilege; it's a group of dedicated people too. The nurses aren't spectators in their own lives. They're part of a great drama. (Neale, 1983: 14-5)

The TUC unions were very reluctant to take outright industrial action and professional

associations who had adopted the legal status of a
trade union faced the same ethical dilemma. (The
RCN's constitution, for example, contains a clause
precluding the 'withdrawal of services' by its
members). Complete withdrawal of labour rarely
occurred (except in extreme local actions) during
the 1970s and the scale and frequency of partial
withdrawals were generally subject to negotiation
(and therefore influenceable) by local managements.

Second, a large proportion of staff employed in
the NHS (particularly in the ancillary sector) are
both part-time and female. Trades unions in the NHS
had managed to overcome the recruitment problems
associated with this type of worker (Bain and Price,
1983), but still faced the difficulties of
participation in union affairs raised by part-time,
female labour (Fryer et al., 1978). The role of
women in trade unions in the public sector is
analysed further in Chapter 2.

Third, despite heavy criticism of its
structural deficiencies, the Whitley system remained
intact. The pressures exerted by employment
legislation had led to a number of initiatives
within health authorities to create local industrial
relations structures. However, pay remained a
matter for determination by the Whitley Councils.

Fourth, while there was a much higher union
density among all groups of staff (see Table 4.1),
large sections of the workforce, such as ancillary
staffs, experienced a deterioration in the relative
value of their pay during the final half of the
1970s (IDS, 1984).

Taking these four elements it can be argued
that, despite a series of unparalleled disputes,
both nationally and locally, successive governments
had maintained a broadly comparable level of control
over pay determination to that noted by Clegg and
Chester in the 1950s (op. cit.).

Against these factors this chapter will examine
how the Conservative government, with a different
philosophy towards the public sector from that of
its post-war predecessors, has confronted industrial
relations in the Health Service since 1979. It will
examine the principal issues under three broad
headings: first, the restructuring of the national
system for pay determination; second, the role and
impact of government ideology on NHS industrial
relations since 1979; third, the consequences and
reactions at local level to government initiatives.

RESTRUCTURING THE SYSTEM OF PAY DETERMINATION

The Clegg Commission

The rash of public sector disputes that occurred in the winter and spring of 1978/79 were popularly held to be a key factor in the Conservatives' electoral success in May 1979. In April, immediately before the general election, the Labour government appointed the Comparability Commission (chaired by Professor Hugh Clegg) as one means to resolve the disputes. It began work in June of that year with a very tight timetable for reporting.

The Commission's short-term brief was to seek to resolve the dispute over pay in the public sector. Its longer-term task was 'to report on the possibility of establishing acceptable bases of comparison for most of the public services sector'. The groups of NHS employees for which the Commission had a remit were ambulancemen, ancillary workers, professions allied to medicine, and nurses. The Commission produced its first report in August 1979 (Clegg, 1979). Other reports soon followed and recommended pay increases on average above the five per cent norm set by the previous Labour government, but they did not meet any of the unions' claims in full, excepting the ambulancemen. Increases for NHS ancillaries ranged from 3.8 to 16.9 per cent, whilst ambulancemen ranged from 12.8 to 25.8 per cent. Professor Clegg enraged the professions allied to medicine by awarding an average 15.3 per cent increase, whilst making it conditional upon staff changing their working hours to 35.5. (Physiotherapists worked 36 hours, radiographers 35, and speech therapists 33 (Gray, 1980)). Further 'days of action' were held by the Chartered Society of Physiotherapists and the Society of Radiographers when the report was received in March 1980. Clegg gave substantial increases to nurses based on internal relativities — the average increase was 19.6 per cent to be paid in two equal stages. This did not restore the salaries to their 1974 post-Halsbury level, which the nurses had requested.

The Commission was doomed to a short life once the Conservative government reached office. In September 1979, it announced that the Commission would be abolished once it had completed its present references. During its short, controversial career, the Commission had emphasised the complexity of pay in the public services. In this sense, it was a

R. Mailly, S. J. Dimmock and A. S. Sethi

rational voice in the forthcoming debate concerning
the best method of deciding pay in the National
Health Service.

Affordability versus comparability

The Conservatives' election manifesto had declared
that public sector pay should not be decided on the
basis of 'comparability' but 'affordability'. This
represented a radical departure from one of the
essential principles of pay determination that has
long been operated in the public sector. Traditionally, pay of NHS employees had been linked, with
varying degrees of formality, with both internal and
external comparators.

Given the occupational complexity of the NHS's
workforce, the comparisons employed were diverse:
encompassing links with local government; the Civil
Service; and sections of industry. A few examples
will suffice. Ancillary workers had links with
local authority manuals. Administrative and
clerical staff, and scientists and technicians, were
linked respectively to administration and scientific
grades in the Civil Service. NHS craftsmen had the
only comparison with the private sector by being
linked with electricians' pay rates in the
electrical contracting industry (Dyson, 1982).
Ambulancemen became part of the NHS in 1974, but
continued their links with local authority manual
workers. However, these analogues were only broad
ones, and internal relativities also influenced pay
awards in some occupational groups.

Following the 1979 dispute, the Conservative
government translated their manifesto into policy
and broke the link between local authority manual
workers and NHS ancillaries by bringing them into
line through a common settlement date, rather than
the local authority settlement which preceded the
NHS. The government also pushed for a common
settlement date of 1st April for all NHS employees -
presumably to tidy up the negotiating process and
provide stronger links with the system of
determining the amount of cash limits. This
assisted the government in its wish to break outside
links with the Civil Service and local authorities.
In April 1980, the various Civil Service analogues
were broken. NALGO balloted its members but there
was insufficient support for action against this
breach.

In the following year - 1981 - the government
abandoned the idea of not stipulating a pay element

120

within cash limits, and set a pay 'norm' for the
public sector. Although the pay factor did not
require all public sector settlements to be based on
the norm, in practice settlements within the public
services had been remarkably similar (Winchester,
1983: 712). That same year, the government pay
allowance within cash limits was set at six per cent
and, in December, ancillary staffs settled for a
flat rate increase of £4.60 (worth between 6.1 and
8.4 per cent) to last 15.5 months. The nurses
received six per cent and the 37.5 hour working week
for nurses was implemented (IDS, 1985). The pay
provision within cash limits for 1982 was set at
four per cent.

The 1982 pay dispute

An unwished for consequence, for the government, of
the common settlement date for NHS staff was the
united action over the 1982 claim for a 12 per cent
increase 'across the board'. The government's
counter offer in April of four per cent to ancillary
and clerical staffs and 6.4 per cent to nurses was
rejected as being divisive. Throughout the long
dispute that followed there were tensions between
the unions which were only partially resolved by the
decision to co-ordinate action through the TUC
Health Services' Committee. A minority of nurses
played some role in the early national stoppages but
this tended to diminish as the dispute developed. A
critical factor on the union side was the position
of the RCN. As an unaffiliated union it did
nevertheless support certain actions taken by the
TUC unions; most notable was its decision in July
to join in the boycott of the Whitley Councils.
Despite a series of actions, commencing initially
with a one-day stoppage in May and culminating in a
five-day stoppage in August, the government's
increased offer was comparatively modest - 7.5 per
cent for nurses and 6.4 per cent for other health
workers. While support was provided by other TUC
unions and sections of the public, the ethical
dilemma in moving towards an all out strike was
clearly apparent in the debates within and between
the NHS unions. As in the pay disputes of the 1970s
a firm stance by the Conservative government kept
the eventual settlement close to its declared pay
norm. A principal outcome of the 1982 dispute was
the decision to determine a system for settling
questions of pay in the longer term for certain
staff groups.

R. Mailly, S. J. Dimmock and A. S. Sethi

In the autumn of 1982, the government commenced talks with the nurses over a system for settling their pay in the long term. In January 1983, the Secretary of State for Health announced to the House of Commons the setting up of review bodies for nurses and midwives and professions allied to medicine. A condition of involvement in the review was that staff had not participated in industrial action in the past and would not do so in the future. Any possibility of similar bodies being set up for other groups of staff was quickly quashed by the Secretary of State.

> It has been clear from the beginning that there will be no question of the review body covering, for example, ancillary workers, administrative workers and clerical workers. We have made our position clear. (Hansard, 18th January 1983)

The employees whom Mr. Fowler excluded from the review system achieved little from the long dispute. Moreover, the decision to create review bodies threw into doubt the future of the Whitley machinery.

The NHS Whitley system has been heavily criticised since its inception. The central issue of government's role in NHS Whitleyism was diagnosed by Lord McCarthy (McCarthy, 1976) as 'employers who do not pay and paymasters who do not employ'. McCarthy's report, 'Making Whitley Work', published in 1976, made a total of 65 recommendations for the reform of Whitley. In particular, it emphasised the problematic role of departmental representatives on Whitley Councils. Each council consists of a management and staff side. Management sides were made up mostly of chairmen or members of health authorities and representatives of the DHSS who provide the secretariat. McCarthy received evidence from both management and staff side that Health Department representatives had a disproportionate influence on the outcome of negotiations. The report proposed that the Health Department's representatives should be concerned with the overall cost of pay offers, while health authority representatives were to concentrate on detailed matters of pay structure and priorities. Most of McCarthy's other proposals for reform centred around improving communications between NHS management and the Whitley Councils' management sides; decentralisation of Whitley through regional Whitley Councils; and the rationalisation of representation on staff sides. Some of McCarthy's recommendations for improving the briefing system for Whitley Councils' management sides were implemented by 1980. However, the system remained heavily centralised.

The 1982/83 dispute reactivated and widened the debate on a new system of pay determination for the NHS. All parties seemingly agreed that the NHS could not go through a similar dispute again. The debate had commenced in 1981 with the TUC's report 'Improving Industrial Relations in the NHS' (TUC, 1981). This report (which had developed from the Royal Commission's Report on the NHS, 1978) suggested an independent pay information system to which both management and unions would have access and whose results would be fed into government formulation of cash limits for the NHS. There would also be an independent system of arbitration. A King's Fund paper published in 1983 (McCarthy, 1983) favoured a pay board consisting of equal numbers of management and unions, and an independent chairman. The board would issue a report which would be the basis of Whitley Council negotiations. The paper also recommended a standing arbitration tribunal to settle disputes. However, the Secretary of State's representative on the management side would have a veto over any agreement to go to arbitration. This proposal thereby recognised the government's likely wish to want to control the use of arbitration. In the same year the National Association of Health Authorities also produced a paper (NAHA, 1983) advocating (by a majority) a joint pay information system for the public services and access to mediation rather than arbitration.

The King's Fund group (7) (which noted the deliberations of Megaw (1982)) wanted NHS management to be able to influence ministers on cash limits and the size of NHS expenditure. The group argued that the regional chairmen of health authorities should be given the responsibility for formulating a strategy on NHS pay (in consultation with district chairmen and regional groups of officers). They also suggested that the regional chairmen should appoint the chairmen of Whitley Councils as a method of ensuring their accountability to the Service. NHS managers argued that the proposals gave too much influence to regional chairmen. Subsequently a joint NAHA/King's Fund seminar (NAHA/King's Fund, 1983) produced a revised proposal for an NHS Pay Policy Council consisting of six RHA chairmen, a DHA chairman from each of the 14 English regions, the chairman of a Scottish health board, one from Wales, the chairmen of the management sides of Whitley. With hindsight, the debate conducted by the service about the future of Whitleyism and pay determination appears largely peripheral to government policy decisions.

Developing a corporate strategy for pay within the Whitley framework - government's action

Central to this debate was the notion that a reformed system of Whitley could provide a rational method of pay determination. In contrast, the pay review bodies for nurses and midwives and professions allied to medicine removed a majority of employees from pay determination within the Whitley framework. Following the establishment of these bodies in 1983, the government instituted discussions between RHA chairmen and a small number of NHS managers. Th new arrangements introduced by the government did reflect some aspects of the King's Fund Report.

There was, for example, limited movement towards allowing NHS management to influence pay strategy. Three RHA chairmen were to form a pay strategy sub-group, supported by a secretariat consisting of a regional administrator, treasurer and personnel officer. The group was charged to:

> . . . develop objectives for pay policies which reflect the manpower requirements of the NHS; provide a view to the Secretary of State on future pay policy options and their consequences in anticipation of public expenditure sub-committee discussions; advise on strategy within which management sides have to operate (Leopold and Beaumont, 1986: 39)

The total number of Whitley Council members was cut from over 200 to less than 40, and the representative system of appointment suggested by McCarthy (1976) was abolished. The declared reason behind the changes was the need for a more professional and committed management side on the Whitley Councils. Appointment of management side members is now made by the Secretary of State on the basis of their personal qualities, their experience of the NHS, and for their specific knowledge of industrial relations and personnel management (Trainor, 1984). The majority of NHS appointments are regional or district chairmen, with health service managers in the minority - the ratio being approximately two to one in favour of health authority members. A new briefing system has been introduced whereby each regional health authority with a council member identifies a briefing officer (usually a personnel officer) who is responsible for organising briefing of the member.

Those regions without a member are 'clustered' together with represented regions and a single contact point is identified to gather the views of that region to feed into the briefing officer. Preliminary impressions of the new system suggest members are happier now that they are receiving the views of NHS managers on topics under discussion (Leopold and Beaumont, 1986: 38). There is however uncertainty whether the views of the briefing officer are representative of NHS management as a whole within a region. In addition, Leopold and Beaumont point to a feeling that briefing officers and contact points were being 'reactive' rather than 'pro-active', in the sense of responding to management secretariat papers and staff side proposals rather than assisting in the production of a pay strategy. The creation of 'Whitley conferences' was intended to meet these concerns. Each English region is to hold a conference to which Whitley members, briefing officers, contact points, all personnel officers from districts in the region and a personnel officer representative of the RHA chairmen's secretariat would be invited. These conferences should enable NHS management to examine the broad sweep of a pay strategy which overarches the sectional concerns of Whitley Councils.

Even with these new arrangements, it is difficult to envisage how NHS management can formulate a pay strategy within the constraints of the cash limits system. As Leopold and Beaumont comment:

> The real test of the new relationship between the two groups representing NHS management views and the government representatives very directly representing the Secretary of State's position will come over the implementation of pay strategy. (1986: 42)

Their discussion concentrates on the effects of 'intra-organisational' and 'multi-lateral' bargaining on pay determination in the NHS. They argue that these reforms have attempted to reduce the impact of intra-organisational bargaining - specifically in regard to differences between DHSS and NHS representatives. A second aim has been to

R. Mailly, S. J. Dimmock and A. S. Sethi

increase the influence of NHS management over decisions taken on pay, and to assist them in formulating a pay strategy.

An alternative interpretation of these reforms is possible. This would view these changes as attempts to reduce intra-organisational bargaining between central government and health authority representatives at the expense of an independent, truly representative management side. Hence, whilst an overt intention of the changes may have been to strengthen the hand of NHS management, their impact in the most important arena - of pay - seems not to have been increased by these changes. Indeed, the increasing influence of regional chairmen (who are appointed for terms of two years and four years by the Secretary of State); district chairmen (who are similarly appointed); and the direct appointment of NHS managers to Whitley Councils, has been criticised by NHS trade unions. They claim the system makes management side members 'creatures of government' (NAHA, 1983: 51). There is little hard evidence to support this claim. While the briefing system aims to maintain a link between the service and Whitley members, it will only prevent them from becoming remote in so far that it works efficiently. Further research into the role and accountability of Whitley Council members is necessary for, as Leopold and Beaumont comment:

> RHA chairmen are clearly accountable to the Secretary of State who appoints them, but also see themselves as the voice of NHS Management. Whitley chairmen now also are accountable to the Secretary of State, and likewise see themselves as the voice of management. (1986: 41)

Staff side representation on Whitley

By comparison the system of representation on the staff sides of Whitley Councils has hardly changed since their inception. It is based on the principle that the staff sides should determine their own composition, and that any recognised organisation with members in a particular staff group should have representation on the appropriate functional Whitley Council. McCarthy's (1976) recommendation that staff side representation should be based upon proportional representation has not won support. This seems to be principally for the reason that the TUC affiliated unions would lose seats to the single professional trade unions. The number of staff organisations recognised for bargaining purposes has fallen from 48 in 1950 to 39 today. However, it seems unlikely that there will be any major reduction in those numbers in the near future, as the position of the TUC affiliates (as stated in the TUC report (TUC, 1981)) is that the single professional unions should amalgamate with TUC affiliates since they do not have the resources to serve their members adequately. The professional unions, on the other hand, wish to remain independent and - by and large - unaffiliated. While the elements of the Whitley Council structure remain, the new pay review bodies have removed many of the principal decisions from the Whitley arena. In this sense, too, their establishment has overtaken the debate on Whitley reform. The functional councils for ambulancemen, ancillary and administrative and clerical staff still remain. In the case of the Ancillary Staffs' Whitley Council it is argued by Neale (1983) that its composition with four seats allocated each to COHSE, NUPE, GUMBATU and TGWU has led to stagnation in terms of decision-making and leadership amongst ancillary workers. The TGWU and GUMBATU have a tiny minority of members in the NHS, and they therefore carry little power within the decision-making levels of these unions. In addition, their leadership are unlikely to take risks in committing themselves to industrial action. NUPE finds that it is quite often in a minority of one in rejecting pay deals and calling for industrial action. Neale argues that the NUPE leadership exploits this position in order to present a militant appearance.

Extra-Whitley arrangements for pay determination

The creation, in 1983, of the pay review bodies for nurses and midwives and health visitors, and professions allied to medicine dealt a severe blow to the notion of a Whitley bargaining structure designed to cover all staff groups. The bodies work on a similar basis to those already established for doctors and dentists, armed forces (up to the rank of brigadier) and the 'Top Salaries' Review Body. It is serviced by the Office of Manpower Economics, which provides a secretariat and research facility. The bodies consist of eight members appointed by the government for limited but extendable periods. Two new committees were created to negotiate on other terms and conditions, chaired by departmental representatives, 'with advice and assistance from NHS management'. These were the Nurses and Midwives

R. Mailly, S. J. Dimmock and A. S. Sethi

Joint Negotiating Committee and the Professions Allied to Medicine Joint Negotiating Committee. The staff side of the former Whitley Councils initially refused to recognise these bodies, and there was considerable delay before they met, particularly in the case of the professions allied to medicine.

These two review bodies, together with the Doctors' and Dentists' Review Body (which was first instituted in 1960), mean that the pay of over half the staff in the NHS is decided outside the Whitley structure. Consequently, managerial influence over the pay of a further section of staff has been seriously weakened. They are not negotiating bodies (Thomason, 1986). While management can submit evidence to them, along with the staff side and the government, the final decision on a recommendation to government lies with its members. Whether the award is implemented in full, in part, or in stages, lies in the hands of the government.

Following the introduction of the review bodies the King's Fund produced a further paper suggesting reforms of the payment structure (King's Fund/NAHA, 1985). The proposals recognised the continued existence of these bodies within a system in which three new groups would contribute to decisions about pay in the NHS: a pay policy committee to determine policy and negotiating strategy; a pay negotiation unit to brief the policy committee; and, an NHS negotiation council to negotiate new pay bands. This system would see the abolition of the occupationally-based Whitley Councils, although it would allow greater flexibility whilst still maintaining central control. The report also advocated the introduction of a 'spinal columnm' for NHS salaries, thus producing broad pay bands to enable reward for merit and performance. However, its proposals received a hostile reception from most organisations representing NHS staff.

The appointment of general managers, as chief executives of health authorities, which followed from the Griffiths Report (1983) saw other pay developments taking place outside the Whitley arena. In the first instance, salaries of the new general managers were determined by the DHSS without reference to Whitley. Following this, a differentiated salary structure was introduced based on a complex formula attaching weight to 'restructuring' and development activities to be carried out within the manager's region, district or unit. Lastly, a system of merit payments was introduced, awarding pay enhancements to general managers dependent upon their performance. Both of these were constructed and implemented independently of Whitley.

Clegg and Chester (1957) pointed out that free collective bargaining was something of a chimera in the NHS. It is a moot point how far it has been further undermined by the developments of the pay review bodies and the general management pay arrangements. Equally, the long-term future of the Whitley system is debatable. Some have suggested that it is now time to stop debating its future, particularly because of its inability to rectify anomalies in pay (Dyson, 1985). For Dyson, the key element in any alternative to Whitley (whatever that may be) should be the right of staff to choose the organisation that represents them (1985: 6).

Underlying any discussions about its future is the fact that NHS labour costs represent 70 per cent of revenue expenditure. In 1957 Clegg and Chester pointed to this as a principal determinant of government policy on pay bargaining in the NHS. This point was re-emphasised by Lord McCarthy in his 1976 report on Whitley. Irrespective of the policies of the political parties and short-term expediencies, the need for government to maintain control over pay (and, by implication, spending on the NHS) seems likely to remain a critical factor in shaping its attitude towards remuneration of health staff. Moreover, the tensions inherent in government's role of paymaster for the NHS and manager of the UK economy act to further constrain the development of coherent pay strategies (Dimmock, 1982a). In this context, the new arrangements designed to encourage the development of a management pay strategy almost immediately encountered the three per cent limit on public sector pay for 1984. Perhaps, as Clegg and Chester (1957) implied, government pay strategy is often reduced to simply minimising labour costs.

Pressure for further reform of Whitleyism
Pressure to reform the Whitley system has been greatly reduced by the establishment of the pay review bodies. In particular, that for the nurses and midwives has provided a number of benefits. It enables the RCN (in common with the single profession trade unions) to distance itself from the ethos of trade unionism whilst still preserving its role as representative body on industrial relations matters. In this sense, it allows the RCN to model itself more closely on the BMA (Dimmock, 1979). In

placating the nurses, government (at least in the short term) has recognised public sympathy aroused by nurses' pay. It has also removed the likelihood of concerted action over pay between the TUC and the non-affiliated unions in which any action by nurses is especially critical to the functioning of hospitals. In addition, the impact of competitive tendering on the membership of ancillary staffs unions has served to reduce their influence. Following the establishment of the NHS management board and the appointment of Mr. Len Peach as personnel director (8), there was considerable speculation within the NHS about the future of Whitleyism with regard to the introduction of local pay bargaining and the extension of merit pay throughout the Service. Some form of regional as opposed to national rates of pay to reflect local labour markets and a marginal extension of merit pay to cover senior managers remain as possible developments (9). However, it can be argued that the changes introduced by government since 1983 have been sufficient to placate the demands for further reforms to the system of pay determination from more powerful interests, such as the RCN. It therefore seems likely that, for the immediate future, the present shape of NHS Whitleyism will remain unchanged.

The measures introduced by government to restructure the system of NHS pay determination have to some degree been influenced by ideology. In particular, the creation of review bodies can be depicted as a 'reward' for 'moderate' staff organisations. However, it is the various initiatives designed to increase organisational and managerial efficiency that most clearly demonstrate the practical translation, in the NHS, of government attitudes towards the public sector.

THE ROLE OF GOVERNMENT IDEOLOGY IN NHS INDUSTRIAL RELATIONS

Efficiency savings

A general strategy of the Conservative government has been to pursue a trade-off between jobs and pay within the public services. This is a particularly important aspect of policy in the Civil Service (see Chapter 3 on Civil Service; and Lloyd and Blackwell, 1985). In the NHS, the trade-off has not been as straightforward, firstly because the government is not the direct employer, and secondly

130

because a health authority's financial position varies depending on its rating within the Resource Allocation Working Party (RAWP) (10) formula. Thus, particularly since the appointment of Norman Fowler as Secretary of State in 1981, the government has pursued a policy of encouraging 'efficiency savings'. Government spokesmen have argued that it is through improving efficiency within hospitals that the 'reduction in the rate of increase of resources' to the NHS will be compensated for and money directed towards patient care. Efficiency savings were to accrue from the increasing drive to contract out NHS ancillary services from savings resulting from the recommendations of the Rayner scrutinies (11), from more efficient working methods and reducing staff costs.

The Conservative government's claim that efficiency savings could be achieved without affecting the service to patients, and that the NHS was adequately funded, has been attacked by trade unions, opposition parties and professional groups such as NAHA. As Winchester notes (1983: 174), there is considerable controversy about the existence or extent of government cuts in public expenditure, and this is particularly acute in the NHS:

> The complexity of data provides almost unlimited opportunities for the government, management and trades unions to develop arguments in defence of their interests and contradict the other's assessment of the impact of public expenditure changes.

Those who argue that the NHS has suffered real reductions in funding point to the particular effect of inflation in the NHS, the increasing demands made upon the NHS by an ageing population, and the need for constant medical innovation (Social Services Committee, 1986) (12). Equally, the evidence of savings from increasing efficiency measures such as contracting out is less than conclusive. It seems reasonable to conclude therefore that, if projected efficiency savings are not being made, and in some health authorities can only be achieved by reducing actual or potential services to patients (especially in authorities whose funds are being reduced through the RAWP formula), the level of expenditure serves to act as a 'cut'. The government has intensified this pressure on health authorities through the underfunding of pay awards.

131

R. Mailly, S. J. Dimmock and A. S. Sethi

Underfunding of national pay awards
From 1980 onwards, government refused to fund national pay awards above the percentage norm for the public sector. This policy became particularly important following the creation of the review bodies in 1983. The first report of the Review Bodies on Nurses and Midwives, chaired by Sir John Greenborough (1984), recommended an average increase of 7.5 per cent on basic salaries. The government funded approximately 80 per cent of the award (Leopold and Beaumont, 1986: 36). The 1985 pay award was implemented in stages (recommendations ranged between 4 and 14.7 per cent, averaging 6.6 per cent). In 1986, it accepted the recommended increase but delayed implementation from April until July, effectively reducing the value of the award to 5.9 per cent for 1986/87. Moreover, 1986 was the sixth successive year that government failed to implement the full increase from the date recommended by the Doctors' and Dentists' Review Body (Industrial Relations Review Report No. 329). By comparison, ancillary staffs during this period received increases on average some one to three per cent below those of nurses and paramedics (e.g. £3.14 flat rate increase in 1986, worth on average 4.7 per cent), but again any amount above the government's norm was not funded (0.7 per cent in 1986).

The 1987 reports for nurses and midwives and professions supplementary to medicine recommended an average increase of 9.5 and 9.1 per cent respectively. In the case of nursing, those qualified staff employed in patient care received larger increases in recognition of the need to retain trained staff. Unlike previous years, and with a general election looming, the awards were implemented in full from 1st April. Their total cost was £488 million, of which £25 million had to be covered from cost improvements to be achieved by health authorities (DHSS Press Release 87/181, 23rd April 1987).

A policy of underfunding awards may have been judged as attracting less publicity and therefore being more politically acceptable than rejecting awards which were nearly double government's advised norms. Its impact upon health authorities has not been uniform. However (particularly in those health authorities whose rate of increase in funds is being reduced due to the RAWP formula), the underfunding of awards has placed further pressure on NHS management to produce savings, usually in the middle

132

of the financial year. The impact of government policy on NHS manpower is more easy to determine.

Manpower levels

Between 1975 and 1984, NHS manpower rose by 27 per cent from 0.8 million to 1.2 million (Office of Health Economics, 1986). The constant rise in manpower, with its implications for increased expenditure, has been of concern to the government. Critics of the NHS within the Conservative Party have pointed to the rise in the number of administrative and clerical staff - even though the actual numbers of managers employed in the NHS measures favourably as compared with other health systems. Indeed, it is a curiosity of government policy that, amidst simultaneously calling for better management, it has tried to reduce managerial manpower. In 1983, manpower 'targets' were set for all staff. Regional health authorities were asked to monitor staff numbers closely and achieve a reduction in overall staff numbers of between 0.75 and 1.0 per cent from the total employed at 31st March 1983. Administrative, clerical, maintenance and ancillary staffs were expected to fall more sharply, between 1.35 and 1.8 per cent (Health Circular (83)6). In particular, health authorities were asked not to fill vacancies automatically. It seems that some authorities exaggerated their likely manpower needs for the forthcoming years and therefore the impact of these targets was probably minimised in those authorities. Other authorities based their figures on their establishments rather than staff in post. Regional health authorities reminded districts of what is required of them each year, and revised targets are set from the baseline given by authorities at the beginning of each financial year. However, the greatest drive for efficiency has been the policy of contracting-out of hospital services (13).

The competitive tendering process for ancillary services has resulted in an instant loss of manpower when contracts have been awarded externally. As is clear from Table 4.2, a decreasing number of outside contracts were awarded during 1985/86. Despite this, in those cases where contracts have been awarded in-house, there have generally been reductions in manpower. Between 1983 and 1985 there was a reduction of approximately 20,000 in the number of full-time equivalent ancillary staff employed in England. Aside from shedding labour through competitive tendering, many authorities, in

Table 4.2 Competitive Tendering Cleaning Contracts awarded by English Health Authorities

	CONTRACTS AWARDED MAY-NOV 85				CONTRACTS AWARDED NOV 85-MID APR 86			
	In-house	Out-house	Total	% awarded in-house	In-house	Out-house	Total	% awarded in-house
Northern	8	1	9	89	7	–	7	100
Yorkshire	8	4	12	67	9	1	10	90
Trent	22	4	26	85	11	–	11	100
East Anglia	5	1	6	83	3	–	3	100
NW Thames	5	5	10	50	–	2	2	0
NE Thames	7	3	10	70	4	2	6	67
SE Thames	10	2	12	83	2	–	2	100
SW Thames	10	6	16	63	4	3	7	57
Wessex	1	1	2	50	10	1	11	91
Oxford	5	1	6	83	4	–	4	100
S Western	9	0	9	100	3	–	3	100
W Midlands	18	5	23	78	14	4	18	78
Mersey	8	1	9	89	4	2	6	67
N Western	7	1	8	88	10	–	10	100
TOTAL	123	35	158	77	85	15	100	82

Cleaning contracts awarded in the NHS (taken from Health Services Journal, 24.4.86)

preparation for the tendering process, have been freezing vacancies as they arise in ancillary jobs during this period. In addition, a small number of authorities have been changing working practices and, consequently, shedding labour in place of tendering. In these cases, the option of going out to tender has proved an effective lever for management in persuading the unions to agree changes.

Contracting out

One of the newly-elected Conservative government's 1979 manifesto commitments was a reduction of public expenditure in absolute terms. Its policy was not simply directed towards public spending by the state, but to reduce the intrusion of state-controlled enterprises in the general economy (i.e. the 'crowding out' thesis; see Chapter 1). This has been loosely termed 'privatisation', but can be broken down into three main strategies: first, decentralisation of public corporations and the sale of public assets (e.g. British Telecom); second, liberalisation, or removing restrictions on private competition for public services (e.g. Transport Act, 1985: deregulation of public passenger road transport); third, contracting-out (e.g. competitive tendering in the NHS and local government). As regards contracting-out, the strategy has taken one of two forms: a direct instruction to tender for services, with no opportunity for the direct workforce to put in its own bid (as in the Ministry of Defence); or, allowing the in-house service to bid against outside tenders with the lowest bid being awarded the contract (as in the NHS and local authorities).

In the case of the NHS, there was a determination to see areas of its 'hotel services' being provided by private enterprise. This was in part an ideological commitment based on the belief that these types of service could be delivered more efficiently and cheaply by private companies. However, it also offered the prospect of reducing labour costs, and therefore NHS expenditure, in one single process.

In August 1981, the then Minister of State for Health, Dr. Gerard Vaughan, wrote to the chairmen of regional and area health authorities and suggested they consider the idea of contracting out their 'hotel' services, as this would save money. There was little, if any, response to this. In fact, the percentage of services contracted out by health

authorities during the first three years of the
Convervative government actually fell (NHS
Unlimited, 1984; Social Services Committee Reports,
1984). In the absence of a positive response from
health authorities, a draft circular on the subject
was prepared in May 1982. However, this was leaked
to the press in the middle of the 1982 pay dispute,
and then subsequently withdrawn. A further draft
circular was issued in February 1983, confirming
that government now wished to replace direct
approaches to private companies with a system of
'competitive tendering'. Although government did
not publish responses from health authorities, it
became clear that the majority would have wished to
be allowed to seek tenders for their ancillary
services and use these as a baseline cost for
examining and running their own in-house operations.
The official circular was issued in September 1983
(HC(83)18). It rejected the use of tenders for this
purpose and, whilst not limiting the coverage of
services, required authorities to seek bids in the
areas of laundries, cleaning and catering. The
circular indicated that authorities were to draw up
programmes by February 1984, stating when and how
these services were to be tested. Initial
resistance was experienced from Labour-controlled
authorities (nine authorities in England and
Scotland had not drawn up a programme by September
1984 (Guardian, 18.9.84)). Eventually, nearly all
English health authorities drew up a timetable, but
resistance in some meant that this was long after
February 1984. Districts that refused to
participate in the process received 'active
encouragement' to comply from regional health
authorities.

The government was keenly aware (through strong
lobbying from the Contract Cleaners and Maintenance
Association (CCMA), the trade union for contract
cleaners) of the need to eradicate 'unfair'
practices for companies competing for contracts in
the NHS. In the budget of 1983, the government had
made provision for health authorities to claim back
VAT paid to outside contractors. The Fair Wages
Resolution, requiring government contractors to
comply with pay and conditions of employment within
state owned enterprises, was abolished in September
1983. This seems to have further encouraged non-
unionised or weakly organised companies with poor
terms and conditions to bid for contracts. However,
many authorities continued to stipulate adherence to
Whitley terms and conditions. In October 1984, the

Health Minister wrote to health authorities instructing them not to require companies to offer Whitley wage rates or conditions of employment. The Secretary of State's legal powers were threatened if authorities failed to comply. Ironically, and to the government's chagrin, members of the CCMA agreed not to pay less than the bottom grade NHS ancillary workers' Whitley Council rate when bidding for contracts (IPM/IDS, 1986: 25).

The health circular stated categorically that contracts should be awarded to the lowest tender and compelling reasons would be needed to convince the DHSS in cases where an in-house tender, which was not the cheapest, was offered the contract. In order for in-house bids to be made more competitive, it has been necessary for authorities to make drastic cuts in costs. Health authorities are legally obliged to pay the Whitley negotiated rate and adhere to Whitley terms and conditions. Therefore, savings have been made through cuts in staff hours; by re-examination of bonus schemes; and, in some cases, redundancies. Many staff were asked to take cuts in hours which brought them below 16 hours a week (thereby obviating the need for national insurance payments). Some bonus schemes were terminated or altered drastically.

Most Health Service managers appear not to have relished the task of putting their services out to tender (IPM/IDS, 1986). They have attempted to involve staff as much as possible in the drawing up of the in-house tenders. This has not meant the exclusion of full-time officials or stewards, but a dual approach through trade union channels and directly to staff. Full-time officials tended to be involved at the specification stage and in the process of drawing up a timetable for competitive tendering. A crucial stage in the tendering process was the drawing up of the contract specification. According to HC(83)18, staffing levels were not to be set down in the specification. Some unions, particularly NUPE, attempted to oppose this. In general, authorities were successful in resisting union pressure aimed at involving them in negotiations over contract specifications.

Some health authorities have attempted to temper government policy. A range of devices have been used to maintain in-house services, ranging from charging for the use of energy, to stressing the importance of adequate pay and ability to recruit quality labour when evaluating tenders. In some cases, in-house tenders have been successful,

137

even though they were not the lowest bid. However, the DHSS inquires into most of these cases, and has generally insisted on the lowest bid being awarded the contract. There are varying reasons why the number of contracts being awarded to external bids is declining (see Table 4.2). Some firms have withdrawn from competing because of the low profit margin; others have made complaints concerning the number of contracts let during a short space of time as health authorities have delayed tendering for the largest contracts until the end of their programme. The CCMA claimed that the market has been flooded and its member companies could not cope. Most importantly (with reference to the tactics of health authorities mentioned above), information exchanges within regions have been instituted, and health authorities have been able to calculate what reductions in costs are necessary to enable in-house bids to be competitive. These sorts of tactics have provoked a strong reaction from the CCMA, with claims of 'rigged' contracts and unfair competition. A letter from the Secretary of State to regional health authority chairmen seemed to be the result of lobbying by the CCMA. This letter, issued in December 1985 (the letter was marked 'confidential' but was leaked to the press) requested, inter alia, regional chairmen to ensure authorities considered amalgamating cleaning and other contracts and offering comprehensive 'hotel services' contracts. Further, that unnecessary questions were not asked in invitation to tender documents - particular emphasis was placed upon questions concerning company recognition of trade unions (Health and Social Services Journal, December 1985). It is clear that NHS managers have had an underlying preference for their existing workforce and have been able to ameliorate, to a degree, government policy in this area (Key, 1987).

Trade unions: tactics and strategy
The reaction from trade unions to these efficiency measures has been muted compared with the anti-cuts campaign of 1975-78 (Fryer, 1979; Winchester, 1983). Job losses amongst other non-ancillary staff groups have not yet been significant, but the RCN has voiced concerns about the under-staffing of wards and recruitment problems.

The principal success of the RCN in this context has been the government's decision to discontinue its plans to sell off accommodation for hospital staff. Its campaign to demonstrate the implications of these proposals on nursing staff, given both the shortage and high prices of private rented accommodation, seems to have been one factor in the resignation of Victor Paige — the first general manager for the NHS. Indeed, the leaders of the RCN have come to recognise the need for greater involvement in politics as a means to further their members' interests.

The ancillary staffs' unions have been concerned to defend jobs whilst simultaneously resisting privatisation. Of the four unions representing ancillary staff, COHSE and NUPE have by far the largest membership. NUPE was particularly active in its opposition to competitive tendering. The national policy on contracting out was contained in a TUC document (1983). This called for trade union nominees on health authorities to resist privatisation at every stage and for trade unionists to lobby members of health authorities. Once the health authority agreed a timetable for competitive tendering, it was envisaged that trade union representatives would be closely involved in the drawing up of the specification, but not in negotiating in-house tenders. By negotiating in-house tenders, it was felt that trade union representatives would be agreeing to a deterioration in members' terms and conditions. Trade unions locally were thereby placed in a dilemma. Despite the efforts of the TUC, many stewards were unprepared for competitive tendering and did not understand all of its implications. Many staff were equally bewildered. Some wished to stay and work for the health authority while others were attracted by redundancy awards (not very far in excess of the state minimum). Faced with an ambivalent attitude amongst many of its members, but with the prospect of losing membership if the contract went outside, many local union representatives (with the increasing involvement of full-time officials) agreed, against their personal principles, to negotiation or consultation on the form of the in-house tender (Mailly, 1986; see also Chapter 2).

In general, the union campaign became a 'damage limitation' exercise. There were areas where the local membership resisted. For example, at Addenbrookes Hospital in Cambridge, and at Barking in London, where cleaning staff went on strike in opposition respectively to the incoming contractor and to cuts in wages made by the private contractor. During these and other disputes, there were attempts to publicise poor services provided by contractors and the possible dangers to health (TUC, 1984). However, in all cases, the unions were eventually defeated. In the case of the Barking dispute, staff lost their jobs.

Although many NHS staff have obtained jobs with private contractors, their terms and conditions are generally far inferior to the NHS. Sick pay is often not payable within the first year of employment and holiday entitlement within the first year is extremely limited. Some recruitment amongst contract workers by NUPE and COHSE has taken place; in particular, NUPE has changed its constitution to enable recruitment of non-public sector employees.

Recent analysis suggests that the actual savings from competitive tendering fall well short of the forecasts of ministers (Key, 1987). However, the long-term implications of the tendering process seem to be quite significant in industrial relations terms. The most immediate implication is the resultant fragmentation with the ancillary staff workforce. This may provide difficulties for both management and unions. Management may well have to cope with a mix of services in their authority: some being provided externally and others internally, with the consequent different styles of management. Unions may find themselves with a high density of membership where the work is provided in-house, but a low density of membership amongst employees working for private companies. It may prove difficult for unions to win back external contracts even with a change of government committed to a reversal of the present policy (Health and Social Services Journal, 1.5.86).

It could be argued that the undeclared aim of competitive tendering was to reduce the influence of the ancillary trade unions. It is a matter for speculation. One continuing factor in government philosophy has been (and declared as such) to reduce the role and influence of trade unions in the general economy. In this context, given the frequency of industrial action within the NHS throughout the 1970s, it would not be unreasonable to perceive competitive tendering which, while a primary weapon against union power, could be cloaked in the guise of a measure to increase efficiency. Since the actual implementation of the complex process of tendering can only be undertaken within individual health authorities, its introduction would be gradual. This militated against a sustained national response, either individually or collectively by the four ancillary unions. Offers of redundancy pay and lack of understanding of the complexities of competitive tendering probably served to fragment individual work groups affected by the process. The relative victory of the government in the long-running 1982 pay dispute reduced the likelihood of any sustained national industrial action either over competitive tendering or pay bargaining. By maintaining a vigorous posture over ancillary pay nationally, and pressing forward locally with competitive tendering, the government caught the weakened unions in a pincer movement. It is easy when discussing events with hindsight to depict strategies that never existed at the time. There is some evidence to suggest that in other contexts within the public sector the government 'planned' for national strikes. Whether competitive tendering was intended as a means to reduce and fragment the membership of the ancillary staffs and their unions, thus ensuring the circumstances in NHS industrial relations in the 1970s would not be repeated in the 1980s, can only be a matter for speculation. As the figures for COHSE and NUPE do not allow identification of the effcts of competitive tendering on its ancillary membership, it is difficult to determine its full impact, although the data in Table 4.3 shows there has been a decline (14).

INDUSTRIAL RELATIONS AT LOCAL LEVEL

Industrial relations machinery
Perhaps the most prominent feature of local industrial relations in the NHS by the late 1970s was the formalisation of relations between management and staff organisations. This was manifested by the introduction of local joint negotiation/consultation committees, largely at district level - although they were also introduced at hospital and area health authority level (Brand and McGill, 1978; Dimmock and Mailly, 1982a). The nature of these committees varied between health authorities: in some, prehaps a minority, they were fora for genuine negotiation of issues of concern to management and staff: in others, they were a channel of communication whereby management passed information on to the trade unions (Dimmock and Mailly, op. cit.). The subject matter of local negotiations/consultation includes such issues as local bonus schemes, staff rotas, health and safety, statutory holidays, gradings, discipline, grievance

Table 4.3   Membership of the four largest NHS Trade Unions 1974-85

Union	1974	1976	1978	1980	1981	1982	1983	1984	1985
NUPE	400,000	650,530	712,392	699,156	703,998	702,159	689,046	673,445	663,776
NHS	163,000	220,000	250,000	-	-	-	-	225,000 approx	-
COHSE (almost all NHS)	143,749	200,689	215,246	216,482	230,709	231,504	222,869	214,321	212,980
RCN	90,616	90,000	134,389	181,111	196,813	223,324	230,786	245,000	251,127
NALGO	541,918	683,011	729,405	782,343	739,013	726,441	780,037	766,390	752,131
NHS	-	-	84,087	-	-	-	-	-	71,249

Figure are taken from the reports of Certification Officer 1974-86. Membership figures for NUPE in the NHS are an estimate based upon information given to the National Health Service Yearbook (1986) edited by M. Chaplin; membership figures for NALGO came direct from the union. Where there is a blank, figures are not available.

and other procedures. The growth of procedural agreements was perhaps one of the most important developments in this period, as local management - required by legislation and the ACAS Codes of Practice - negotiated procedures on discipline, grievance and time off for trade union duties and activities. The 'proceduralisation' of local industrial relations was given national encouragement through the negotiation of 'enabling agreements' by the General Whitley Council (GWC). In particular, the GWC agreed a framework for consultation in 1979 and for a local disputes procedure in 1980. However, throughout this period local management was forced to take the initiative given the relative absence of advice from the Whitley machinery (Dimmock, 1982b).

Despite the apparent growth of procedures, both ACAS (1978) and Bosanquet (1979) criticised health authorities for lack of order in their industrial relations. To quote Bosanquet: 'In 90 per cent (of health districts) the main problems were objective ones to do with the lack of a system - of procedures for dealing with change'. However, in the case of ACAS, the timing of their collation of evidence was perhaps the very period when procedural arrangements were becoming common and, as Barnard and Harrison (1986) point out, in the case of both Bosanquet and ACAS, the assessments were based upon limited evidence and might have been more difficult to sustain in the face of more comprehensive knowledge. Even by 1986, however, the presence of procedures in the NHS could not be said to be comprehensive, particularly with reference to the implementation of the national disputes procedure (Swales, Collins and Walden, 1986) and, as Dimmock and Mailly (1982b) reported, many health authorities had good, local reasons for not having some procedures. Moreover, a lack of procedures did not necessarily mean the conduct of industrial relations was not formalised.

The ACAS evidence to the Royal Commission made other criticisms of industrial relations in the NHS which were perhaps more valid. It pointed to the lack of professionalism in industrial relations in NHS management, the absence of a district personnel officer in some health districts, and a general lack of industrial relations policy in many of the old area health authorities. Following the ACAS Report, the DHSS initiated a considerable investment in training for NHS personnel in industrial relations. In the 1982 reorganisation, most health authorities appointed a district personnel officer. Batstone

(1980) argues that over recent years there has been a 'professionalisation' of the personnel function which has led to the 'institutionalisation' of trade unions (1980). The process of institutionalisation in the NHS had reached its peak prior to the 1982/83 dispute. The extent to which the personnel function has reached a position of influence in the determination of management policy-making, however, is unclear. McCarthy (1985) has argued that this is not the case, due in part to lack of local bargaining over the remuneration package. The actual position probably differs between health authorities. Certainly, the appointment of personnel directors within health authorities following the introduction of general management implies the influence of personnel within management has been consolidated.

ACAS criticised the trade unions for lack of co-ordination locally (through joint shop steward committees) and inter-union rivalry, particularly between NUPE and COHSE (1978). In the late 1970s, there was also an unwillingness in some area health authorities among TUC affiliated unions (particularly NUPE and ASTMS) to sit with non-TUC affiliates (such as the RCN) on joint negotiation and consultative committees. This issue seems to have diminished by the early 1980s (Dimmock and Mailly, 1982a). The rapid growth of both NUPE and COHSE over these years (see Table 4.3) led to competition for membership and reduced levels of co-operation locally. In addition, the differences between the professional trade unions (generally not affiliated to the TUC) and the ancillary staffs unions over the issue of industrial action led to a lack of co-ordination through joint shop steward committees, more commonly present in industry (Neale, 1983). It is estimated that trade union membership reached its highest density in 1981. Workplace organisation, although considerably more developed than a decade before, had not shifted the balance of power between management and staff. The circumstances favouring job control and work group power are not commonly present in the NHS, as Bosanquet (1982b) points out. In the arena of 'management relations' (Fox, 1966), the ancillary unions had made little impact whereas, in 'market relations', they had suffered serious defeats and seen their relative pay decline over the first half of the 1980s.

Local consequences of national disputes
The national disputes during the spring of 1979 highlighted the difficulties inherent in maintaining a consistent management response at health authority level. Equally, action was not very well co-ordinated on the unions' part. Overtime bans were difficult to continue for any length of time without breaks in the ranks of the trade unions representing ancillary staff, and sectional strikes were not conducive to solidarity (Neale, 1983). While sections of the army were mobilised at one point in the 1978 dispute in case of a complete withdrawal of labour by ambulancemen, in general the Labour government was ambivalent in its attitude towards the way management should respond to the industrial action. The Secretary of State initially wished to maintain control over the manner in which health authorities responded. Discretion was subsequently given to authorities to react in the manner they saw fit - later, that discretion was removed (Dyson, 1979). Generally speaking, few staff were suspended for not working normally, and most staff were paid unless they withdrew their labour completely. This prompted Dyson (op. cit.) to comment:

> Is the maintenance of patient services in the short term the one major objective of the management side, irrespective of its long-term consequences? If the answer is 'yes', the NHS is doomed to go through future industrial conflicts in ways that will be similar to this year's experience. Those who answer 'no' are not automatically sacrificing the short-term interests of patients. If trade union action forces the closure of even emergency services, it would be possible to consider major deployment of staff as well as the more extensive use of public volunteers.

Dyson's reflection on the 1979 disputes was a harbinger of developments which followed the election of the Conservative government in May 1979. In December of that year, the DHSS issued a circular entitled 'If Industrial Relations Break Down' (HC(79)20), partly in response to requests from regional personnel officers for some national guidance on the handling of disputes. The only instruction within the circular was that staff taking full strike action should not receive pay. The bulk of the advice was contained in an appendix to the circular, which suggested alternative

145

responses to industrial action which fell short of a
full strike. One alternative was to send staff home
until they were prepared to work normally; another
was the deduction of pay when full services were not
provided; another the use of volunteers. The
circular acknowledged that its suggestions, if
applied by hospital management, could provoke an
escalation of the dispute. There was no discussion
of the movement towards a negotiated settlement in
the context of local disputes towards which the
advice was also presumably aimed (Harrison, 1980).
The circular was greeted with hostility by the trade
unions (with whom it was not discussed), but was
welcomed by some NHS managers (Button, 1980). Its
impact on local management behaviour during
subsequent disputes has been less certain.

Although the employers' response to the 1982
dispute was more determined than in 1979, a survey
of 31 districts in the south-east of England (Morris
and Rydykowski, 1984), following the dispute,
discovered that responses to the industrial action
varied between health authorities. All managers
followed the only mandatory provision of HC(79)20 -
that staff on strike should not be paid or receive
bonus payments. However, the new 'freedom' provided
by circular HC(79)20 did not appear to produce a
comprehensive harder line among health authorities.
Of the 15 districts that experienced restrictive
working during the dispute, in only three cases were
deductions made from pay, and in only five were
staff actually sent home. Although the circular
suggested the use of volunteers, none of the
districts in their survey used external volunteers,
although they did employ managers and nurses on
duties not normally carried out by those members of
staff (though an increased reluctance to carry out
these duties was noted among some members of
management). In general, there seemed to be a tacit
agreement between management and staff that, if
management agreed to give exaggerated reports to the
press of the impact of the dispute, then unions
would not hit them so hard.

The 1982 dispute produced ripples locally which
did not die away immediately. The impact of the
dispute was not uniform. In those authorities in
which there had been close co-operation between
management and unions over implications of
industrial action for services to patients and
relations with the press, industrial relations did
not tend to suffer greatly as a consequence of the
dispute. However, in those authorities which took

action, such as sending home staff who refused to work normally or who used internal volunteers (the minority), industrial relations tended to be adversely affected (Morris and Rydykowski, op. cit.). Many local managers felt intensely frustrated by a dispute that was not within their remit to settle and in which they felt a degree of sympathy for the staff side's case. The wish for stability in industrial relations perhaps prompted the 'middle way' which seemed to be steered by management within most health authorities, despite strong government advice for management to take a hard line approach in response to industrial action (Morris and Rydykowski, op. cit.).

The introduction of general managers

One of the more significant government initiatives has been the introduction of general managers following the Griffiths Report (1983). As previously discussed, issues in regard to their pay and associated matters were determined outside the formal industrial relations structures. The appointment of district and general managers appears to have had only a superficial effect on local industrial relations. In local disputes, general managers, perhaps inevitably, have become the personification of management sides. While the new general managers have spoken about the need to seize the initiative in communicating with and involving the workforce in decision-making without reference to local trade union organisation, there is little evidence to suggest that consultative machinery has been dismantled. It seems more likely that, in circumstances where local union organisation has been significantly weakened by national initiatives, such as competitive tendering, general managers have found it easier to re-draw the local agendas for consultation. Experience since the early 1970s suggests that, in general, government rather than management plays the principal role in NHS industrial relations. In the context of industrial relations since 1979, the Conservative government can be said to have taken virtually all the initiatives, with only limited reference to NHS management. Its role has been to translate (albeit not unthinkingly and on occasions relatively unwillingly) the Conservative government policies at local level. The introduction of general management, while it fostered considerable uncertainty within health authorities, encountered little national or local opposition from generally

147

weakened trade union organisations. Indeed, the consequent management restructuring created considerable uncertainty within management itself. In terms of the turbulence created within management, the process of injecting new managerial philosophy was probably experienced as a more fundamental change than the 1974 NHS reorganisation.

One of the more significant responses to general management came from the RCN. Deeply concerned about the loss of nursing influence at senior management level, it conducted a major publicity campaign against the new philosophy. Newly appointed general managers may have found it necessary to placate nursing opinion in designing their management structures, but the role of the RCN was generally muted at local level - possibly it preferred political channels that were less public to achieve its interests.

CONCLUSION

After two terms in office, the Conservative government can reflect on sustained progress (in its own terms) in achieving a different climate in NHS industrial relations. Whether the changes to the industrial relations system of pay determination and the measures to increase organisational efficiency have been the outcome of a deliberate strategy or merely incremental opportunism remain a matter for speculation. However, its approach towards introducing these changes illustrated the relatively limited influence exercised by NHS management on national issues.

The 1982 dispute significantly weakened staff organisations, particularly the TUC unions with major NHS interests. By comparison, the single professional unions fared much better, especially the RCN, in achieving their longer run objectives for 'independent' methods of determining their members' remuneration. Nevertheless, the eventual settlement of the 1982 dispute; government's re-scheduling of subsequent awards to accommodate pay norms and public spending plans; and its almost cavalier attitude towards the TUC unions representing ancillary workers over the introduction of competitive tendering, all serve to re-emphasise the relative fragility of unionism in the NHS. Whether this approach is effective in the longer term given the manpower shortages envisaged for nursing and professions allied to medicine in the

1990s must be open to doubt. However, short-term expediency appears to be a traditional feature of government policy towards NHS pay (Clegg and Chester, 1957; Dimmock, 1982a).

The growth of trade union workplace organisation and influence was a concomitant of the aggressive bargaining strategies by the unions at national level during the 1970s. In consequence, by 1982 local management and unions had generally determined forms of industrial relations machinery and a relatively wide range of procedural and local substantive agreements. The evidence suggests that management were reluctant to place them in jeopardy in the 1982 dispute (Morris and Rydykowski, 1984). It is too early to tell how the introduction of general maangement has weakened local industrial relations arrangements. It seems likely that established local patterns of behaviour between unions and management will continue, albeit in a more muted form. However, this owes more to the impact of the initiatives on the part of Conservative government rather than to a conscious policy on the part of NHS managment.

NOTES

1. This figure is from the Office of Health Economics, Compendium of Health Statistics, London, 1986. The whole-time equivalent figure for those employed in the NHS is well below one million, indicating the amount of part-time employment there is in the NHS (the structure and make-up of the workforce in the public services is discussed more fully in Chapter 2).

2. The sums allocated are not to be exceeded (since the introduction of cash limits in 1976).

3. Originally nine functional councils were created: Administrative and Clerical; Ancillary Staffs; Community Dental; Medical and Hospital Dental; Professional and Technical 'A' (i.e. scientists, chaplains, professions supplementary to medicine other than laboratory scientific officers, speech therapists, and helpers in these professions); Professional and Technical 'B' (i.e. medical laboratory scientific officers, technicians in a wide range of departments, and works officers). A tenth council was added in 1974 when ambulancemen were transferred from local authority control to the NHS. The Medical and (Hospital) Dental and Community Dental councils exist in shadow form as

149

R. Mailly, S. J. Dimmock and A. S. Sethi

the pay and conditions of doctors and dentists are
decided by the Prime Minister on the recommendation
of the Doctors and Dentists Review Body formed in
1960. The creation of the review body for nurses
and the majority of the professions supplementary to
medicine has effectively replaced the Nurses and
Midwives Council and the Professional and Technical
'A' Council. Scientists, chaplains and speech
therapists have not been included in these
arrangements and a new Whitley Council - the
Scientific and Professional Staffs Council - has
been formed.

4. The NHS (Conditions of Remuneration) Order
1951 requires all health authorities to pay neither
more nor less than the rates agreed by Whitley
Councils.

5. Since the early 1970s the number of
hospitals as workplaces has declined, with a
continuing trend to close outlying (often smaller
and older) institutions and to concentrate acute
care in central district general hospitals.

6. The Trade Union and Labour Relations Act
created the Certification Officer whose duties
included issuing certificates of 'independence' to
organisations that fitted certain criteria. Only
'independent' trade unions have the protection of
the various 'rights' given in the auxiliary
legislation, e.g. time off for trade union duties
for their officers.

7. The King's Fund is an independent
charitable trust which researches into the provision
and management of health care in the United Kingdom.

8. Mr. Leonard Peach was seconded to the NHS
management board from IBM for a period of three
years. On the sudden resignation of the first
general manager of the board - Victor Paige - he
took over the duties of general manager in addition
to his personnel responsibilities.

9. There are already great divergences
between the grading of similar jobs between the
south-east and the rest of the UK, due to the effect
of the labour market. The likely introduction of
regional pay in the Civil Service makes this an even
stronger possibility.

10. The formula was introduced by the Labour
government in 1976 and is based on weighting systems
taking into account the birth rate, morbidity level
and age profile of a population within a particular
region. Broadly speaking, resources have been moved
from the London and south eastern regions towards
the northern regions.

11. Lord Rayner, following his investigations
into efficiency in the Civil Service, was asked by
the Prime Minister to examine methods of reducing
costs and bureaucracy in the NHS in 1982. Ten areas
of scrutiny were announced but not all of these have
been produced.

12. The Office of Health Economics Compendium
of Health Statistics report for 1987 points out that
resources have risen by only 26 per cent in volume
terms since 1973.   Wage and price inflation have
absorbed much of the increased NHS spending.

> Hospital spending has risen by one per cent a
> year in volume terms since 1980, one half less
> than the target growth needed to keep pace with
> rising demand from the increasing number of
> elderly people and medical advances, as well as
> to meet the government's policy objectives.

This shortfall, reports the OHE, indicates a
cumulative total underfunding of hospital resources
by about £400 million between 1980 and 1986.

13. The government has been favouring an
increase of manpower for 'direct' services as
opposed to 'indirect' services. Hospital manpower
rose by 13 per cent to nearly a million over the
decade. Doctors, nurses and midwives accounted for
most of the rise (OHE, 1987). The OHE point out,
however, that the figures are in part a statistical
artifact, as some of the increase was due to a
reduction in nurses' working hours in 1980.

14. This sub-section relies heavily on
research conducted by one of the authors, the
results of which are analysed in more detail in
Mailly, R. (1986) 'The Impact of Contracting-Out in
the NHS', Employee Relations, Vol. 8, No. 1, to
which readers are referred.

REFERENCES

ACAS (1978) Evidence for the Royal Commission on
    the NHS: Report No. 12, Advisory, Conciliation
    and Arbitration Service
Bain, G. and Price, R. (1983) 'Union Growth', in
    Bain, G. (ed.) Industrial Relations in
    Britain, Blackwell, Oxford
Barnard, K. and Harrison, S. (1986) 'Labour
    Relations in Health Service Management', Social
    Science and Medicine, 22(11), pp. 1213-28
Batstone, E. (1980) 'What have Personnel Managers

R. Mailly, S. J. Dimmock and A. S. Sethi

done for Industrial Relations?', _Personnel Management_, June, pp. 36-9
Bosanquet, N. (1979) 'The Search for a System', in Bosanquet, N. (ed.) _Industrial Relations in the NHS: The Search for a System_, King Edward's Hospital Fund for London, London
Bosanquet, N. (1982a) 'Industrial Relations in the NHS after the Breakdown of the Old Colonial System', _Public Administration Bulletin_, 40, pp. 40-55
Bosanquet, N. (1982b) 'What is the Impact of Trade Unionism on the NHS?', _Health Service Manpower Review_, 8(2), pp. 11-4
Brand, C. and McGill, I. (1978) _A Review of the East Sussex AHA Machinery for Joint Consultation_, Brighton Polytechnic, Brighton
Button, J. (1980) 'Responses to Industrial Action (2)', _Health Services Manpower Review_, 6(1), pp. 17-9
Carpenter, M. (1982) 'The Labour Movement in the National Health Service (NHS) UK', in Sethi, A. S. and Dimmock, S. (eds.) _Industrial Relations and Health Services_, Croom Helm, London
Clay, T. (1987) _Nurses, Power and Politics_, Heinemann Nursing, London
Clegg, H. A. and Chester, T. E. (1957) _Wage Policy and the Health Service_, Blackwell, London
Clegg, H. A. (1979) _Standing Commission on Pay and Comparability, Report No. 1: Local Authority and University Manual Workers, NHS Ancillary Staffs and Ambulancemen_, HMSO
Dimmock, S. (1979) 'Dilemmas of Medical Representation: A View', in Bosanquet, N. (ed.) _Industrial Relations and Health Services_, Croom Helm, London
Dimmock, S. (1982a) 'Incomes Policy and Health Services in the UK', in Sethi, A. S. and Dimmock, S. J. (eds.) _Industrial Relations and Health Services_, Croom Helm, London
Dimmock, S. (1982b) 'Collective Bargaining among Non-Professional and Allied Professional Employees in the Health Sector UK', in Sethi, A. S. and Dimmock, S. J. (eds.) _Industrial Relations and Health Services_, Croom Helm, London
Dimmock, S. and Farnham, D. (1975) 'Working with Whitley in Today's NHS', _Personnel Management_, January, pp. 33-7
Dimmock, S. J. and Mailly, R. (1982a) 'Joint Consultation Arrangements in the NHS', _Industrial Relations Briefing Paper No. 1_,

Leeds University, Leeds

Dimmock, S. J. and Mailly, R. (1982b) 'Time off for Trade Union Duties and Activities in the NHS', Industrial Relations Briefing Paper No. 2, Leeds University, Leeds

Dyson, R. F. (1979) 'Industrial Action 1979: What Can We Learn?', British Medical Journal, 26th May, pp. 1435-7

Dyson, R. F. (1982) 'The Future of Whitley and Pay Bargaining', Hospital and Health Services Review, September, pp. 237-41

Dyson, R. F. (1985) 'Making Whitley Work: Is it Time to Stop Trying?', Health Services Manpower Review, 11(1), pp. 4-6

Dyson, R. F. and Spary, K. (1979) 'Professional Associations', in Bosanquet, N. (ed.), op. cit.

Fox, A. (1966) Industrial Sociology and Industrial Relations, HMSO, London

Fryer, R. (1979) 'Trades Unions and the Cuts', Capital and Class, VIII, pp. 94-112

Fryer, R., Fairclough, A. J. and Manson, T. B. (1974) Organisation and Change in the National Union of Public Employees, NUPE, London

Fryer, R., Fairclough, A. J. and Manson, T. B. (1978) 'Facilities for Female Shop Stewards: The Employment Protection Act and Collective Agreements', British Journal of Industrial Relations, 16(2), pp. 160-74

Gray, P. (1980) 'How to Run a Comparability Commission and Why the Clegg Commission made such a Mess of the Last One', Health Services Manpower Review, 6(3), pp. 16-21

Greenborough, J. (1984) First Report on the Review Body on Pay for Nurses, Midwives, Health Visitors and Professions supplementary to Medicine

Griffiths, R. (1983) National Health Service Management Inquiry: Letter to the Secretary of State

Harrison, S. (1980) 'Responses to Industrial Action - Assumptions and Evidence', Health Services Manpower Review, 6(1), pp. 15-7

Incomes Data Services (1984) Public Sector Unit Report No. 4 - NHS Ancillary Staffs

Incomes Data Services (1985) Public Sector Unit Report No. 2 - NHS Ancillary Staffs

Industrial Relations Review and Report (IRRR) (1984) Pay and Benefits Bulletin, No. 329

Institute of Personnel Management/Incomes Data Services (1986) Competitive Tendering in the Public Sector, IPM/IDS, London

R. Mailly, S. J. Dimmock and A. S. Sethi

Key, A. (1987) 'Contracting Out in the NHS', in
    Harrison, A. and Gretton, J. (eds.) Health
    Care UK, Policy Journals, Newbury
King's Fund/NAHA (1985) NHS Pay - A Time for
    Change, NAHA, Birmingham
Leopold, J. and Beaumont, P. (1986) 'Pay
    Bargaining and Management Strategy in the NHS',
    Industrial Relations Journal, 17(1), pp. 32-45
Lloyd, P. and Blackwell, R. (1985) 'Manpower
    Economics, Management and Industrial Relations
    in the Civil Service', Industrial Relations
    Journal, 16(4), pp. 25-37
McCarthy, M. (1983) A New System of Pay
    Determination for the NHS: A Contribution
    Towards the Debate, King Edward's Hospital Fund
    for London, London
McCarthy, M. (1985) 'Once More with a Feeling:
    The Griffiths Report and Personnel', Health
    Services Manpower Review, 11, pp. 3-5
McCarthy, W. (1976) Making Whitley Work, HMSO,
    London
Mailly, R. (1986) 'The Impact of Contracting Out
    in the NHS', Employee Relations, 8(1)
Manson, T. B. (1977) 'Management, Professions and
    the Unions: A Social Analysis', in Stacey, M.
    (ed.) Health and the Division of Labour, Croom
    Helm, London
Megaw, J. (1982) Inquiry into Civil Service Pay,
    HMSO, London
Miles, A. W. and Smith, D. (1969) Joint
    Consultation: Defeat or Opportunity?, King
    Edward's Hospital Fund for London, London
Morris, G. and Rydykowski, S. (1984) 'Approaches
    to Industrial Action in the NHS', Industrial
    Law Journal, 13(3), pp. 153-64
National Association of Health Authorities (NAHA)
    (1983) Pay Determination in the NHS - A System
    for the Future, Birmingham
NAHA/King's Fund (1983) Pay Determination in the
    NHS: Conclusions of the Strathallan Seminar,
    Birmingham
National Board for Prices and Incomes (1967) Pay
    and Conditions of Manual Workers in Local
    Authorities, the Health Service, Gas and Water
    Supply, Report No. 27, Cmnd. 3230, HMSO, London
National Board for Prices and Incomes (1971) The
    Pay and Conditions of Ancillary Workers in the
    National Health Service, Report No. 166, HMSO,
    London
Neale, J. (1983) Memoirs of a Callous Picket:
    Working for the NHS, Pluto Press, London

154

NHS Unlimited (1984) Contracting Out 'Ancillary' Services - the Health Authority View, NHS Unlimited, London

Office of Health Economics (1987) Compendium of Health Statistics

Office of Health Economics (1980) Compendium of Health Statistics

Royal Commission on the NHS (1978) Report, HMSO, London

Swales, A. I. R., Collins, P. and Walden, R. (1986) 'The Resolution of Disputes', Health Services Manpower Review, 22(1), pp. 2-5

Social Services Committee (1986) Public Expenditure on the Social Services, HMSO, London

Thomason, G. (1986) 'The Pay Review Bodies', Health Services Manpower Review, 11(3), pp. 2-3

Trades Union Congress (1981) Improving Industrial Relations in the National Health Service, London

Trades Union Congress (1984) Contractors' Failures: The Privatisation Experience, London

Trainor, R. (1984) 'A Directory of the National Health Service Whitley Council System', Health Service Manpower Review, Keele

Undy, R. (1978) 'The Devolution of Bargaining Levels and Responsibilities in the TGWU 1965-75', Industrial Relations Journal, 9(3)

Winchester, D. (1983) 'Industrial Relations in the Public Sector', in Bain, G. (ed.) Industrial Relations in Britain, Blackwell, Oxford

Chapter 5

BARGAINING STRATEGIES IN LOCAL GOVERNMENT

I. Kessler (1)

Local Government employs nearly three million workers. Apart from the half million teachers, dealt with in Chapter 6, and police and firefighters, the majority of workers fall within two bargaining groups: manual, and administrative, professional, technical and clerical (APT&C). Each covers a wide range of occupations employed in differing combinations by all authorities.

The ordered regulation of industrial relations for local authority manual and white collar workers through the establishment of bargaining machinery based on the Whitley model, was a long and far from smooth process. It involved the integration of a diverse range of occupations and the co-ordination of around 1,400 independent employing units. Initial attempts to establish unified machinery immediately following the Whitley Reports, 1916-17, were unsuccessful. While regional or provincial level agreements were reached in some parts of the country, the pre-1917 practice of authorities determining terms and conditions for their own employees continued to be widespread. The National Joint Councils for manual and APT&C workers were finally established on a firm basis in 1946 with the legal right of unilateral access to arbitration proving decisive. As MacIntosh noted: 'If authorities could be made to pay the same rates as other authorities were paying then it became crucially important that they should play a part in determining wages' (1955: 152).

The sustained and relatively peaceful operation of the national machinery throughout the 1950s and 1960s owed much to a favourable context character-ised by increasing local government employment and expenditure and, in particular, public expenditure planning mechanisms which provided for the absorption of increased labour costs by central government. Bargaining became highly centralised with comprehensive agreements reached nationally and, partly as a consequence, local management and trade union organisation remained largely undeveloped. There was certainly little scope for the kind of workplace activity which the 1968 Donovan Report had identified as undermining national agreements in the private manufacturing sector.

The consensual Whitley machinery came under pressures from the late 1960s which were sustained for much of the next decade. These pressures derived from a number of inter-related factors. Pay conflict emerged in 1969-70 largely in response to the perceived discriminatory impact of incomes policy. Amongst APT&C workers there was particular concern at the difficulties in taking advantage of the scope for expanding earnings opportunities through increased productivity, available to many groups under the 1965-69 incomes policy. This frustration was reflected in the repudiation by local government delegates at a National and Local Government Officers Association (NALGO) Group Conference in September 1969 of a two-year nationally negotiated agreement (Newman, 1982).

In the case of the local authority manuals, the National Board for Prices and Incomes (NBPI) had made a suggestion for linking pay and productivity through the introduction of local bonus schemes. In practice, however, these schemes related to a small proportion of the workforce and were slow to be implemented. The limited scope for most manuals to improve on low basic pay levels prompted the unions to pursue national minimum pay targets. Unofficial action, primarily by London refuse collectors in 1969, was succeeded the following year by the 'dirty jobs strike' with the TUC minimum target of £16.50 as a key objective. The Scamp Committee set up to settle the dispute after four weeks of action endorsed the NBPI analysis of the low pay problem but within its terms of reference was unable to make any fundamental proposals on the issue.

More general changes were to take place from the mid-1970s as local government was reorganised. A rationalised two-tier local government structure of shire and urban counties and districts introduced in 1974 reduced the number of authorities by around two-thirds to 456 in England and Wales (518 including the Scottish regions and districts). This reorganisation was accompanied by an attempt to

provide a coherent and streamlined model for
management organisation in which the personnel
function was to figure significantly (2). Yet
within this changed context many of the tensions of
the late 1960s were to reassert themselves.

The uneven impact of incomes policies again led
local authority pay to fall relative to private
sector groups. But to this was added the
considerable impact of high inflation on living
standards. Union concerns in this respect were
reflected in the manuals' claim for 1977 which noted
that:

> In a period of high inflation, it is even more
> essential to ensure that the low paid do not
> suffer. Local authority workers cannot afford
> to take further cuts in real pay. Their
> starting point is too close to the breadline.

Local authority trade unions were becoming more
assertive, campaigning organisations. The action
taken by local authority white collar workers in
pursuit of their London weighting claim in 1974
represented the first industrial action taken by
NALGO in pursuit of a major claim. This was
followed in 1978 by a period of prolonged action by
local authority social workers. The National Union
of Public Employees (NUPE) was to achieve a more
prominent reputation as a 'militant' union, rooted
in the leading role it had played in the 1970
strike. This reputation was to linger long in the
public mind, finding its fulfilment in the events of
the 'Winter of Discontent' in 1978-79.

The industrial action of 1979 was launched in
the face of the Labour government's five per cent
pay limit as set out in its White Paper, 'Winning
the Battle Against Inflation'. The action again
coalesced around the TUC minimum pay figure which,
since its achievement by the manuals in 1974, had
continued to represent an important benchmark for
the unions. The 'Winter of Discontent' marked a
major breakdown in the manual bargaining machinery
and was only finally resolved by the establishment
of the Standing Commission on Pay Comparability with
the local authority manuals as its first reference.
The consequence of the action, however, went well
beyond local authority industrial relations. The
action contributed to the defeat of the Labour
government and its replacement with a government
committed to a philosophy inimical to the
development of the public service sector.

Furthermore, it created a climate in which the new government could more generally seek to weaken the trade union movement.

It has been argued that the change in government policy objectives from the 1970s, as commitments to growth and full employment were replaced by a concern to reduce inflation, with attempts to restrain public expenditure and introduce new control mechanisms, marked a watershed in the development of public sector industrial relations (Winchester, 1983). As is pointed out in Chapter 1, it is equally apparent that while these changed policy objectives remained central after 1979, their pursuit from a fundamentally different ideological base resulted in significant qualitative changes in both the general and public sector industrial relations context.

Accounting for around a quarter of all public spending, it was inevitable that a government committed to reducing public expenditure would exert considerable pressure on local government (Douglas and Lord, 1986). Three analytically distinct, albeit closely related, developments emerged from this pressure combining to significantly change the bargaining context for local authority manual and white collar workers in the post-1979 period. The first was a central government emphasis on the importance of reducing local authority manpower. As a means of highlighting changes in employment levels, Manpower Watch figures have since been produced on a quarterly basis. In the main, however, the Secretary of State for the Environment has had to rely on exhortations to authorities which remain possible for decisions on patterns and levels of employment (Travers, 1982).

The second development was the increased importance attached to the need for local authority services to be 'efficient', providing 'value for money'. This can partly be related to the financial constraints imposed on authorities. It is also associated with the government's ideological belief that these principles are best pursued through the testing of services in the market place. This juxtaposition of financial imperative and ideological commitment was captured in the government's consultative paper, 'Competition in the Provision of Local Authority Services' (1985), which stated:

> At a time when it remains of paramount importance to restrain public expenditure, local authorities' resources must be used so as

> to secure the maximum value for money. With
> this end in view, it is the Government's
> declared and continuing intention to promote
> the extension of free competition in the
> provision of local authority service.

Although clearly stated in circulars sent to
authorities from the Department of the Environment,
this approach has also been supported by statutory
mechanisms. The Planning and Land Act 1980
introduced compulsory competitive tendering for
buildings, highways and maintenance work. The Green
Paper proposals extending this process over a wider
range of service were temporarily shelved before the
1987 general election, but have since been
resurrected.

The third and most fundamental development was
the change in the financial framework within which
local authorities operate. It has three dimensions.
Firstly, there has been a significant shift from
central government to local authority financing of
local services as sizeable reductions have been made
in the percentage of authority expenditure met by
central government grant. Thus, between 1979 and
1985 relevant expenditure financed by grant fell
from 61 per cent to 46 per cent. Secondly, central
government has attempted to exert an increasingly
tight control on local authority expenditure. From
the imposition of cash limits on the money provided
centrally, the government has sought to exert a
control over total local authority expenditure
introducing penalties, targets and rate capping with
varying impact on individual authorities. Thirdly,
the introduction of control mechanisms designed to
impose the discipline of the market on local
authorities has produced an extremely close
relationship between employee terms and conditions
and local expenditure plans. In the absence of
central financial adjustments to meet unanticipated
labour costs, improvements in terms and conditions
have implications for levels of employment and the
provision of local services. The establishment of
these links has rendered the process of bargaining
of importance not only to politicians and trade
unionists in their ability to pursue policy
objectives, but also to wider local community with a
stake in the level of service provision.

In the changed context which has developed
since 1979, the central issue has become the
functional viability of national bargaining given
the special and distinctive features and needs of

the different types of authorities covered. The changes outlined above have not had a uniform impact or elicited the same responses from authorities subject to differing local economic and political forces and varying structurally in terms of their geographical size and complexion, the functions they perform and the nature of the workforce employed. Consideration of this central issue gives rise to three questions: what kind of pressures have been exerted by local authorities on national representatives and negotiators; how has the shape or direction of bargaining strategies on employer and trade union sides been affected by these pressures; and what kind of developments have taken place at the local level in response to national settlements?

This chapter is structured around these three questions. It is suggested, however, that the answers will not be the same for the two bargaining groups. It is argued that variation in the structure of collective bargaining for manuals and white collar workers will influence employer and trade union behaviour at national and local levels. More specifically, analysis of differences in four dimensions of collective bargaining - coverage, level of bargaining, scope of agreements and representation - will help explain variation in local and national processes (Kessler and Winchester, 1982) (3).

THE STRUCTURE OF COLLECTIVE BARGAINING

Coverage
The National Joint Council for local authority manual and white collar workers covers two of the largest bargaining units in the United Kingdom. They both incorporate around 450 independent employing authorities and cover diverse ranges of occupational groups. There are, however, important differences in the compositions of these units. The manual group is characterised by a predominance of part-time women workers and includes mainly unskilled and semi-skilled occupations. Thus, around two-thirds of the 890,000 manuals in England and Wales are part-time women, employed mainly in the two largest local authority services - education and social service - as school meals workers and cleaners and as home helps and care assistants. The remaining mainly full-time male workers are employed in refuse collection and disposal, road-works,

transport, leisure, parks and housing. The white collar group, in contrast, has well under a quarter of its 646,000 workers in England and Wales employed on a part-time basis. It encompasses occupations ranging from those characterised by minor status and low qualifications - clerical and secretarial staff - to those of a professional and quasi-professional nature such as solicitors, architects, surveyors and social workers. The bargaining unit therefore spans very different levels of managerial authority.

The salary and grading structures developed for these two groups have inevitably differed markedly in response to the workers covered. A simple seven grade manual structure introduced in 1969, reduced in 1985 to five grades, can be set aside a much more complex white collar salary structure. Six unified APT&C scales plus senior office and principal officer scales range across a 49-point spinal column. Provision is also made for 'miscellaneous grades' which cover employees perceived as not wholly white collar or manual as well as for prescribed grades which cover specific occupational groups and take a number of points from the spinal column for their incremental scale. Furthermore, while the national manuals agreement allocates each occupational group to a grade, the white collar agreement allows authorities to adapt most job requirements to fit the salary scale they wish to pay.

Level and scope of bargaining

National negotiations on pay and conditions provide the most important level of collective bargaining for manuals and white collar workers. National agreements are comprehensive, covering basic pay rates, holiday entitlements, hours, premium payments and allowances. The 14 manual and 13 APT&C provincial councils represent an intermediary level of bargaining dealing with disputes and forming an integral part of the employers' consultative machinery rather than playing a direct role in pay determination.

There are, however, important differences between the two groups in the scope and level of bargaining. For manuals, the watershed in the development of local bargaining was the 1967 NPBI Report (No. 29) with its proposal to introduce bonus schemes as a means of bolstering earnings opportunity and productivity. Yet these schemes, as already suggested, had no impact on the majority of manuals. They were applied mainly to full-time, male, occupational groups - refuse collectors and roadmen - whose work lent itself to work measurement more easily than that of part-time women in the caring service. As important, some male manual workers had the power to push for these schemes and the resultant increases in earnings. In 1978, 72 per cent of full-time workers were in receipt of bonus payments, while only one per cent of part-time workers received them. Indeed, in 1979, basic pay still represented 92.8 per cent of average weekly earnings for part-time women, whereas the equivalent figure for men was 70.5 per cent.

For white collar workers the scope for local bargaining has mainly been based on the discretion available to authorities on the grading of most occupations. There were pressures in the mid-1970s for the greater development of bargaining opportunities: in 1976 the NALGO conferences passed a motion calling for the introduction of a shop steward system and, in 1977, demanded consideration to be given to abandoning Whitleyism. The latter proposal was averted with the leadership successfully arguing that Whitleyism had the flexibility to allow stronger branches to bargain locally while retaining a 'safety net' of national conditions for those that were weaker. Indeed, recent survey findings (Ingham, 1985) suggest that a significant proportion of authorities bargain over white collar holiday entitlements and hours, certainly a far higher proportion than those who bargain over these issues for manuals.

Representation
A wide variety of organisations have representatives on the employer and trade union sides of the NJCs, as indicated in Table 5.1. The table, however, cannot provide a complete picture of the dispersal of power between organisations or the potential lines of division and conflict. Indeed, in relation to the trade union side of the APT&C NJC, the table is slightly misleading; NALGO's dominance is uncontested despite the presence of four other unions. NALGO, originally created as a local government trade union, organising from 'tea boy to town clerk' (Spoor, 1967), has around 430,000 local government members. It has established its dominance on the NJC through its control of the provincial council seats which, in turn, reflects its membership strength within local authorities. This dominance has inevitably tended to shift the focus of interst in discussing the trade union side

163

I. Kessler

Table 5.1   Composition of National Joint Councils

NJC for Manuals		NJC for APT&C Staff	
EMPLOYERS' SIDE	Seats	EMPLOYERS' SIDE	Seats
Association of Municipal Authorities	7	Association of Municipal Authorities	6
Association of County Councils	6	Association of County Councils	6
Association of District Councils	6	Association of District Councils	4
Provincial Councils	20	Provincial Councils	16
Scottish Council	4	Scottish Council	4
Northern Ireland Council	2		
	45		36
TRADE UNION SIDE	Seats	TRADE UNION SIDE	Seats
GMBATU	12	Provincial Councils	16
NUPE	9	Scottish Council	4
TGWU	9	NALGO	8
		GMBATU	2
		NUPE	2
		TGWU	1
		COHSE	1
	30		34

from inter-union relations to the internal decision-making of a single union.

The manual trade union side has, in contrast, been subject to periodic inter-union rivalry. The number of General Municipal, Boilermakers and Allied Trade Union (GMBATU) and Transport and General Workers Union (TGWU) seats in comparison to those of NUPE reflects the traditional strength of the general unions in local government rather than existing membership levels. Thus, NUPE has around 400,000 local authority members, GMBATU 220,000 and TGWU 60,000. NUPE's strength reflects 'aggressive' recruitment drives particularly amongst isolated and relatively inaccessible part-time women workers. The consequence of these drives has been to unsettle inter-union relations (4) on occasions, with NUPE resenting that its membership strength is not reflected in the NJC composition and the two general unions being concerned at NUPE's 'opportunistic' recruitment tactics. They have also resulted in a marked difference in the membership composition of the unions with the predominance of full-time men in the TGWU being set against NUPE's part-time women. Nonetheless, the scope for inter-union conflict remains limited when compared with the underlying divisions apparent on the employer sides of the NJCs.

The potential divisions within the employer sides of the two NJCs present major problems of co-ordination for the secretariat of the Local Authority Conditions of Service Advisory Board (LACSAB), the employers' association covering all local authority bargaining groups. These divisions can in large part be related to the distinctive features of individual authorities discussed earlier and, emerging at the national level, they have added a degree of intra-organisational conflict (Walton and McKersie, 1965) unusual amongst employer sides in British negotiations. Potential division can be identified along three lines.

The first is the party political line. It is a unique feature of collective bargaining in local government that representatives - councillors - from different political parties are directly involved in industrial relations with the result that party differences naturally encroach upon the bargaining process. Secondly, divisions of interest can develop around the composition of local authority workforces. Differences in functions performed produce variations in the occupational make-up of workforces with the result that the terms and

conditions of particular groups are not of equal
interest to all authorities. Finally, divisions may
be related to size of authorities. The number of
manuals and white collar employees will vary
significantly between authorities of different
sizes. This may, in turn, be associated with the
character of personnel and broader management skills
which are likely to be more developed in larger
authorities.

The differences between authorities are to some
extent linked to authority type and, as a
consequence, are represented through the three local
authority employer associations: the Association of
Metropolitan Authorities (AMA); the Association of
County Councils (ACC); and the Association of
District Councils (ADC). All authorities employ
manuals and white collar staff and all three
associations are, therefore, represented on the two
NJCs. The situation is, however, complicated by the
fact that certain divisions cut across the formal
institutional machinery of the employer sides. For
example, the Conservative controlled ACC delegations
who represent authorities carrying out the social
service and education functions, have many shared
interests with the Labour dominated AMA delegations.
Moreover, both organisations, employing the
overwhelming majority of manual and white collar
workers, share a concern at the level of ADC
representation on both NJCs (5).

Two further sets of relationships are worthy of
note. The first concerns the relationship between
central government and the respective employer
sides. In contrast to the teachers, where central
government can now determine terms and conditions on
the manual and the white collar NJCs, influence can
only be exerted indirectly through public
pronouncements of government wishes or the more
covert use of local government connections.
Attempts to exert such influence can have a variable
impact; in certain circumstances it can exacerbate
party political divisions with representatives using
the employer side as an arena for displaying the
strength of opposition or support for broader party
political policies. On other occasions, such
influence may be seen as central government
'interfering' or 'undermining' the local government
community, so producing a more unified response.
The second relationship of interest is that between
LACSAB secretariat and the councillors. As
suggested, LACSAB face significant difficulties in
seeking to co-ordinate the employer sides, but with

this concern to co-ordinate, the secretariat becomes an interest group in its own right with objectives to pursue during the negotiating process.

The bargaining machinery for manual and white collar workers thus shares a number of common features. The comprehensive agreements reached in both NJCs cover diverse ranges of occupational groups employed in varying combinations by all types of authority. However, important differences in the structure of collective bargaining remain. The concentration of mainly part-time female manuals in unskilled and semi-skilled jobs contrasts with the predominantly full-time white collar employees in posts ranging across skill and managerial levels. Moreover, significant variations are also apparent in those issues subject to local negotiation and in inter-union relations. The next section considers the way in which these differences have affected the process of collective bargaining.

THE PROCESS OF BARGAINING

Bargaining strategies
In the changed bargaining context after 1979, the responses of the union and employer sides of the NJCs have displayed certain similarities. Following the initial implementation of the Clegg Commission award for the manuals and the settlement arising from the 'in-house' comparability exercise for the APT&C staff in July 1979, the respective sides were forced to contemplate their future approaches. For the union sides, the succeeding years were characterised by the pursuit of traditional objectives through changing strategies. The 1980-82 period of nominal adherence to the TUC co-ordinated public service strategy gave way to a more parochial concern with attempts to seek improvements through careful review and adaptation of employment terms and conditions. The employers were moved to place increasing emphasis on 'ability to pay' in their response to claims. They began to develop their own sets of demands which could be put to unions as a return for the concessions they granted. This also involved a close examination of the total employment package as a means of identifying cost saving measures. Yet, while common features can be noted, there were marked differences between the two groups in the detailed shape and success of the union and employer side strategies.

Manual Trade Unions and Employers. In the early
1980s, the manuals, with a settlement date in
November and representing a large, visible group,
occupied an important strategic position in the
annual wage round. In the context of the public
sector, this position became particularly
significant as the manuals assumed the vanguard in
challenging cash limits and, from 1981, effectively
led the TUC co-ordinated public service strategy.
Union negotiators generally saw this position in the
wage round as a major handicap. The manuals had
limited bargaining power and, despite attempts to
isolate them as a 'special case', it was inevitable
that the employers were conscious of the likelihood
that the manual settlement could become a 'going
rate'. These concerns help explain the tenacity
with which the unions pursued a change of settlement
date, succeeding in 1983 when it was moved to
September.

The public service strategy of the TUC had a
presentational effect on the manual trade union
bargaining strategy; it scarcely influenced the
substantive objectives pursued in the negotiating
process. The manuals were required to present their
traditional objectives in terms of the 'core' TUC
aims in their claims. In 1981, for example, the
minimum low pay target was replaced by an increase
in line with inflation. As bargaining commenced,
however, the manual negotiators were quick to argue
the 'special' low pay position of the manuals in
support of their case, so detaching themselves from
other local government groups. Even this limited
impact of the co-ordinated strategy was, however,
shortlived.

The call to mobilise across the public service
sector in 1982 was made in response to the needs of
workers in the National Health Service rather than
in local government. While considerable support was
displayed, the action pointed to some of the
problems faced in achieving a unified approach. The
campaign revealed the difficulties which were always
likely to arise in seeking to mobilise workers for
sustained periods where their interests were not
directly at stake. Although public service unions
continued to exchange information through the TUC
and make token reference to increasingly loose core
aims, the NHS dispute marked the high point of the
strategy. As financial controls tightened, the
response of the unions was to turn more inwards.

The change in the manual union strategy from
1983, closely associated with the succession of John

Edmonds of the GMBATU as trade union side secretary, was characterised by a more overt recognition of the financial realities facing the employers. Although the traditional low pay target was formally reinstated in the 1983 claim, fundamental and wide-ranging proposals were also put forward. These had some attraction to the employers in helping to make cost savings as they moved towards this target. Three proposals, in particular, were suggested: a revision in the pay structure allowing re-grading to follow change in duties which would increase flexibility; a simplification of bonus schemes and a streamlining of the associated administration; and changes in methods of wage payment.

The former proposal, a revision in the pay structure, remained a central union concern in succeeding years. It was based on a union belief that the old structure was outdated, failing to reflect the changing nature of certain jobs, especially those of the home help and the care assistant. The potentially discriminatory nature of the grading structure within the terms of the equal pay for work of equal value legislation provided an added pressure for change to which the employers were as concerned to respond as the unions. With a shared interest in revision, progress has been made. In 1984, agreement was reached to carry out a job evaluation exercise, the results of which would provide the basis for the new structure. By February 1987 the job evaluation exercise had been completed and agreement reached on a new six grade structure (6). At the time of writing, pay rates for the new grades have yet to be agreed.

The manual trade union side has displayed considerable unity since 1979. The alacrity with which unions were prepared to allow their traditional objectives to be subsumed, albeit cosmetically, into the TUC core did vary. Nonetheless, union negotiators, charged with formulating a unified claim, retained considerable freedom of manoeuvre in bridging differences. Whether more fundamental conflicts will emerge in relation to discussions on the new grading structure remains an open question. The manual employers, in contrast, have had major difficulties in formulating a unified approach. Party political differences have emerged in relation to employer responses to pay claims. Despite a degree of genuine concern across the employer side for the low pay problem, Labour councillors have shown particular sympathy for the manual workers' plight. This has regularly produced voting along strictly party lines on employer discussions of pay offers. More fundamentally, however, divisions have arisen preventing the manual employers from developing a coherent set of objectives which could be brought to the negotiating table.

In the changed bargaining context of the 1980s, local authorities have expressed concerns about the functional viability of the national negotiating machinery. These concerns have been expressed in terms of the restrictive and outdated nature of some parts of the agreement. However, in the LACSAB secretary's words, these views emerged as 'slogans and grumbles':

> The lesson we must have learned is that we cannot bargain on slogans and grumbles about what exists. That is fine as a starter but it has to be converted into hard terms in an agreement. That is where we have failed. (LACSAB, 1983)

This 'failure' arose from attempts to develop objectives which exposed some of the divisions highlighted earlier in this chapter. Between 1980 and 1982 the employers' side of the NJC was particularly concerned with two issues: ways of reducing the cost of bonus schemes which in 1981 represented 8.6 per cent of the total manual paybill; and amendments to the national school meals agreement which included such costly provisions as the payment of a retainer fee to school meals workers over holiday periods. The latter issue, in particular, was clearly of concern only to the 104 education authorities. There was a natural reluctance on the part of those representing the vast majority of non-education authorities to jeopardise a pay settlement in pursuit of such objectives. In a discussion document entitled 'Changing the National Agreement', produced by LACSAB and circulated to all authorities at the end of 1983, it was concluded: 'The lesson to be drawn perhaps is that Employers should only pursue matters on which they can guarantee majority support'.

Prompted by the 'constructive' union approach and 'drawing the lessons' from previous efforts, the employers embarked on a much more systematic review of the scope for change, seeking to develop more broadly conceived objectives. In 1984, the LACSAB secretary identified the following aims:

1)   A pay settlement within the financial means of
     authorities;
2)   Productivity and better value for money;
3)   Flexibility at local level;
4)   Changes in outdated national agreements;
5)   Lower administrative overheads;
6)   A pay deal for manual workers which is fair by
     comparison with other groups.

This list of aims represented an attempt by LACSAB
to set out an all-embracing agenda for change,
incorporating the genuine concerns perceived to be
of importance to authorities. In seeking to develop
these objectives, eight specialist groups were set
up to review manpower utilisation and working
practices in the major manual occupations. The
reports of these groups, circulated to all
authorities, were followed by a paper asking for the
views of authorities on 'flexibility, harmonisation
and working time'.
     Whether the national agreement can adapt in
ways which meet the objectives remains an open
question. Certainly, fundamental issues remain to
be addressed by the employers' side. The process
has so far been concerned to identify areas of
potential change and divisions are more likely to
arise in seeking agreement on solutions, although
the scope for changes may have been severely
restricted by the decision to carry out the job
evaluation exercise before agreement had been
reached on altering working practices.
     The employer difficulties in developing a
coherence contrasts with the unity of the trade
unions, but it is equally apparent that both sides
have striven hard to adapt and revise their
approaches during the post-1979 period in attempts
to find more effective bargaining strategies. On
the union side, the changes have largely been
presentational. The consistently held aim of
improving low pay has been pursued through TUC co-
ordination, by putting forward manuals as a 'special
case', and then by providing proposals which address
the financial concerns of authorities. On the
employers' side it is the objectives which have
altered as a means of capturing more general
support. Specific and narrowly conceived aims,
appealing only to particular types of authority,
have had to give way to much more broadly based
concerns related to such concepts as 'flexibility'
and 'value for money'.

I. Kessler

APT&C trade unions and employers. The white collar
trade unions with a settlement date in July, at the
end of the annual wage round, have faced major
difficulties in linking with earlier groups as part
of the co-ordinated strategy. In one of the most
thoroughly argued trade union publications on the
common pay strategy, NALGO noted:

> The main problem with the development of the
> strategy in local government has been that,
> while it was designed to allow separate
> negotiating groups to campaign jointly and
> bring their full collective strength to bear in
> negotiations, the spread of the pay year from
> November to July has itself split up the
> different groups and allowed the employers to
> approach each set of negotiations separately.
> (NALGO, 1983: 23)

The APT&C trade union or staff side attempts to deal
with the resultant difficulties involved the early
submission of claims and calls for a change to an
April settlement date. Yet, as with the manuals,
adherence to the strategy had a presentational and
procedural effect rather than diverting attention
from traditional concerns.

Two related themes spanned the post-1979 years.
The first was an attempt to accommodate the
interests of members with widely ranging earnings
levels. Although consistent attempts were made to
restore the real value of earnings agreed following
the comparability exercise in July 1979, the exact
formulation of claims reflected the ebb and flow of
internal NALGO debates on the question of flat rate
or percentage increases and whether the union should
be pursuing egalitarian principles or seeking to
maintain differentials. Thus, in 1983, the claim
was for £15 plus three per cent, in 1984 for seven
per cent, in 1985 for a flat rate of £15, and in
1986 12 per cent or £900.

The second theme has been the staff side
attempt to use reform of the salary structure to
further the interests of its low paid members. Two
main areas of low pay have been distinguished: the
'miscellaneous grades' and the bottom end of the
spinal column. Consistent calls have been made for
the deletion of the six nationally designated
miscellaneous grades which provide little scope for
incremental progression, overlap with one another,
and are misapplied by authorities. Reform of the

172

lower end of the salary structure has concentrated on seeking payment of the adult rate at 18, rather than 21, and scale shortening.

Following a degree of success on structural reforms, particularly in relation to scale shortening 1, the NALGO bargaining strategy underwent a further change in 1986. A much 'higher profile' campaigning style was adopted, largely engineered by the leadership responding to a mixture of pressures. Lay activists and certain sections of the membership had been calling for a stronger line on pay for a number of years. Given the white collar position in the wage round, there was often limited scope for discussion on the level of the pay increase with a 'going rate' already well established. The national leadership had already laid the groundwork for a more determined campaign as early as October 1985. However, this approach was given added impetus by major developments amongst other groups of local government workers in subsequent months. The impact of these developments was emphasised in a statement at a full NJC meeting in January 1986. The staff side noted that within weeks of being offered 5.6 per cent:

> 7.4 per cent had been offered to the Chief Officers on top of the 4 per cent given for restructuring in the previous year. The staff side has also been told that a phased settlement was out of the question but then the teachers had been offered a deal costing 8.5 per cent in total. In addition, manual workers had been offered an 8.4 per cent increase following a ten-month settlement in the previous year. It seems as if there was no justice and that the APT&C staff were local government's poor relations.

The campaign was finally halted when NALGO failed to receive a majority vote for industrial action. The high vote for action, however, suggests that attempts will be made to build upon this more determined approach.

The employers' side of the APT&C NJC, in marked contrast to the manual employers, has displayed considerable success in developing a coherent strategy. A number of factors explain this relative success. There has not been the same degree of sympathy amongst Labour councillors for the demands of white collar workers with the result that party

political divisions have been less sharp. The
position of the white collar workers in the wage
round has also reduced the likelihood of party
political polarisation; with a 'going rate'
established, conflict over pay offers has been less
prevalent. The employers have, in addition, shared
certain broad objectives with the staff side on
reform of the salary structure which has encouraged
them to put forward proposals. Finally, the APT&C
agreement has provided authorities with considerable
flexibility in meeting local needs. Reform, thus,
involves more a 'fine tuning' rather than a
wholesale restructuring.

The employers' strategy gained real momentum in
1982 following a comprehensive consultation exercise
with local authorities. The widespread belief in
the need to rationalise and simplify the salary
structure was one shared with the staff side; and,
over the years, the separate technical, clerical and
administrative and professional divisions have been
merged into unified scales. Less agreement was
apparent on the position of the low paid. It
emerged from the consultation that authorities felt
themselves to be 'up market' at the bottom end of
the spinal column. This initially produced employer
proposals for restructuring to meet this concern.
Clearly, this approach was diametrically opposed to
that of the unions, and these proposals were quickly
forced off the negotiating table. Nonetheless, the
views of authorities on low pay have remained
largely unaltered.

Attempts to increase further the flexibility of
the national agreement have concentrated almost
wholly on removal of national prescriptions for
certain gradings. Indeed, reflecting a general
belief that there is limited scope for further
fundamental revisions to the national agreement,
very few authorities responded positively to the
most recent proposal to introduce further
flexibility in the form of performance pay. A
consultation document was circulated to authorities
in May 1985. Of 232 authorities responding, almost
half did not favour any further action on the
matter. Many of those prepared to accept work on
developing the concept were certainly not committed
to the idea, indicating that they still felt their
objectives could be achieved locally without change
to the national agreement. Faced with such a
response, the concept of performance pay has
disappeared from the bargaining scheme for the
immediate future.

Bargaining outcomes

Cash limits, unsupported by incomes policy after 1979, provided the Conservative government with a self-regulating means of controlling public sector pay. While different public sector employers and unions had some flexibility in the level of settlements reached, operating with an overall cash constraint meant that decisions made on pay had significant implications for jobs and the level of service provision. Under the cash limit regime, therefore, the outcome of the bargaining process came to constitute more than just the increase in pay rates and other improvements, but also included the impact of settlements on employment levels and other working practices.

This section considers bargaining outcomes in this broader context, considering first settlement levels and then their wider effects on employment and working practices. While similarities in pay increases are apparent between manual and white collar workers, the impact on employment levels has differed markedly.

While the cash limit system appeared to free central government from the need to intervene in the pay bargaining process, it has nonetheless retained a strong interest in local government negotiations. This partly stems from a belief that local government settlements, particularly the manual settlement, can have a significant impact on pay increases throughout the economy. In addition, the local government sector is not totally dependent on central funds and, consequently, not totally constrained by cash limits. In the absence of direct representation on most local government bargaining bodies, attempts to influence negotiations have been through public exhortation and 'semi-private' warnings to negotiators. The report of attempts by the Environment Secretary to influence the 1986 manual pay negotiations (Financial Times, 11.9.86) was certainly not an isolated example. It is questionable whether this kind of intervention has carried much weight in influencing settlement levels; the tightening constraints of the government's financial framework, however, certainly have.

Although the announcement of a pay assumption within cash limits was not designed to undermine the scope for some flexibility in settlement levels, for several years public service settlements displayed a considerable degree of uniformity (Winchester, 1983). Table 5.2 indicates that the estimated

Table 5.2 Bargaining Outturns, 1980-86

Date	MANUALS Settlement	Estimated paybill cost (actual paybill increase in brackets)	PAY FACTOR	Estimated paybill cost	APT&C settlement	Date
Nov 1980	£4.60 pw	7.5% (1.8%)	6.0%	7.5%	7.3% plus restructuring worth 0.2%	Jul 1981
Nov 1981	£4.60pw (1)	6.9% (5.9%)	4.0%	5.7%	5.7% (arbitration)	Jul 1982
Nov 1982	£3.25-£3.75 pw	4.8% (2) (5.0)	3.5%	4.894%	4.6-5.5%	Jul 1983
Nov 1983	£3.40 pw (3)	4.5%	3.0%	5.13%	4.6-5.6% (arbitration)	Jul 1984
Nov 1984 (4)	£4.00 pw	5.1% (3.7%)		5.6%	£309 pa for scales 1 and 2: 5.25 all others	Jul 1985
Sep 1985	£6.00 pw (plus merging bottom 3 grades)	8.0% (N/A)			5.95%	Jul 1986

(1) Hours also reduced from 40 to 39 with effect from 4.11.82.
(2) Excludes effect of reduction in working week
(3) Includes effect of reduction in working week
(4) 10-month deal, new review date September

increases in paybill costs for manuals and APT&C settlements have been similar for much of the period. The pay assumption figure has been breached each year but not by a significant amount suggesting that, while inevitably becoming the minimum for any increase, the figure has at the same time lowered expectations. Certainly the pay of manual and white collar workers has fallen since 1979 relative to both the cost of living and the earnings of other groups of workers. NALGO has calculated that between July 1979 and December 1985 purchasing power of white collar employees declined by nine per cent and, relative to earning in the rest of the economy, by 14 per cent. In the case of manuals, LACSAB figures indicate that, while average earnings in the whole economy rose by 62.0 per cent between November 1979 and November 1984, full-time manual earnings increased by 41.5 per cent over the same period.

Yet alongside similarities in the estimated paybill increases arising from settlements, there have been major differences between manuals and white collar workers in terms of the impact on jobs and working practices. Table 5.2 gives some indication of developments in employment practices for manuals. With the exception of 1982, when the cost of a reduction in hours had to be absorbed, each year has seen the <u>actual</u> increase in the paybill significantly lower than the settlement level.

Such a difference can arise from reductions in jobs, hours and overtime, as well as from a shift from full-time to part-time employment. Table 5.3 indicates that there have indeed been sizeable overall reductions in manual employment while also providing clear evidence of shifts from full-time employment to part-time. Thus, the relatively small overall fall of only 6.0 per cent in part-time women, in the context of strong impressionistic evidence of major reductions amongst this most vulnerable of groups, suggests that some of the losses may have been compensated for a change in the status of full-time women.

Although comparable figures for the actual increase in the paybill are not available for the APT&C staff, it is clear that the outturn increase has been considerably closer to the settlement level than for manuals. Average APT&C earnings have been rising slightly higher than the cost of annual settlements. In 1983, for example, while the estimated cost of the settlement was 5.7 per cent, the increase in average APT&C earnings was 6.4 per cent, a difference explained by changes within and between grades, promotions and regradings. In stark contrast to the manuals, the number of APT&C staff employed has been consistently increasing; between 1983 and 1985 the number of full-time equivalents increased from 553,500 to 574,300.

Table 5.3 Employment of Manual Workers by Group 1979-84

	Jun 1979	Jun 1983	Jun 1984	% change 1979-84
Full-time men	240,678	207,571	203,094	-15.6
Full-time women	119,052	86,706	86,132	-27.7
Part-time men	25,284	18,899	19,606	-22.5
Part-time women	623,092	590,421	585,418	-6.0
TOTAL	1,008,106	903,597	894,250	-11.3

Source: LACSAB, 19.10.84

It is important to appreciate that these aggregate figures on changes in employment levels, and indications of other changes in working practices, are based on a multitude of decisions made at local authority level. These decisions will not invariably be in line with the general trend, being designed to meet the specific circumstances of the authority and deriving from the interaction of a range of political, managerial and union pressures. More detailed consideration is given to the local decision-making process in the next section.

Bargaining Strategies in Local Government

In a period of cash constraints the ability to
pay has become the key criterion in pay
determination, overshadowing any broader conceptions
of comparability. For the unions, the shared
experience of these constraints in an economic and
legal environment which has weakened their
bargaining power initially produced an attempt to
co-ordinate across the sector. However, as the
organisational problems of such a strategy emerged
even its limited, presentational effect began to
wither. It became increasingly apparent that more
effective progress could be made through specific
changes to the salary and grading structures.
Significant developments have taken place in this
direction, but there have also been costs for the
unions over this period. Both manual and white
collar pay has fallen in real terms and relative to
other groups, as settlements have only just breached
pay assumption figures usually set well below the
inflation rate and movements in outside earnings.
For manuals some success on reform of the grading
structure has been countered by significant falls in
employment. The staff side have felt excluded from
special pay treatment although this must be weighed
against more buoyant employment levels.

Amongst the national employer representatives,
the increasing importance of 'ability to pay' has
prompted an increasing sensitivity to local
authority concerns about the outdated parts of the
national machinery and its failure to accommodate
their specific needs. The strategies pursued by the
two employer sides have been based upon these
concerns but there have been marked differences in
the extent to which coherent strategies have been
developed. The contrast between the manual
employers' representatives' difficulties and the
white collar employers' success in bringing
objectives to the bargaining table cannot solely be
accounted for by variations in the degree of
political divisiveness within the two sides. It is
certainly the case that, although a greater
politicisation of employer procedures has been
apparent on both NJCs, the sympathy of Labour
councillors for the manuals has sharpened political
differences. But equally significant has been the
fact that, in seeking to reform a much more rigid
and prescriptive grading structure, the manual
employers have exposed the major differences of
interest between authority types largely channelled
and expressed through the national local authority
associations. For the white collar employers, the

potential sharpness of conflict has been blunted by
a more flexible agreement requiring less fundamental
change.
    In developing their strategies both the
employer and trade union sides of the two NJCs have
been seeking to respond to the pressures on their
respective members at the local level generated by
the post-1979 financial and statutory frameworks.
There are, nonetheless, limits on the extent to
which national agreements, however much they are
modified and revised, can meet the interests of
employing organisations with such differing
structures, needs and policy objectives. In
voluntarily adhering to national agreements, local
authority employers and trade unionists commit
themselves to using the resources at their disposal
within the constraints imposed by those agreements.
The manner in which resources have been used and
constraints have been accommodated can be expected
to vary and it is to this process of accommodation
at the local level that attention now turns.

INDUSTRIAL RELATIONS AT LOCAL AUTHORITY LEVEL

The local authority constitutes a markedly different
employing unit from the factory which for so many
years formed the focus of analysis and theorising on
workplace industrial relations. The geographical
areas covered by the local authority and the
consequent dispersal of the workforce, the range of
self-contained services, and the identity of
employers' locally accountable party political
representatives suggests that direct comparisons of
local authority and factory workplace industrial
relations are of extremely limited value.
    It is also important to re-emphasise that local
authorities do not represent a homogeneous set of
employing units. The structural differences between
authority types in terms of the areas covered, the
urban-rural balance, the services performed and the
character of their workforces, have already been
seen to generate differences of interest which,
channelled through local associations, have had a
significant effect on the national bargaining
process. These same differences have also been
extremely influential in shaping industrial
relations at the local authority level. While they
have obviously not determined the character of local
union and management organisation, they have imposed

significant constraints, and influenced the types of issues unions and management have been forced to confront and the way they have been handled.

This section is divided into three parts. The first and second consider, in turn, the development of union and management organisation, focusing in particular upon variation in the character of such organisation. The third looks at how these organisational variations are translated into behavioural differences, concentrating on how unions and management have responded to the pressures of the 1980s in terms of actions and policies on local employment practices and procedures.

Local union organisation

The pressures of the post-1979 period have impacted upon the relatively new emerged and fragile steward organisation. Shop stewards were not officially recognised in local government until 1969 and, although worker representatives certainly existed before that date, it was not until the early 1970s that the number of manual stewards grew significantly. Thus, Fryer et al. (1974) reported that, whilst in 1970 39 per cent of NUPE branches had no stewards, with just 21 per cent having five or more, by 1974 only 11 per cent noted no stewards with 40 per cent having five or more. On the white collar side, although NALGO had passed a conference resolution in 1977 calling for the implementation of full steward systems, the late development was reflected in a further conference motion in 1983, noting the urgency of this matter and calling for a campaign to encourage all branches to adopt a steward system.

The rapid emergence of steward organisation remains all the more noteworthy given the fundamental difficulties which have always faced manual and white collar unions in organising members in local government. It will be recalled that the number of part-time women workers is particularly high amongst manuals and not negligible amongst white collar staff. These workers have traditionally shown a limited commitment to trade union organisation, in large part a consequence of domestic responsibilities but, in the local government context, equally a result of their involvement in the 'caring services' with a concomitant concern for their clients. The dispersal of workers over significant geographical areas has additionally presented major problems of contact between members, lay activists and full-time union officers.

The dramatic increase in steward numbers in the face of these organisational difficulties gives rise to three main questions: how have stewards emerged; how have they related to one another; and what role have they played? Recent research (Terry, 1982; Kessler, 1986) suggests that the fragility of steward organisation in local government lies not only in the obvious inexperience of the stewards, but also in the difficulties they face in performing all but a limited number of functions and in organising in a co-ordinated and unified manner across the authority. Yet this same research warns against the dangers of generalising about steward organisation. There is no single, straightforward answer to these three questions; the processes by which steward organisation develops varies considerably.

These variations can be related to the fact that manual and white collar workers in local government carry out a wide variety of tasks requiring very different working practices and places of work. For full-time male depot workers involved in refuse collection and road work, steward representation developed relatively early and spontaneously. Bonus schemes provided some scope for decision-making while employees were in contact with each other at the depot from which they left and returned, usually on a daily basis. Moreover, these were workers with a degree of industrial muscle who could, as a consequence, mobilise effectively in pursuit of objectives.

Similarly, problems of contact did not arise for white collar staff concentrated in large offices and consequently the collective consciousness needed to elect a representative could develop with relative ease. For many occupational groups in social services and education, however, the work involved employees being scattered as isolated individuals. Home helps and social workers, for instance, serviced clients on a one-to-one basis, while dinner ladies, cleaners and secretarial staff in schools as well as care assistants and administrative staff in residential homes worked in small establishments.

The emergence of a steward has had to rely far more on a 'key' outside figure - a senior steward, branch or full-time union official - to stimulate the appointment of a steward, often in the wake of a disruptive event like industrial action (7).

The stimulation of steward representation amongst many social service and education workers in this way raises major questions about the effectiveness of steward representation; it is one thing to impose a steward, it is another to ensure that members are effectively serviced. The structural conditions which inhibited the emergence of the steward continue to inhibit the effective performance of the steward's role. For the majority of stewards who have not been integrated into the formal joint negotiating or consultative machinery, the bargaining function, for so long associated with the traditional steward, is not performed. Spasmodic contact with members hinders steward appreciation of grievances and concerns, while irregular contact with line management and even rarer contact with senior, decision-making levels, prevents the effective resolution of issues. Moreover, this tenuous relationship with constituents serves to strengthen management's unwillingness to involve figures who inadequately represent employee views and cannot assure adherence to agreements reached. For many of these stewards, communication of national and branch information remains the sole function although even this can present difficulties. NALGO's 'Guide to Steward Systems' (undated) notes:

> In December 1983 an independent opinion survey carried out by the Market and Opinion Research International . . . showed that, while 46 per cent of members said they got information about NALGO from their steward or representative, 73 per cent said they would prefer to obtain information this way.

Limits on the ability of most stewards to play a full role in turn suggests difficulties in stewards associating effectively at levels above the immediate place of work. Yet while in certain authorities steward organisation has fragmented, with stewards interacting exclusively on a geographical, occupational or departmental basis, and articulating issues of parochial concern, in others unity and co-ordination at authority level have been achieved as different types of stewards have become integrated into authority-wide committees pursuing interests of concern to the whole workforce.

The type of authority has been important in shaping the ways in which stewards have associated. The shire district, carrying out a limited range of services and therefore producing a small, relatively homogeneous steward body able to meet with comparative ease, can be contrasted with the occupational diversity of stewards scattered across a large geographical area in the shire county. The urban districts fall between these types, for although they perform a wide range of functions, thus producing a heterogeneous group of stewards, they also cover a compact area which facilitates contact. The formal institutional machinery within which stewards meet, in particular branch and joint union-management consultative/negotiating structures, has been equally significant in influencing steward organisations. NUPE and NALGO, as sector specific unions, have been able to develop branch machinery with far greater sensitivity to local government structure than the general unions. Thus the creation of branches which have mirrored employing authorities has certainly aided the emergence of an authority-wide approach (8). Similarly, the existence of strong and effective joint union-management machinery covering the whole of the workforce has integrated different occupational stewards and encouraged the articulation of issues of wide concern. The fragmentation of steward organisation is most apparent, however, where joint committees based on occupation or department dovetail with branches based on the same boundaries, therefore reinforcing division.

Although it has been stresssed that the pressures of the post-1979 period have affected recently emerged and fragile steward organisation, few systematic attempts have been made to assess how effectively stewards have withstood these pressures. Nonetheless, this section has dealt at length with the structure of steward organisation because, in so doing, it is at least possible to suggest how organisation might have developed in the Thatcher years. As will be seen later in this chapter, the ways in which authorities have responded to financial and statutory pressures have affected different occupational groups with varying degrees of intensity. This differential impact of change is likely to have encouraged a marked preoccupation with group specific concerns, hence undermining the creation or continuation of broader workforce unity. It is also likely to have given certain newly emerged and inexperienced stewards a greater chance to develop and strengthen their roles than others. It is probable that the gains in steward organisation amongst some occupational groups, for example school meal workers, in the 1970s may have become casualties of the 1980s.

Local management organisation

The development of the personnel function and the emergence of specialist management techniques is also relatively recent in local government. Until the mid-1970s personnel was viewed primarily in establishment control terms. Personnel practices remained fragmented and informal, being based upon individual service departments and resting largely on 'custom and practice' (Fowler, 1975; Walsh, 1982). However, many of the general changes in the local government context and more specific changes in the industrial relations climate in the late 1960s and early 1970s increased the need for a much more broadly based and centralised personnel function.

The industrial unrest associated with pay policies and the extension of employment protection legislation highlighted the importance of stable industrial relations for the successful implementation of council policy objectives and emphasised the need for more formalised personnel practices and procedures. The major stimulus to the development of personnel, however, was the reorganisation of local government in 1974. The process of reorganisation gave rise to many substantive personnel issues which inevitably boosted the importance of the function, but it also provided a change to reconsider management structure generally and the role of personnel within it. From this general reappraisal increased significance was attached to the personnel function with a realisation that, within such a labour intensive sector, personnel had a key role to play in increasing efficiency and effectiveness (Bains, 1972).

But reorganisation marked not only an opportunity to develop the role of personnel but also provided a chance to introduce a new style of management. As Walsh has stated: 'The discontinuity of reorganisation has provided the opportunity to move from the old "administrative way" to the new "managerial way"'; this new way involving the use of more 'rational techniques and cost conscious patterns of organisation and operation' (1982). Certainly, the introduction of bonus schemes on a limited scale had prompted the need for such management techniques as work measurement and organisation and methods, while the 1973 Audit Code of Practice for Local Authorities obliged the auditor to ensure that a local authority's accounts did not 'disclose any significant loss arising from waste, extravagance, inefficient financial administration, poor value for money, mistake or other cause'. But at a time when the local government sector was still expanding, the adoption of these techniques appeared to owe as much to styles of management prevailing in broader public and private sectors in the era of productivity bargaining as to the immediate needs of most authorities.

The pressures associated with the introduction of the post-1979 financial and statutory frameworks for local government have further prompted increased specialisation in the field of personnel management and extended the use of management techniques as a matter of necessity rather than convention. The financial stringencies imposed on local authorities would, in themselves, have required reviews in the level and organisation of service provision. However, greater urgency has been added by central government exhortations, backed by statutory mechanisms, for local authorities to reassess the way in which they provided services with a view to increasing 'value for money'. This search for 'value for money', somewhat akin to a holy crusade pursued by the government through the public service sector, has been reinforced by two developments.

First, the institutional machinery for assessing 'value for money' has been increasingly formalised and strengthened. The Audit Code of Practice, quoted above, listed a broad set of principles which might be deemed to apply to any publicly accountable body. The Local Government Act 1982 went considerably further in extending the role of the auditor. The Audit Commission was established with a statutory responsibility to appoint auditors in all local authorities, with a brief to ensure that 'proper arrangements had been made for securing economy, efficiency and effectiveness of resources' (Section 12). Furthermore the Commission was charged with undertaking studies 'to improve economy, efficiency and effectiveness' (Section 26).

The second development has been the statutory support provided by this government for its belief that the efficiency and effectiveness of local authority services is best tested in the market place. Attention has already been drawn to the provision of the Local Government Planning Act 1980, which introduced compulsory competitive tendering for services carried out by local authority direct labour organisation, new building work, maintenance and highways work. The government's 1985 consultative paper, 'Competition in the Provision of Local Authority Services', envisaged the extension of competitive tendering to five new services: school meals and other catering; refuse collection and street cleaning; cleaning of buildings; vehicle maintenance; and ground maintenance.

Having concentrated on the pressures which have encouraged increased centralisation and specialisation in the field of personnel management, it is important to stress that, as with steward organisation, developments have been far from even. Variations have arisen both within and between different types of authority in the accommodation of personnel policies and practices within council committee and council office management structures.

Personnel has not traditionally been an area which has generated much interest amongst councillors; broader social and economic concerns usually stimulate involvement in local politics. Interest in the subject has, however, grown as councillors have come to appreciate that personnel decisions can profoundly affect the pursuit of their wider concerns in a period of financial constraint. Nevertheless, differences remain in the status of councillors involved and the extent to which they directly participate in industrial relations by meeting with personnel specialists and trade unionists rather than dealing with related issues. Any explanation of the variation between authorities may be found in the shape and role of their own committee structures.

The main distinction within the management structure lies between the centralised and decentralised personnel function (Hinnings and Walsh, 1979). Responsibility for personnel usually lies with an independent department or a section of the chief executive's department. Nevertheless, there are differences in the extent to which authorities have appointed specialist personnel

officers within departments and the relative power
balance between them, line managers and central
personnel staff.
    The shape and role of the personnel function
has usually been conceived as part of the broader
organisational structure of the authority (Greenwood
et al., 1980) and clearly discussion of the
development of this structure is beyond the scope of
this chapter.   Nonetheless, it is apparent that
characteristics associated with different types of
authority have had specific impact on the
development of personnel.   Walsh (1982), for
instance, points to the likelihood of personnel
becoming better established in urban districts than
shire counties, with the former not only subject to
greater change on reorganisation but also subject to
more extensive environmental complexity and
instability.   The political complexion of
councillors can also be significant.   Labour
councillors tend to be more willing to become
involved directly in the handling of industrial
relations issues than Conservatives and also more
suspicious of sanctioning the development of certain
management techniques (Kessler, 1982).
    Following 30 years of highly centralised
bargaining after 1945, the scope for local decision-
making has broadened significantly. This was partly
as a consequence of attempts to introduce more
flexible payment systems for selective groups, but
more generally in response to the pressures for
change in employment practice and conditions
generated by financial constraints and the drive for
greater 'efficiency and effectiveness'.   While this
increased scope for local bargaining has allowed for
the development of steward organisation and
personnel management, these developments have not
been even.   Not only have different types of
authority constituted very different kinds of
workplaces but the political control of authorities
has varied as have the range of environmental
pressures faced.   Variations in the structure and
role of steward organisation and personnel
management leads one to look for differences in
local union and management policy and activity.   It
is to such differences that attention now turns.

Changes in local employment practices and procedures
For local authorities responding to the pressures
associated with post-1979 financial and statutory
frameworks, the nationally negotiated agreements for
manual and white collar workers have had a

significant regulatory effect upon behaviour. Faced
with nationally agreed terms and conditions which
imperfectly reflected local circumstances,
authorities have taken two broad approaches: they
have sought ways to avoid the perceived constraints
of the agreements by moving outside them or they
have adapted local employment practices and
conditions within the scope provided by those
agreements.

The former approach comprises a number of
different strategies, most of which have involved
moving away from the manual, rather than the white
collar, agreement. First, there are examples of
authorities, exclusively Conservative, which have
ceased to perform a particular service altogether.
Given statutory obligations, the opportunities for
authorities to take this course of action are
strictly limited. The only significant development
in this direction has arisen as a consequence of the
Education Act 1980 which, in allowing considerable
flexibility in the provision of school meals,
prompted a small number of shire counties, including
Lincolnshire and Dorset, to cease providing meals in
primary schools.

The 1980 Act also encouraged a second strategy
of continuing to provide services using council
employees, but employing them on terms inferior to
those in the national agreement. The attempts made
by Hertfordshire and Kent County Councils to
terminate the contracts of school meals workers, re-
employing them on terms which departed from the
national agreement, were widely reported following
legal action taken by the employees concerned. Yet
moves to worsen national terms remain rare and are
more than countered by examples of authorities which
have supplemented national terms seen as
perpetuating low pay in their areas. The most
concerted and sustained move to 'top up' national
basic rates has been taken by Sheffield City Council
as part of a broader attack on low pay in the
authority, although there are additional examples of
low pay supplements particularly in Labour-
controlled London boroughs (Pay and Benefits
Bulletin, No. 171, 1986).

Encouraged by the statutory support for
competitive tendering, the strategy which has
received most attention within this first broad
approach has been privatisation or contracting out
of services. Savings on labour costs have been
available to authorities through the use of outside
firms providing terms and conditions inferior to

those agreed nationally and especially through the employment of fewer workers to carry out the service. Alongside the concerns raised about the quality of the services provided by contractors, it is this under-cutting of national terms which has been highlighted by trade unions in attacking privatisation. The limited research available into the employment practices of contractors certainly lends weight to union concerns. A survey conducted at York University indicates that in 14 out of 25 local authority and NHS contracts won by firms, the contractors paid lower wage rates. Moreover, Hartley and Huby (1985: 24) note: 'Contractors often "economise" on conditions of service, especially superannuation, holiday pay and sickness benefits'. The same survey also revealed that not one outside firm awarded a contract re-employed all council staff on a full-time basis.

Yet, while it is clear that certain authorities have sought savings by side-stepping national terms, it is equally apparent that, in total, the number of authorities resorting to privatisation or contracting out has remained small. The Local Government Chronicle (LGC) privatisation survey carried out in each of the last four years has revealed between 11 and 16 per cent of authorities annually reporting privatisation of a limited range of services, in the main refuse collection, catering and cleaning. The use of contractors and attitudes towards them can be related to the party political complexion of the council, but distinctions should not be too rigidly drawn. The LGC 1985-86 survey revealed that 34 of the 60 authorities privatising were Conservative and 10 Labour. Yet, it is a reflection of general disenchantment with the process that the leader of the Conservative-controlled ADC has warned the Environment Secretary that grass roots Conservative support would be lost if the government forced authorities to put more services out to tender (LGC, 19.9.86).

Although it is clear that relatively few authorities have favoured the three strategies which involve moving outside national agreements, the influence of these strategies should not be under-estimated. The threatened resort to one of them, with such drastic implications for workforces, has certainly acted as a stimulus to change in many authorities. Yet, the essential point remains that the pressures generated since 1979 have largely continued to be handled within the framework of national terms and conditions. The strategies

190

adopted by authorities within this second broad approach remain under-researched. Nonetheless, evidence available (Quintas, 1986; Walker, 1986; Audit Commission, 1984, 1985, 1986) suggests four interrelated strategies: renegotiation of locally determined payment systems; changes in the levels and patterns of employment; administrative rationalisation and reorganisation; and increased managerial control.

As suggested earlier, within a highly centralised system of pay bargaining, bonus schemes, in the main confined to selected groups of manuals, remain the sole payment system open to local reform. From the outset, these schemes were not always tightly constructed, being seen as a way of bolstering earnings opportunities as well as increasing productivity. Over the years, however, schemes deteriorated further as authorities failed to readjust time and work values to compensate for new machinery and working methods. In 1979 the former Chief Inspector of Audit noted:

> Many bonus schemes have become little more than a complicated and expensive method of calculating a man's pay and have weakened local authorities' financial control over an important part of their budget. (Audit Commission, 1984: 24)

The Audit Commission in 1984 also singled out bonus schemes as an area where savings could be made and warned that its auditors would pay close attention to their operation. It states:

> There can be no excuse for paying more in bonuses than is earned by performance as demonstrably such a local authority is not obtaining value for money. Moreover, a weak bonus scheme is unfair to those employees who are working to earn their pay; it pre-empts resources which could be put to better use in the service of the community; it encourages a cynical attitude among other council employees; and, if the facts become known locally, public confidence in the integrity and effectiveness of local government and its officers will be undermined. (1984: 25)

Certainly, case study evidence does suggest that authorities are renegotiating and tightening bonus schemes (Terry, 1982; Kessler, 1986; Walker,

1986), moves given added urgency by the fact that those employees most threatened with compulsory tendering are, in the main, those covered by schemes.

The renegotiation of bonus schemes can be linked to the other strategies as its main purpose is to reduce costs and/or increase competitiveness through changes in levels and patterns of employment, administrative rationalisation, and increased managerial control. However, these strategies have involved more fundamental changes across authority workforces. Attention has already been drawn to reduction in total manual staff levels contrasting with buoyant levels of employment amongst white collar employees. In aggregate terms, it is also important to note that changes in employment levels have varied markedly between different local authority services. Thus, employment has fallen significantly in refuse collection and ancillary school services over the last decade, whilst in the social services and recreation it has been rising (Quintas, 1986: 175). Although compulsory redundancies have taken place the contribution they have made to lower manual numbers should not be overestimated. Other practices, used for many years in other sectors of the economy, have been introduced to control and reduce employment, in particular recruitment freezes and voluntary redundancies. Changes in patterns of employment can also be related to the extension of broader trends to local governments. For instance, attempts to increase flexibility have seen not only the substitution of part-time for full-time employees but also the greater use of temporary and casual employees (Walker, 1986).

The scope for administrative rationalisation and reorganisation has certainly been increased by the introduction of new technology to local government. Moreover, Quintas (1986) has noted, albeit on the basis of one case study authority, that efforts have been concentrated on using new technology for 'process innovation' - speeding up routine clerical tasks - rather than 'product innovation' - providing new types of service. But, in addition to savings gained in administrative costs from the exploitation of new technology, there is also evidence of administrative reorganisation to place the operation of certain services on a more commercial basis. This appears more prevalent amongst direct labour organisations subject to the pressures of compulsory tendering. Walker (1986)

192

points to one authority where the DLO was reorganised into four service-based divisions, each operating as separate profit centres and utilising commercial accounting procedures.

The final strategy - attempts to increase managerial control - has seen authorities seeking to identify 'managerial objectives' and to establish clear lines of managerial accountability and responsibility. However, perhaps the most fundamental development has been management efforts to control the use of resources. It is in this respect that new technology appears to have had its most significant impact, increasing the quantity and quality of information available and enabling the maximisation of use of all resources.

How extensively these four strategies have been used by authorities and the ways in which they have been combined must await further, more systematic, research. There is also a pressing need for research which examines the relationship between the structure of local union and management organisation and all of the strategies distinguished in this section. At a general level, a number of relationships can be suggested. Labour-controlled councils, for instance, have been less inclined to use contractors than Conservative councils. It is also possible to relate the character of steward organisation to campaigns waged against certain management strategies. Thus, one can contrast the effectively co-ordinated strike action conducted by the compact, service-based NUPE and NALGO steward organisation in Birmingham against the introduction of management consultants in 1982 (Kline, 1985) with the failure of the dispersed and weakly organised school meals workers in Dorset to take coherent action against the closure of the primary school meals service (Kessler, 1982).

Nevertheless, there are more searching questions which need to be asked: to what extent does the involvement of senior councillors affect management pursuit of different strategies? Are strategies within the framework of national agreements more or less successfully pursued by centralised personnel functions? Is resort to a strategy outside national agreements a reflection of a personnel function with a low status and/or lacking the requisite management techniques? How sucessful have local union organisations been in influencing management strategies? Can union opposition to a strategy within the framework of national agreements backfire and result in resort to

a strategy outside of agreements? These are
questions which deserve consideration through more
detailed research work.

SUMMARY AND CONCLUSIONS

In the changed bargaining context of the post-1979
period, local authority employers and trade unions
at both the national and local levels have been
forced to review the manner in which they conduct
industrial relations. Both sides have modified and
developed their objectives and strategies in
response to the limited financial resources
available and to a statutory framework which forces
the testing of the 'value' provided by services in
the market place. Within such frameworks high
labour costs have come to have a significant impact
upon the level of employment and the quality and
range of service provided. Two themes have,
however, been proposed as central to an
understanding of union and employer responses:
differences in the structure of collective
bargaining between manual and white collar workers,
and variations between different types of authority
in terms of their needs and interests.
     The pressures of the post-1979 period have
raised major questions about the viability of
national negotiating machinery in meeting the
specific needs of individual authorities. For
manual and white collar union negotiators, initial
attempts to override the parochial interests
generated by distinctive, group-based bargaining
machinery, through a co-ordinated TUC strategy,
quickly gave way to a recognition that objectives
were more effectively pursued by concentrating on
modifications to the specific conditions of
employment of their members. Amongst the employers
attempts to develop a coherent approach in response
to concerns voiced by authorities about the
flexibility of machinery have achieved mixed
results. For the white collar employers seeking
minor, uncontentious adjustments to an already
flexible agreement, objectives were successfully
brought to the negotiating table and pursued with
some effect. For the manual employers, however,
efforts to reform a more rigid and prescriptive
agreement resulted in the emergence of divergent
interests between representatives from different
types of authority, inhibiting the formulation of
consensus on any proposals for change.

At the local level it was clear that, despite any perceived concern at the inflexibility of national bargaining, very few authorities had actually decided to opt out of agreements. It was noted that individual authorities faced with absorbing nationally agreed changes in terms and conditions within financial constraints and controls had adopted a range of strategies primarily related to manual rather than white collar workers. Whilst one of the broad approaches distinguished involved moving outside of national agreements by ceasing to perform a service, paying council employees below nationally agreed rates or contracting out, most authorities had responded to the pressures for change by reviewing and modifying employment levels and work practices within the framework of the national agreement.

The scope for further fundamental modifications to the manual and white collar agreements may now be limited. Certainly, at the time of writing, the manual NJC is discussing a major departure from the national agreement on working time. It is likely, however, that this development and indeed others nationally will take the form of setting flexible criteria within which authorities have scope to design employment practices and procedures to meet their own resources, needs and policy objectives. From the limited amount of evidence available, it is already clear that authorities have adopted a myriad of different personnel responses to meet the pressures of the post-1979 period. It is likely that the dynamism and variation in local government industrial relations will continue to be found at the authority level.

NOTES

1. The author would like to express his thanks to David Winchester for reading and commenting on earlier drafts of this chapter.

2. A working group under the chairmanship of M. Bains, Clerk of Kent County Council, was set up in May 1971 to consider management structures appropriate for the new authorities. Its report was published in 1972 under the title, 'The New Local Authorities: Management and Structure'.

3. Much of the information used in this chapter was gathered during a research project carried out at Warwick University with David Winchester between 1981 and 1983. The research

project looked at government influence on national collective bargaining in the local government sector and selected four local authority bargaining groups for study: manual; APT&C staff; primary and secondary school teachers; and firemen. The relationship between the structure of collective bargaining and its differences was analysed in these four groups. The value of this relationship was much clearer in analysing across all four groups where sharper differences in the structure of collective bargaining were apparent between manuals and white collar staff on the one hand and teachers and firemen on the other.

4. The quality of inter-relations has fluctuated over the years. Certainly one of the more recent lows in relations occurred during the 'Winter of Discontent' when the then GMWU national officer reported to his conference that NUPE leaders 'were determined to demonstrate their virility in pursuance of a recruitment drive . . . their strategy was to organise chaos and pick up the pieces'.

5. Shire counties and urban districts employ over 70 per cent of all local authority staff. The distribution of seats on the employer sides of the NJCs does not, however, reflect this situation, the shire district's representative tending to control the provincial council seats. Although this has caused some concern on the part of the AMA and ACC, the ADC counters by stressing that they represent the majority of employing units.

6. The job evaluation exercise was noteworthy for the importance attached to 'equal value principles'. In the design of the scheme care was taken not to include or define factors which could produce results biased against women workers. For example, 'physical effort' incorporated not just the strength needed to do a job, but bending, kneeling and other aspects of physical effort; in the 'skill' factor, account was taken not only of formal training and qualifications, but also informal training, acquired experience and caring. Moreover, the Equal Opportunities Commission was closely involved in the process, approving for instance the weightings attached to the factors. Partly as a result, major occupational groups where women predominated scored well. In particular, home helps and care assistants scored highly relative to, for instance, refuse collectors, with a consequent reversal of their positions when a revised grading structure was designed.

7. The author's case study work (1982) suggests that the national industrial action during 1979 provided the stimulus for the emergence of a considerable number of stewards.

8. Although NUPE and NALGO branch structures have in general tended to mirror employing authorities, there are nonetheless examples of branches based upon occupations and departments and particular difficulties have been faced in establishing branches which covered shire districts.

REFERENCES

Audit Commission (1984, 1985, 1986) Report and Accounts

Bains, M. (1972) 'The New Local Authorities: Management and Structure, London

Douglas, I. and Lord, S. (1986) Local Government Finance, A Practical Guide, Local Government Information Unit, London

Fowler, A. (1975) Personnel Management in Local Government, IPM, London

Fryer, R., Fairclough, A. and Manson, T. (1974) Organisation and Change in the National Union of Public Employees, NUPE, Warwick

Greenwood, R., Walsh, K., Hinnings, C. and Ranson, S. (1980) Patterns in Management in Local Government, Martin Robertson, Oxford

Hartley, K. and Huby, M. (1985) 'Contracting-Out in Health and Local Authorities: Prospects, Progress and Pitfalls', Public Money, 5(2), September

Ingham, M. (1985) 'Industrial Relations in British Local Government', Industrial Relations Journal, Spring, 16(1)

Kessler, I. (1982) Steward Organisation Amongst Local Authority Manual Workers, (PhD Thesis), Warwick University, Warwick

Kessler, I. (1986) 'Shop Stewards in Local Government Revisited', British Journal of Industrial Relations, November, XXIV(3), pp. 419-41

Kessler, I. and Winchester, D. (1982) 'Pay Negotiations in Local Government', Local Government Studies, November/December, 8(6)

Kline, R. (1985) 'There's Gold in Them Thar Audits', Background Paper No. 11 - National Conference on Privatisation of Council Services, Sheffield Council/Local Government Information Unit

I. Kessler

LACSAB (1983) Changing the National Agreement
MacIntosh, M. (1955) 'The Negotiation of Wages and
    Conditions for Local Authority Employees',
    Public Administration, XXIII
McSweeney, B. (1985) 'Value for Money, Alchemy or
    Science', Background Paper No. 11 - National
    Conference on Privatisation, Sheffield/LGIU
National Board for Prices and Incomes (1967) 'Pay
    and Conditions of Manual Workers in Local
    Authorities, the Health Service, Gas and Water
    Supply', Report No. 27, Cmnd 3230, HMSO, London
National and Local Government Officers' Association
    (1983) Co-ordinated Public Service Pay
    Strategy, NALGO
National and Local Government Officers' Association
    (undated) Pay Strategy, NALGO
National and Local Government Officers' Association
    (undated) Steward Systems, NALGO
Newman, G. (1982) Path to Maturity, Co-operative
    Press, London
Quintas, P. (1986) 'Information Technology and
    Employment in Local Government: The
    Quantitative and Qualitative Effects on Jobs in
    the Late 1980s', New Technology Work and
    Employment, 1(2), pp. 172-84
Spoor, A. (1967) White Collar Union: Sixty Years
    of NALGO, Heinemann, London
Terry, M. (1982) 'Organising a Fragmented
    Workforce: Shop Stewards in Local Government',
    British Journal of Industrial Relations, XX,
    pp. 1-19
Travers, T. (1982) 'Pay Versus Jobs: The Choice
    Facing Local Authorities', Public Money, 2(3)
    December
Walker, J. (1986) Local Authorities in Britain:
    Model Employers of the 1980s?, Seminar Paper
    for Urban Research Unit
Walsh, K. (1982) The Role of the Personnel Manager
    in Corporate Management, Society of Chief
    Personnel in Local Government
Walton, R. and McKersie, R. (1965) A Behaviour
    Theory of Labour Negotiations: An Analysis of
    a Social Interaction System, McGraw Hill, New
    York
Winchester, D. (1983) 'Industrial Relations in the
    Public Sector', in Bain, G. (ed.) Industrial
    Relations in Britain, Basil Blackwell, Oxford
Wright, M. (1981) 'Big Government in Hard Times:
    The Restraint of Public Expenditure', in Hood,
    C. and Wright, M. (eds.) Big Government in
    Hard Times, Martin Robertson, Oxford

Chapter 6

INDUSTRIAL RELATIONS IN THE SCHOOL SECTOR

R. V. Seifert

INTRODUCTION

The history of industrial relations in the school sector from 1979 illustrates many of the general themes identified with changes in the public services. As Winchester (1983) noted: 'By 1980 it had become commonplace to consider the major source of instability in British industrial relations as lying in the relationship between governments and the public sector trade unions' (p. 155). The central unresolved problem remains the determination of pay. Cuts in public expenditure have been chosen as one method of achieving a lower wage bill, and the strategies followed to implement those cuts have included large scale reorganisations, centralisation and greater managerial specialisation (including forms of work study such as performance indicators and performance appraisal). Other strategies of importance to education have also been applied on a wider scale such as the weakening of the ability of trade unions to resist job losses, and the reduction in powers and financial independence of local authorities.

Two of the most important outcomes of these strategies of the 1980s have been the extensive use of industrial action by schoolteachers including the largest and longest national strike ever held between 1985-86; and a major reassessment by all those involved of school-based terms and conditions of employment. These strategies of government aimed at securing the objectives of greater financial and political controls over the operation of state schools, and the outcomes of these policies in terms of strikes and new definitions of teacher professionalism have been made both more difficult to achieve and less easy to sell to the public

199

because of the existence of a complex set of institutional bargaining arrangements, and because of extensive differences within each side of the negotiations.

While institutional analyses based on traditional industrial relations' approaches are of real importance in understanding developments in the 1980s and while they are well illustrated by the following account of events in the school sector since 1979, they are nonetheless secondary to the dominant and determinant ideological and economic conditions. These include the renewed commitment to private provision of education and the recognition that the labour markets require more narrowly trained and less well educated units of labour time. They also include the drive towards greater state authority in order to control the social and political forces that threaten to undermine the economic objectives of lower wages, fewer employment rights, weaker trade unions and a generally more flexible and docile workforce. There is also an ideological objective to remove the 'left' from any position of power or credibility within the country through assaults on its strongholds; trade unions and public services.

The 1980s, therefore, have proved to be the decade when school teachers, among other public service workers, received the full force of attacks from the central state under the control of an ideologically right-wing central government. These attacks were aimed at dividing and weakening their defence organisations (trade unions) and hence their role in the collective bargaining machinery; at the undermining of their labour market protections (through unemployment, low pay, restructuring of pay, and merit pay); at their professional independence (through performance appraisal and control of the curriculum); at their freedom at work (through contractual definitions of conditions of service); and of the rights to negotiate pay (Teachers' Pay and Conditions Act 1987). The final objective of these policies is the reduction in quality and quantity of state education and its funding in favour of the private sector.

The teachers and their organisations responded through campaigning with publicity and pressure on local and national political parties, and a series of strikes. But their lack of unity at vital moments hampered any consistently coherent approach to the tactics and strategies of the employers; this disunity and incoherence is made worse in light of a famously phrased difficulty of dealing with 'employers who do not pay and paymasters who do not employ' (McCarthy, quoted in Leopold and Beaumont, 1986: 32). It was not until 1984 that sustained local industrial action combined with growing public concern of parents to allow real pressure on employers and government which led to the largest and longest national teacher strike in history in 1985/86. This was itself a sign of what Brian Simon (1986: 5) recently noticed; that 'the alienation of the teachers from government policies now goes very deep indeed'.

Several commentators, from different perspectives, have argued that the teacher strikes in the 1980s both provide evidence for, and help to promote, a new relationship between state and teachers. Lawn (1985a: 29) invokes the plans for regular assessment and 'the new structure of work and pay' as evidence of the replacement of consensus by control in the government's strategy, while Rhodes (1985) examines and rejects corporatism as a useful tool for analysing pay negotiations in local government. A more helpful approach may be to consider what teachers do: their work purpose. They have simultaneously two distinct tasks: to educate the children of predominantly working class origins; and to supply qualified labour to the employers of labour through various markets. The demand for the latter determines, under Conservative government policies and assumptions, the demand for teacher labour time and therefore its value in pay terms and its control at the point of operation by local managements. The demand for the former comes from parents, children, teachers and the organised labour movement: only to the extent that these groups are employers or can put pressure on employers will their demand for the full qualitative experience of education be met. In other circumstances their views are discounted and largely ignored.

In these conditions there is a growth in the political content of professional activity, and as governments exercise their labour market options more forcefully, so public sector trade unions are more likely to move to the left, affiliate to the TUC, consider affiliation to the Labour Party, take more industrial action, develop workplace bargaining rights, and become part of the traditional working class trade union organisation whose prime aim is, as Max Morris (1984: 446) reminds us: 'The one immutable principle is, in the immortal words of

Jack Dash: the job of the union is to separate the boss from his cash'.

This chapter takes up these general themes of the centralising drive from the government, the intra-organisational bargaining within the management and union sides, the forces undermining traditional bargaining relationships and the removal of traditional 'impasse resolution' mechanisms, the political aspects of pay determination, and industrial action by teachers. It seeks to illustrate their applicability to the specifics of the public sector in education through a story of events since 1979 divided into three sections: the pressures to reform Burnham and intra-organisational bargaining between the parties; the determination of national pay and conditions of service; and the local strikes against cuts leading to the development of workplace industrial relations.

INTRA-ORGANISATIONAL BARGAINING AND THE ABOLITION OF BURNHAM

The Burnham Committee to determine pay was forged after the Great War as a compromise between the centralising urges of the government, the financial dependence of local employers on the central state, and the demands of the unions for consistent pay bargaining. The central element of Burnham is that representatives from the national organisations of teachers and employers provide members of a teachers' panel and a management panel. The composition of each side is determined by the Secretary of State, but each side arrives at its own policies through voting and informal pressure group meetings. The two sides then meet across a table with an independent chairman (Table 6.1); in practice more time is spent arguing within each side than between the two sides. This is because the membership of the panels have deep-seated and structured differences of interest.

The changed context of bargaining in the 1980s has led to 'dissatisfaction and consequently conflict among these participants, which has manifested itself in attempts to change the system of bargaining itself' (Walsh, 1981). Within the management side the actual employers are divided politically and geographically into local education authorities (LEAs). The LEAs have forced themselves into two national groupings: Association of County Councils (ACC, usually Tory-controlled), and the

Association of Metropolitan Authorities (AMA, usually Labour-controlled). On the Burnham Committee for pay they are joined by two representatives from the DES who have 15 votes under the 1965 Concordat.

Table 6.1 Burnham in 1986

TEACHERS' PANEL		----------	MANAGEMENT PANEL	
NUT	13		ACC	13
NAS/UWT	7		AMA	10
AMMA	4	Independent chair	WJEC	2
NAHT	2		DES	2*
SHA	1			
PAT	1			
Formal meetings to decide policy by majority vote			Formal meetings to decide policy by majority vote	

*DES have two seats but 15 votes under the Concordat 1965-85

The DES is not represented on the other negotiating body for teachers, the Committee of Local Education Authorities, nor on its school teacher section (CLEA/ST) which settles conditions of service only. This example of voluntary bargaining is favoured by some unions and some political groupings as a possible model for a body which would negotiate pay and conditions together. This suggestion became a concrete proposal when four of the teacher trade unions (NUT, NAS/UWT, AMMA and SHA) agreed to a National Joint Council for negotiations with the majority on the employers' side in June 1987.

The Teachers' Panel of Burnham also represents a major centre of divergent interests. The unions are divided between the organisations for head teachers (National Association of Head Teachers (NAHT) with about 20,000 members), and those representing mainly classroom teachers. This latter group is itself divided; there is a new union based on opposition to strike action and encouraged by the government, the Professional Association of Teachers (PAT), with about 20,000 members. Then there are the TUC affiliates which are the two largest and most representative of the unions (the National Union of Teachers (NUT) has about 220,000 members, and the National Association of Schoolmasters and Union of Women Teachers (NAS/UWT) has about 115,000 members). There is another classroom teacher union not in the TUC with a more moderate image which represents teachers in the private sector and ex-grammar schools, the Assistant Masters and Mistresses Association (AMMA) with 65,000 members.

Each union has separate policy objectives, traditions and political divisions (Manzer, 1970; Coates, 1972a; Gosden, 1972). The NUT and NAS/UWT compete for members and for the moral high ground in debate; as Winchester suggests:

> Inter-union conflict between teachers' unions is deeply rooted in differing conceptions of status, professionalism, and the legitimacy of industrial action, but ministerial power to alter trade union side representation in collective bargaining has undoubtedly exacerbated the problem. (1983: 162)

The main developments noted above of intra-organisational (Walton and McKersie, 1965) and multi-lateral bargaining (Thomson and Beaumont, 1978) which Leopold and Beaumont (1986) applied to the NHS can certainly serve with equal vigour for the education sector. Another important parallel with the health service was the ending of normal pay comparisons and alterations in the rules about arbitration which they argue led to the 1982 strikes in the NHS, and which certainly contributed to the 1984 and 1985/86 strikes among teachers. In addition, the restrictive union laws, especially those elements about strike ballots, had the now familiar unintended consequence that union leaders hold ballots for tactical reasons in order to threaten action with public proof of membership backing.

Attempts to reform Burnham
The dominant legislation which determined the bargaining over teachers' pay was the 1965 Remuneration of Teachers Act (RTA). It came into existence as a result of an earlier Conservative

government's efforts to centralise control of teacher pay and educational expenditure (Coates, 1972b). It allowed the Secretary of State to vary the representatives of the various bodies (para. 1.3), to crucially allow either side to go to arbitration (para. 3.1), and to veto any settlement (para. 4.21). A few days before this act was passed the management panel made a 'secret' deal with the DES called the Concordat which immensely increased the powers of central government (Saran, 1985: 22-3), and which was published for the first time in Education (19/26.12.80: 571). Its major provisions include the statement that 'no claim will be accepted or offer made or agreement given . . . if the Secretary of State objects to the total cost involved'; and later 'the Secretary of State's vote will be cast in each Committee with the weight indicated in the Schedule' (i.e. 15).

The attempt to reform Burnham was firmly linked with dissatisfaction and the separate forms for negotiating pay and conditions; this meant the repeal of the RTA, and a revised form of arbitration. In May 1980 the Secretary of State, Mark Carlisle, proposed both these reforms with management backing, but the unions (especially the NUT) were against. The NUT took a strong line on mixing pay with conditions of service negotiations urging in their April NUT News that progress was being made in the CLEA/ST working party (which NAS/UWT refused to join) on the need for a job description, contact time and other duties, but that there must be no link with pay. These talks paralleled those about to commence formally on a new pay structure.

The management panel view changed with Labour winning control of AMA and opposing reform of the negotiating machinery while the Tory ACC pushed for a restriction on the right to arbitration. By the end of 1980 the government had announced further cuts and a six per cent cash limit which provided the NUT and the NAS/UWT with an excuse to boycott talks on new conditions of service. Meanwhile Mark Carlisle had moved towards reducing the NUT's national control of Burnham by granting PAT a seat on Burnham and upping the NAS/UWT representation from six to seven while increasing the total teachers' side from 30 to 32 with NUT keeping their 16.

The new Secretary of State, Sir Keith Joseph, started in September 1980 and immediately took the line that the RTA should remain and that pay and conditions should not be brought under one negotiating body to the fury of the management panel. This decision put the squeeze on the Concordat and foretold of the coming years of confusion, frustration and incompetence from management and DES alike. As it was, the government amended the RTA in February to permit arbitration if, and only if, both sides agreed to go. This was the major institutional rule change which led to the strikes later in the decade. A system whereby either party can go to arbitration is a form of compulsion and is a policy statement that, while such references tend to be inflationary, that is the price to be paid for industrial peace in schools. The new rules reflected the change in policy which put the fight against inflation before disruption of the state schooling system.

The Conservative government had in fact inherited an agreement within CLEA/ST to set up a working party on conditions of service. Its basis was the fear by the unions about pressures on professionalism and their demands for a proper job description and stricter controls over teaching time, while the employers demanded more controls over teachers' duties and pay (NUT Annual Report 1980: 119). The NAS/UWT alone of the unions refused to join the working party on the grounds that any agreement would jeopardise the voluntary nature of many duties (Schoolmaster and Career Teacher, September 1980: 4). This position was maintained by the NAS/UWT right through these years and included its refusal to agree to the 1986/87 voluntary accord between unions and employers. Scottish teachers had worked under contractual conditions for some years and, although they found it a two-edged sword, the CIS considered it of some help in defending jobs in a period of contraction (Ozga, 1985).

Negotiations over the next seven years were to be constantly hampered by the employers' insistence that any final deal on conditions of service should be directly linked with pay and pay structures. The NUT and AMMA strongly resisted such calls for a merger of negotiations, although the NAS/UWT favoured them as a means of bypassing the NUT majority on Burnham. As Peter Smith of AMMA argued:

> At the heart of the controversy about linking the 1980 Burnham award to a new conditions of service agreement lay an apparent paradox . . . when presenting their evidence for salary increases, teachers cite all they do outside

class contact hours . . . in dispute with the
authorities, they claim the work to be
voluntary and assert the right to stop
volunteering. (Times Educational Supplement,
9.5.80)

Also, there were further changes in the
representation of the union side of Burnham. In
1985, the Secretary of State, Sir Keith Joseph,
reduced the NUT's representation on the Teachers'
Panel based on new membership figures: NUT 13 (216,
138); NAS/UWT 7 (115, 611); AMMA 4 (64, 636);
NAHT 2 (19, 52); PAT 1 (21, 260); SHA 1 (3, 39).
This meant that the NUT had lost its majority for
the first time. Rather than create a vehicle for
moderation, the changes produced a mixture of
paralysis and unrepresentative decisions from the
Teachers' Panel which resulted in further discredit
to the system and prolonged the status.
    The paralysis within Burnham being worsened and
the unions further divided through government
policies, the government finally decided to
legislate and abolish Burnham. At the time the act
was passed, a Labour majority on the employers' side
and a majority on the Teachers' Panel (NUT and AMMA)
had agreed a deal in a form which had effectively
brought pay, pay structure and conditions of service
negotiations into a single bargaining form. The
agreement, however, came too late and was
unacceptable to the Cabinet. The act replaced
Burnham with an Interim Advisory Committee on School
Teachers' Pay and Conditions. This committee
provides for a minimal input from employers and
unions, and comes under great ministerial control.
The heart of the act allows the Secretary of State
to vary any award: 'an order may make different
provision for different cases, including different
provision for different areas' (para. 3.4), and on
pay an order 'may confer discretion in the local
education authority with respect to any matters'
(para. 3.5) thus paving the way for the end to
national pay bargaining.

Pay outcomes and strikes
The Clegg Commission came five years after the
Houghton inquiry into teachers' pay which awarded
them a substantial rise. The fact that there were
two major inquiries into teacher pay within the
lifetime of one Labour government suggested a
serious crisis in pay determination methods as well
as Labour's wish to avoid a teachers' strike.

R. V. Seifert

In 1974 the Labour government set up a committee of inquiry into pay under Lord Houghton (Cmnd. 5848). The estimated salary cost for 1974/75 for full-time school teachers in England and Wales was £1,019.6 million (para. 4) which provides a good reason for increased government concern in the outcome of negotiations. The central issues were the recognised and agreed fall in teachers' pay compared with general movements in pay (para. 42), and the Clegg Commission itself (Cmnd. 7880) was set up in the shadow of Houghton (para. 2). It was noted that the NAS/UWT did not co-operate with the study (para. 17). The NAS/UWT wanted arbitration, and their national treasurer later referred to 'the absolute chaos into which our salary negotiations have fallen as a result of the Clegg exercise' (Schoolmaster and Career Teacher, March 1980: 7).

The management evidence to the Clegg Commission argued against automatic indexation (para. 20); they also stressed changes in the labour market for teachers (para. 21) and down-graded notions of teachers' managerial responsibility (para. 22). They also strongly urged on the Commission a link between pay awards and duties such as covering for absent colleagues (para. 25).

The teacher evidence emphasised the importance of education to the nation (NUT Submission to the Clegg Commission on Pay Comparability, October 1979: 1), great increases in stress and strain, and the greater difficulty of the job (p. 2). Most of the NUT evidence (over 100 pages of it) concentrates on the nature of the job with a detailed analysis of class time and of time during breaks (for example only 26 per cent of time allocated to breaks was spent on personal matters, p. 72). They also were very concerned with career prospects and promotion at a time of falling rolls (p. 118), and that pay levels should be restored to Houghton awards (p. 120).

After an embarrassing inability to achieve their original objectives, the Commission fell back on the comparisons made by Houghton: a comparison of salaries of graduate entrants to teaching with others, and then to use internal relativities upwards (para. 61). In the end they recommended a 17 to 24 per cent pay rise with more for those at the top (para. 74). Later they discovered a four per cent error in favour of the teachers but it was too late and too humiliating to alter the settlement.

The Clegg decision went to Burnham for agreement and then on to government who swallowed it with difficulty, and by June 1980 it was all settled.

Clegg's Commission was surrounded with controversy and a sense of entering a dark tunnel. Management, with government backing, wanted a new salary structure linked to defined conditions of service and packaged up with pay levels. At this time, all sides said they wanted a reform of the Burnham system, and the generally established view of Clegg was summed up in a Times Educational Supplement editorial (18.4.80: 2): 'Only fairly good, fairly difficult to pay, and just about fair to an underpaid profession which is expected to improve standards in the face of increasing public and financial pressures'.

By the start of 1980 the government cuts in education and their cash limits on local authorities had reinforced the effects of falling rolls (especially in primary schools) to create an atmosphere of resentment and panic. The panic, or at least the search for purely mechanical devices to resolve political issues, was shown by the reaction to reform of Burnham and the unsatisfactory arbitration pay award for April 1980. All of this was compounded by the four per cent Clegg error and the sharp divisions within each side of Burnham. Whilst most of the unions gave a cautious welcome to Clegg as the best deal available, the NAS/UWT continued its violent opposition. In the words of its assistant general secretary: 'The Clegg report destroyed Houghton and placed an albatross around our necks' (Schoolmaster and Career Teacher, November 1980: 10).

As the Clegg settlement was implemented the teachers put in for a 20 per cent pay rise for 1980 but, after some wrangling, the management offered 9.3 per cent. The claim went to arbitration which ended up awarding 13.5 per cent.

The management also hardened their view of comparability and rejected notions of linking teacher pay with Civil Service pay through Megaw (1982), but still insisted on their long-term aim of linking pay with performance.

National developments on codified conditions ground to a halt in 1981. Some progress was made on a range of ad hoc issues, but the unions were unhappy that many LEAs were not operating the CLEA/ST collective disputes procedure. Better

results had been achieved in persuading nearly all
LEAs to adopt the 'model paragraph' into individual
teacher contracts which refers to nationally and
locally negotiated agreements (NUT Annual Report
1982: 119).

Little happened in the national forum of
CLEA/ST in 1982 with minimal progress only on unpaid
leave of absence.   On major items such as the
collective disputes procedure and travel allowances
nothing developed in the first meeting for over a
year in July.   Nonetheless AMA wanted to resolve
conditions of service matters in CLEA/ST and
government wished to tie them into pay negotiations.
These talks allied to the unions' renewed offer on
hours and duties started the process off again in
October.   This time round the NUT concentrated on
class size and minimum staffing standards to protect
jobs (NUT Annual Report 1983: 115), but NAS/UWT
continued its general opposition to such talks and
in particular to minimum staffing. At the same time
the employers were again challenging the contractual
nature of voluntary duties and claimed in CLEA/ST
that the 1968 school meals agreement put a clear
duty on teachers to support the head in midday
supervision.

In 1983 there were no dramatic developments in
national negotiations on conditions of service,
although over 40 different topics were discussed at
the four meetings of CLEA/ST (NUT Annual Report
1984: 112).   The major issue was the abuse by
authorities of fixed-term contracts: the unions
agreed that these could be used to cover for
teachers and maternity leave, secondment, long-term
illness, and when vacancies are to be filled next
term (NUT News, June 1983, 10).   But the unions
strongly rejected the employers' use of fixed-term
contracts to regulate teacher numbers and to
circumvent redeployment agreements.

The other major concern for the unions was the
call for teacher assessment and merit pay. This had
been one of the main planks of Sir Keith Joseph's
pay policy and had received strong support from
employers and head teacher unions (as long as it did
not apply to their members). With the confidence of
a large parliamentary majority and defensive trade
unions, the education policy-makers in government
focused their attention more and more on merit pay
schemes and annual performance monitoring.   The
NAS/UWT was already on record for its strong
opposition to appraisal: 'No existing objective
criteria can be applied to a definition of minimum

acceptable standards, the current models of teacher appraisal are fatally flawed' (Schoolmaster and Career Teacher, December 1980: 5-7). Later the new president attacked the system in his address to the 1983 Annual Conference when he noted that accelerated increments would be paid for doing extra jobs other than teaching and not for being a good teacher (Schoolmaster and Career Teacher, May 1983: 5-6).

These developments were watched carefully by the government, increasingly concerned to secure cuts in pay and conditions with minimal opposition through public appeals to the failure of teachers and some councils to provide a service that both gave value for money and gave parents what they wanted. Amidst strong calls to rid the system of inefficient and incompetent teachers, and for special pay for maths and science teachers (Cockcroft, 1982), the pay round for 1982 brought a harder position from all parties. The unions wanted 12 per cent to keep up with inflation and to restore Houghton (not Clegg), while the management offered 3.4 per cent with a threat that more would cost jobs and worsen school conditions. In March and April the Labour-controlled AMA wanted to improve the management offer but the Tory-led ACC stuck firm (the ACC had 13 seats to AMA's 10 on Burnham). This deadlock within the ranks of the management panel encouraged the unions to take industrial action in the form of withdrawal of goodwill to force their claim to arbitration, and allowed the NUT and NAS/UWT to co-operate over pay strikes.

A direct result of the government's changes in the Burnham rules meant that the unions had to apply sanctions in order to end up in arbitration. The NUT and AMMA made a major tactical point of exempting those LEAs which publicly supported arbitration; thus strengthening AMA's hand. NAS/UWT were not selective in this way and carried out sanctions across the range of LEAs. Eventually, ACC and AMA agreed a joint informal offer of 5.9 per cent, but the DES blocked that with its veto, which so infuriated the ACC that it was driven into the arms of AMA and a management agreement to go to arbitration against the wishes of both the DES and government. In this way the government, through its DES representatives on Burnham, skewered their ACC allies and forced arbitration in order to end industrial action. In June the arbitration panel awarded a pay rise of six per cent to the teachers.

Meanwhile, the talks on structure became

stranded and further efforts by management to win union support for appraisal and improved conditions of service had led them, by November, to agree to the unions' demands for a merged Scale 1 and 2. This was against a background of promotion blockages and with more cuts and closures every day.

In 1983 the salary structure reforms were the main issue with the management still hoping to link structure to merit pay through assessment and a general trade-off with conditions. The unions were very defensive after the Falklands war and the high showing of the government in the opinion polls. With government projections published in February that the number of teachers would fall to 385,000 by 1985/86 from 438,000 in 1979/80, and with a concomitant real cut in the education budgets, the government was in a strong political position and the unions in general at the nadir of their post-war power. Rising unemployment and the Employment Acts put pressure on the unions for another quick pay settlement. The management dutifully offered 3.5 per cent but settled for 4.98 per cent in April after some half-hearted strike threats. NAS/UWT wanted arbitration again (as part of the campaign for the reform of Burnham and to counter the NUT majority on Burnham; (see Schoolmaster and Career Teacher, September 1983: 6) but the NUT held out for a pay deal which included the setting up of a pay data working party (NUT Annual Report 1984: 134) to compile information of use in comparability arguments next time round.

The Tory win at the general election reinforced the government's policy and the position of Sir Keith Joseph, and their calls for performance measures which delighted both the DES and management on CLEA/ST. This gave renewed impetus to the structure talks but with a stronger line from management that new structures would not entail new money. The tough economic stance of the post-election phase meant real cuts in the rate support grant announced in August. The impending laws on rate-capping combined with high levels of teacher unemployment (Cook and Barnbaum, 1983: 229, concluded that 'the oversupply of teachers in certain subjects . . . will remain and may become more marked') to push management to favour payment by results systems for teachers linked to contractually defined duties and responsibilities. All this pressure further exposed the differences between teacher trade unions with the NAS/UWT favouring a trade-off of conditions for pay if the

price is right; the SHA and NAHT supporting
assessment; and only the NUT with unsure support
from AMMA rejecting the pay conditions link and its
merit pay corollary. The government strategy on pay
structure and its general anti-union propaganda
wedded to severe financial limits and the genuine
crisis of morale within the profession meant that
'teachers are more divided among themselves than
they have ever been' (David, 1983: 225).

In this climate management offered three per
cent in line with the pay ceiling but the unions
rejected that and dug in over any attempts to link
pay with assessment (NUT News, 1983: 13).

The second Thatcher government 1983-87
The massive electoral triumph of June 1983 linked
with the poor performance of the Labour Party paved
the way for the next stage of the government's
education strategy. The encouragement of direct and
indirect private education by starving the state
sector of funds was achieved through the weakening
of both Labour-controlled councils and the trade
unions. The latter were concerned not only with the
pay and conditions of their members but were closely
associated with the spread of comprehensive
education and other progressive developments within
the state sector. The government now embarked on
the eclipse of the NUT within the teacher trade
union bargaining forum, the curtailment of that
forum's relevance, a tight control of teachers'
working day and the establishment of the head as
manager. This view of school management included an
enhanced role for governors and was tied to a
national curriculum in order to bypass local
authority control of education and create an
education service in which schools competed with
each other for pupils and teachers. This opened the
door for USA-style merit pay. These strategies met
with genuine popular opposition mounted by the
teachers of England, Wales and Scotland in a series
of national strikes in 1985/86.

1984 opened with the depressingly familiar
announcements on more cuts in spending, more job
losses and the news that two-thirds of teachers
earned below the average wage. As one AMMA official
suggested, the situation could be described with the
military metaphor of a slow march towards the sound
of gunfire. By February the teachers had asked for
a rise of 7.5 per cent along with progress on
restructuring of salary scales. In March the
management panel offered three per cent under the

pressure of rate-capping and central government's
cash limit controls with the argument that more pay
means less books, and a further push to link pay
with performance and conditions of service. The NUT
restated its salary structure case in great detail
(NUT News, March 1984: 4) and restated its rejection
of any merger of salary and conditions negotiating
machinery. In contrast the NAS/UWT still wanted
more pay and faster promotion in exchange for
assessment and some trade in conditions.

The NUT also rejected the three per cent offer
and reminded their members that they needed 31 per
cent to restore Houghton and that the pay data base
on comparable earnings supported their case. The
unions wanted arbitration again but were summarily
rebuffed and by April the NUT and the NAS/UWT
announced industrial action to force management to
arbitration; a rerun of 1982 but with far more
bitterness and far worse consequences.

In May and June the major teacher unions took
industrial action. The NUT Annual Report 1985: 62
reported:

> The action was necessitated by the attitude
> adopted by the Management Panel to the
> teachers' pay claim, its initial adherence to
> an offer of three per cent, its unwillingness
> to move beyond an utterly unsatisfactory offer
> of 4.5 per cent, and its dogged refusal to
> agree to arbitration once it had become clear
> that there was no hope of a settlement by
> negotiation.

The result was that at the start of the summer term
NUT and NAS/UWT members were called upon to withdraw
from lunchtime supervision and activities connected
with the school meal service; to refuse to attend
parents' meetings outside normal school hours
connected with the running operations of the school.
The unions had clear mandates from their respective
annual conferences at Blackpool and Llandudno to
strike over pay and to press for arbitration, and it
was clear that the action was primarily against
central government and its drive for greater central
control.

What was equally obvious was that the employers
took the line from the Cabinet that they could not
afford to pay more and that no award could conjure
up money that was not there.

214

There was also a one-day national strike by the NUT on 9th May and intense lobbying of local councillors and MPs. In addition the NUT balloted 30,000 members who overwhelmingly voted to strike and between 22nd May and 21st June 23,000 members in 1,400 schools took part in three-day strikes. Further ballots of 100,000 NUT members resulted in large majorities in favour of more strikes planned for 26th-28th June, but on 22nd June the management panel agreed to refer the claim to arbitration. At that time all action ceased.

The management panel's submission (Management Panel Submission to the Arbitral Body on Teachers' Pay from 1st April 1984, August 1984) stressed the need to look at pay alone, and reminded the panel of the obstructing effects of separate pay and conditions negotiating machinery (para. 1.4). Their case was based on four principles: financial resources; the recruitment, retention and motivation of teachers; other local government settlements; and the pay, duties and responsibilities of teachers.

The financial case rested on central government's control over local authorities' budgets and its economic objectives. This control, the management argued, takes the form of making it illegal to levy a supplementary rate, the 'tapering' of grant support, the use of cash limits, and the introduction of targets and penalties. The rate support grant for education was cut by two per cent in cash terms between 1983/84 and 1984/85 (para. 6.12). This financial constraint can only be dealt with through controlling the number of teachers and their pay (para. 6.26). In 1984 6,000 jobs will go, compared with 4,000 in 1983 and 5,400 in 1982. Therefore the LEAs could not afford a pay rise beyond the 4.5 per cent offered and central government would not meet an award higher than that out of central funds.

The teachers in contrast produced a submission (The Teachers' Panel Submission to the Board of Arbitration on the Salaries of Teachers from 1st April 1984, July 1984) based entirely on comparability and the findings of the pay data working party. Page after page of the submission details the erosion of teachers' pay compared to a whole range of comparators. To underline this they say: 'There is one fundamental principle in the 1984 claim which the Teachers' Panel wish to see recognised. That is that teachers' pay should be comparable with other professional groups' (para. 6.2).

The other main argument produced is that the demands of the profession are greater than ever; more work, higher standards, more stress, massive curriculum development (for example, multi-cultural education, new technology), more meetings on planning with advisers, reviews of pupil performance, new acts of Parliament (1980 and 1981), and all this against a background of mass unemployment and falling resources (section 7).

In September the arbitration panel awarded a 5.1 per cent pay rise to the fury of the unions. The NUT expressed profound disappointment and suggested that:

> The award . . . was not the award of the arbitral body, because the Panel itself could not agree. It was the award of the Chairman acting as an 'Umpire', the first time this has happened in respect of teachers' pay. The appointment of the Chairman itself was the subject of controversy prior to the arbitral hearing and the nominee of the Teachers' Panel, Mr. John Hughes, was unwilling to sign the report of the arbitral body. (NUT Annual Report 1985: 63)

The failure of the umpire to understand the true political purposes of the arbitration and to account for the balance of power within the schools system (and his failure to apply the golden rule of arbitration - find out who is the lion and give them the lion's share) resulted in a recommendation that inevitably paved the way for the prolonged strike of 1985/86.

The unions had argued since 1980 that falling rolls and financial cuts had worsened promotion and career prospects and that a radical structural change in salary scales was needed. Over 60 per cent of teachers were on scale 1 and 2 with little hope of promotion. Since 1981 the teachers had pushed for a new salary scale, but in July 1984 the talks halted. In 1981 the Teachers' Panel wanted a common spine for all salary scales, a through scale from 1 to 2, more scale 3 and 4 posts, a reduction in the number of groups of schools, a review of the method of grouping, senior posts to be related to curricular and staffing needs of schools. Only in 1983 did the employers respond in detail: an entry grade which went on to the main professional grade only after satisfactory assessment, a main professional grade with annual assessments and accelerated increments (merit pay) for better teachers, payment for grades above main professional grade and payments for heads and deputies.

The management wanted all teachers to have defined duties and responsibilities which would be contractual and include midday supervision. These would include a whole range of teaching and management functions such as the duty to contribute to and participate in team planning, self-evaluation, in-service training and professional development in assigned areas of the curriculum and pastoral arrangements; and to participate in related staff meetings and school events (What Price a New Salary Structure?, NUT, 1984.

The NUT rejected the management's attempt to make reform of the pay structure dependent on changes in teachers' conditions of service and decided to end its commitment to the working party; this position was carried against the views of all other unions (NUT Annual Report 1985: 63). This again showed the extent of divisions among the unions, and the institutionalised way in which the NUT's majority position was able to determine policy even when efforts to secure agreements with other unions failed.

After the bitter disappointment of the arbitral award in 1984 and the behaviour of the employers, the unions had no option but to fight on with the public support of their members and in parallel with their colleagues north of the border. By October they had formulated a powerful pay strategy for a £1,200 rise with progress on structure and developments on assessment. The initial management responses, however, left all negotiations in collapse by the end of the year. The NUT had already decided at its Special Salaries Conference (Scarborough, 29th September) not to go back to arbitration. This had provoked further divisions among other teacher unions: SHA and NHAT opposed flat rate increases; AMMA was unhappy with premature militancy; and the NUT/UWT only just managed to paper over the cracks in their temporary alliance to take action for pay and resume talks on structure.

The employers felt confident enough to take on the unions as the NCB were doing elsewhere, but the first response was that the NUT walked out of the structure working party at the end of November. The

R. V. Seifert

employers' position soon showed its vulnerability when the Secretary of State and senior DES officials sought to undermine both the unions' and employers' case with a cavalier disregard of collective bargaining processes. Dramatic events followed with Sir Keith Joseph's announcement on 19th February 1985 that there was no prospect of the government finding the seven per cent necessary to fund the employers' salary structure package. This caused confusion among all the unions and also divided the employers' side.

In an unusual publication entitled _Education's 'Crown Jewels'_ (NUT, 1985) the Union comments:

> The NUT has now come into possession of a note of a meeting which proves that the employers knew that their package would not be funded even before they launched it. The Secretary of State met them on 14th November 1984 and the note of that meeting shows that they were firmly told by him that the figure then said to be 7.5 per cent was 'out of reach'. The note is reproduced in full in this document. There could have been no doubt in the minds of either the representatives of the Conservative-led ACC or the representatives of the Labour-led AMA that the government was not prepared to fund the package they were trying to sell to teachers. This document proves that the employers sought to mislead teachers. Their surprise at Sir Keith's statements was not about the content but at the exposure of their description. (p. 1)

This charge illustrated a major contention of the NUT and of its experienced general secretary, Fred Jarvis, that the failure of Labour employers fully to support the teachers helped to create the conditions for both strike action and the abolition of Burnham. This is in sharp contrast to the support given by Labour employers to Scottish teachers and raises major questions about Labour Party policy on public sector pay determination.

Thus the start of 1985 marked the high point of negotiation by threat, subterfuge, media exposure and legal action, and therefore the low point of negotiation by collective bargaining. This was not in any simple way due to the real inadequacies of Burnham since a similar situation of confusion and division existed in the Civil Service and NHS, but it was a result of government policies across the

public service sector in which the function of
unions was bypassed by employers, senior civil
servants and government ministers without a grasp of
the realities which determined the need for the use
of collective bargaining mechanisms to resolve
differences on pay, conditions and funding.

The pay dispute of 1985/86 and the subsequent
large scale strikes by teachers brought together all
the elements that had made up the confusions of the
previous five years; demands for reform of Burnham;
a pay/conditions structure/assessment package;
divided unions; divided employers; and a DES and
Secretary of State either unwilling to or incapable
of agreeing with their own side let alone with the
unions. This deliberate removal of 'impasse
resolution' mechanisms by the government forced the
hands of the teachers and so provoked the strikes
which started in February 1985.

The story starts in January when Sir Keith
Joseph repeated his views on assessment. At the
North of England Education Conference in Chester he
said:

> During the period of continuing contraction
> that lies ahead, I believe that a solution is
> most likely to be found by way of reforms which
> link higher pay to high quality performance -
> in the classroom and in the management of
> schools.

At the same time the employers were offering a new
deal on structure: to clarify and enhance the basic
professional role of the teacher, to help new
entrants, to develop professional performance, to
provide new career paths, to aid head teachers as
professional and managerial leaders, and to provide
professional levels of pay. Many members of the
profession reacted angrily to the proposals, and
these were well captured by Benford (1985) when he
denounced the scheme:

> Apart from their financial dishonesty . . . the
> combined effect of proposals designed to
> improve standards will contribute to a massive
> and sterile conformity.

> It is a hair's-breadth away from 'payment-by-
> results', for how will head teachers judge
> merit in a world of objectives?

In February the Burnham pay talks had broken

219

R. V. Seifert

down after the management offered an extra 7.5 per
cent on pay in return for a new contract. The NUT
backed only by AMMA rejected this and argued for
separate and concurrent negotiations on pay in
Burnham and on conditions in CLEA/ST. The NUT as a
result balloted members for strike action to start
on 26th February with selective three-day stoppages
and the NAS/UWT called a half-day strike on that
day.

The original management offer was four per cent
and/or arbitration with more if there was a package
to present to Sir Keith, but the main unions wanted
12.5 per cent and a common pay scale. As a result
the NUT declared the withdrawal of goodwill from 6th
February and later the NUT called out 4,000 members
in 26 LEAs on three-day strikes after a ballot of
15,000 members in 750 schools produced an 80 per
cent vote in favour of action. The NAS/UWT also
started selective strikes in 11 LEAs and AMMA took
out advertisements to encourage the employers to
negotiate separately in CLEA/ST and Burnham. This
already tense and determined attitude of both sides
was made much worse by Sir Keith Joseph's
insensitive statements and the threat by some LEAs
to dock pay when teachers were in breach of contract
for not carrying out 'voluntary' duties. There is a
detailed account of the teacher strikes of these
years in the second half of my book on the history
of teacher strikes (Seifert, 1987).

The strike soon became one between the
government and the largest teacher unions with the
management panel caught between the indifference of
Sir Keith's tinkering with the mechanics of
negotiations which he never understood or accepted,
and the tactical acumen of the union leaders with
strong support for their members.

The employers, in an increasingly impossible
situation, offered the services of an independent
conciliator, but the teachers rejected it as
pointless. The unions decided to step up their
action and not to move from their original claim.
In late March the NUT called out 7,000 members in 47
LEAs affecting 325,000 pupils in three-day strikes.
The NAS/UWT called out members in another six LEAs
making 22 in all. None of this was in any way
influenced by some LEAs warning of breach of
contracts.

At Easter the teachers' unions prepared for
their annual conferences and settlements became
unlikely as member anger resounded through the

public debates. The NUT had members out in 466
schools in 52 LEAs affecting 375,000 pupils, and
decided to exempt pro-settlement Labour LEAs from
action next term. The NUT executive took to their
conference a call for more action while the NAS/UWT
passed this motion:

> Conference recognises that this campaign will
> require extended periods of militant action,
> endorses the action currently being taken by
> NAS/UWT members, expresses its appreciation of
> the resolute way in which members are
> supporting the action and declares whole-
> hearted support for continuation of the 1985
> phase of the campaign. (NAS/UWT Report No. 8,
> April 1985)

Gordon Green, the NUT president, underlined the
ways in which the government had provoked the
teachers and moved 'from neglect to open hostility'
(NUT Annual Report 1985: 54). The other union
presidents took a different line: Joe Boone of the
NAS/UWT attacked the government but placed great
emphasis on the reform of Burnham; and the AMMA
president Edward Hartley spoke of the need for more
resources if Sir Keith was to achieve his radical
aims. His union decided to withdraw from lunchtime
cover from 15th April.

The case for more pay itself came from the pay
data working party on comparability, and this was
linked to pay losses associated with the lack of
promotion. Calls for a new pay review began to be
made as a way of rescuing the employers from their
predicament, but what was really being suggested was
ways of linking pay with structure and conditions
outside Burnham (Preston, 1985).

May saw a further falling apart of the
management side: the DES and ACC disagreed over
reform of RTA; the management panel wanted to tear
up the Concordat; Sir Keith's public statements
unsettled the employers and angered the unions; and
the Tories lost vital control in the shires after
the local elections. Burnham talks resumed under
presure from the Labour-controlled AMA and with the
employers anxious for a quick deal, but the
Secretary of State claimed on The World This Weekend
that teachers were 'mad' not to accept the
employers' offer. This political message from the
top echoed down to Tory backbenchers; Mrs. Jill
Knight wrote to a teacher constituent: 'It does not

seem to me too bad that four per cent is on offer
this year . . . the demand of 12.4 per cent is
totally unrealistic'.
    Meanwhile the NUT held strikes in 729 schools
in 43 LEAs and the NAS/UWT were to call members out
in another six LEAs. The NAHT said it was becoming
more sympathetic to the teachers, and more LEAs
announced support for the unions after the election
results. This entailed acceptance of the pay data
evidence, the recognition of the value of the job,
acknowledgement that the job is more demanding,
recognition of the inadequacy of the four per cent,
no arbitration, and a substantially increased pay
offer (NUT Formula for Resolving Teachers Pay
Dispute for Adoption by Local Education Authorities
for Removal of Targetting for Two-Day Week
Schooling).
    All this pressure meant movement in the Burnham
pay forum: the ACC wanted to offer five per cent
but AMA thought it too low and the DES too high and
so it fell; but then ACC and DES defeated the AMA
move to offer 6.2 per cent as too much. This
opening up of genuine exchange of propositions was
threatened again by Sir Keith's much publicised
statement that there was no more cash for a
settlement this year. As a result the NUT had
strikes in 825 schools in 42 LEAs involving 12,500
members, and NAS/UWT selection action in 26 LEAs, as
a NUT press release noted (24.5.85):

> When the current rate of inflation is 6.9 per
> cent and pay settlements are averaging 7.5 per
> cent, teachers are incensed that the government
> has blocked any prospect of phasing restoration
> of teachers' pay and metropolitan boroughs and
> county councils have only improved their offer
> to five per cent.

    Again the management tried to improve their
offer with a possible phased deal with end-loading
and a five per cent interim payment. Even with a
Labour majority on the management panel for the
first time and desperate for a deal the unions
rejected it. The NUT called off its action during
the holidays but with the threat of even more
strikes in the autumn - over 100,000 NUT members had
been on strike so far. The NAS/UWT also decided to
call more strikes next term, and AMMA decided to
continue its school meal supervision boycott.
    ACAS tried to create the positional acceptance

of informal talks, but despite some movement from
the employers the strikes went on. The announcement
of the top people's pay awards did much to fuel
teacher support for strikes as did the knowledge
that teachers in Scotland were increasing their
industrial action.

In August these ambiguous signs continued: Sir
Keith announced his £1.25 billion package over four
years tied to new structure (DES News, 5.8.85), but
the NUT thought it did nothing for the 1985 pay
settlement. Indeed the union announced its actions
for the new school year: half-day strikes, local
three-day strikes, ban on co-operation over GCSE,
more no-cover actions. The NAS/UWT also announced
their new selective strikes. All this went ahead
even though Sir Keith had changed some of the rules
of the game by reducing the NUT's representation on
the Teachers' Panel.

Early in September the editorial of the Times
Educational Supplement (6.9.85: 2) proposed the
following: 'It is clear, however, that the only way
out of the present cul-de-sac now involves a deal
which simultaneously covers 1985 and the contract-
salary structure elements of a 1986 settlement'.
Such a DES-inspired compromise was of no use to the
NUT but did attract support from the other unions.
It was clear that management had abandoned their
structure link and were prepared to settle on pay
only, and AMA were pressing ACAS to come up with a
deal. The NUT urged members to vote for more action
given the last offer of 6.06 per cent with strings
and effectively exploiting the propaganda gift of
the top people's award (NUT News, 19), and also
threw out the formal offer of 5.85 per cent with
duties and structure links made at the last Burnham
meeting on 12th September. As one NUT executive
member said: 'Teachers are incensed that once again
the employers have failed to come up with a
realistic offer to stop this year's dispute' (NUT
press release, 13.9.85). The NAS/UWT backed by the
head teacher unions indicated a willingness to
settle for 6.9 per cent, but the NUT blocked that
move (NUT, Employers' Offer: Why It Was Rejected).

The final loss of the NUT's majority on the
Teachers' Panel on 2nd December created the
conditions for a settlement. The NUT was replaced
as chair and secretary of the Teachers' Panel, and
even though the non-NUT majority had difficulty in
agreeing among themselves they still eventually
concluded a deal without the NUT. The NAS/UWT had

'decided to go for a negotiated interim settlement
for 1985' with the result going to a ballot of
members (NAS/UWT Report No. 19, November 1985). The
NUT sensed a deal in the offing and noted that 'the
NAS/UWT abandonment of any commitment to restore
Houghton levels would mean the end of the salaries
campaign' (NUT Executive Report 1986: 106).

The pressure through NUT and NAS/UWT strikes
was still on for a settlement and improved offer:
the NUT held numerous half-day stoppages and were
balloting (No. 10) on extended action (particularly
in marginal constituencies). The NUT's pre-
conditions for a deal (the four principles) were
reiterated up and down the country: an increase at
least equal to the rate of inflation; no erosion of
teacher relative salaries; an element towards the
recovery of the decline outlined by the pay data
working party; and a move towards the restoration
of Houghton.

Throughout this trying period the NUT launched
savage attacks on the NAS/UWT and its attempts to
deal with management without the treasured
commitment to restore Houghton. The phrases
'principles' of the NUT and 'sell-out' by the
NAS/UWT appeared in most NUT News issued in November
and December 1985. The Teachers' Panel finally
voted 15 to 13 (with the NUT alone against) in
favour of seeking an interim settlement without
reference to Houghton, and accepting links of pay
with conditions. The NUT prepared to go on alone
and the year ended with the unions' traditional
divisions working more than ever in management's
favour, and yet management unable to conclude a
realistic settlement without NUT and therefore
unable to stop the industrial action that started in
February. The longest and most serious pay strike
in teacher history thus continued into 1986.

In January 1986 ACAS was helping to secure a
deal between the employers and unions without the
NUT. At the NUT's Special Salaries Conference on
18th January the executive received strong support
from delegates to stay outside the ACAS talks to
insist on the four principles articulated earlier in
the dispute, to keep pay and conditions separate, to
keep up industrial action, and to enter into
structure talks after the 1985 settlement and within
the 1986 negotiations (The Teacher, 27.1.86: 2).
This line was endorsed despite some pressure for
more action from the far left mainly represented by
the Socialist Teachers' Alliance (Seifert, 1984).

This contrasted with the NAS/UWT position to accept the ACAS inspired management offer of 6.9 per cent backdated to April 1985 with 1.6 per cent from March 1986. This deal included statements about the need for increased resources, improved structure, arrangements for training and appraisal, a clear definition of contractual duties, and the procedure for the 1986 negotiations. This was to be under an impartial panel, chaired by Professor Wood, appointed by ACAS:

> . . . to guide, advise and assist as a matter of urgency, the management and teachers to provisional agreements on the pay, structure and career progression and any other related matters, e.g. conditions of service and procedures for negotiations, which either party may wish to bring forward for discussion and negotiation. (Education, 31.1.86: 92)

The unions undertook to stop all industrial action and that the final deal was to be ratified in Burnham and CLEA/ST. The NUT was not party to this agreement, and its task of persuading members to stick with industrial action and shun the ACAS deal was made simpler by Mrs. Thatcher's statement urging LEAs to lock out teachers taking action, as the NUT said her suggestion 'has only strengthened the resolve of teachers to continue their salary campaign' (NUT press release, 7.1.86). The NUT laid its contingency plans with ballots Nos. 12, 13 and 14 and decided 'on targetting of LEAs particularly guilty of retaliation against Trade Unions' (private and confidential memo from a regional officer to local association and divisional secretaries dated 23.1.86).

Meanwhile the AMMA executive ratified the agreement without a ballot, and in a highly charged atmosphere NAS/UWT members voted 43,899 in favour of the deal and 20,407 against. At the same time NUT members were voting in favour of more industrial action with an 87 per cent 'yes' response. The NUT enjoyed real mass support from the membership over their refusal to withdraw from a commitment to restore Houghton and to keep pay and conditions separate. This enabled the NUT to put pressure on the NAS/UWT which could no longer hide behind the NUT's Burnham majority as an excuse for every failure and wrong move. This meant an increase in the bitterness of exchanges between the leaders of the two unions, although amongst the rank and file (especially the NUT) there were moves for merger talks.

March was a month of uncertainty and tactical manoeuvres which reinforced the views of the right-wing leader of the Hereford and Worcester Education Committee: 'Effete and ineffectual leadership of both the ACC and employers' side of the Burnham Committee coupled with the failure to act by Sir Keith Joseph had helped to prolong the teachers' pay dispute' (Education, 17.1.86: 54). These weaknesses among the management were matched by those between the unions. Fred Smithies, NAS/UWT general secretary, wrote an open letter to his members in March stating his two prime objectives: 'to expose to teachers in schools the gross absurdity and stupidity of the negotiations', and 'I deeply regret that the NUT sought, by innuendo and lies, to distort our position'. This argument was taken up by his deputy with an attack on the sincerity of the NUT's position and the 'skin deep' nature of unity with NUT (Schoolmaster and Career Teacher, Spring 1986: 6-7).

The NUT opposed the settlement and tried to spoil it in CLEA/ST (Fred Jarvis argued that it would not settle the dispute nor teacher grievances; see his statement to Burnham in The Teacher, 10.3.86: 8) but it finally went through Burnham to the Secretary of State for ratification on the pay element only. At that stage ACAS had set up its panel under Sir John Wood (with Tony Peers and Bill Kendall) to oversee the 1986 settlement. The employers refused to let the NUT in those talks until it called off all action, but the NUT said it would only do so in return for an interim pay award (NUT News, 12, April 1986). Through April and May the NUT kept up some non-strike sanctions and held out for an interim deal. This pressure further divided the employers from the DES and was mirrored in the NAS/UWT snub to Sir Keith at the annual conference. Even though the High Court found against the NUT on their right to attend the panel talks (The Teacher, 28.4.86: 1) this legal decision was bypassed by the real situation. After intense pressure from the Labour Party on both the employers (especially after the Labour gains in the local elections) and the NUT a deal was struck: the NUT would call off its action and join the 1986 talks in exchange for a 5.5 per cent or £520 interim pay rise (The Teacher, 19.5.86: 14). The NUT School Rep Guidelines (16.5.86) informed them that there was to be 'peace and calm' in schools. The employers brushed aside DES objections and Sir Keith Joseph's reign ended with the appointment of Kenneth Baker to his post.

The end of the 1985/86 strike was followed by months of hard negotiations at Coventry, Nottingham and London which resulted in an agreement between the majority on the Teachers' Panel (NUT and AMMA) and the Labour majority on the employers' side. The agreement, although ratified in Burnham and CLEA/ST was never implemented since the government abandoned its support for the employers and legislated both a settlement and the abolition of Burnham.

After the strikes ended in May 1986 all the parties began a detailed series of negotiations in four working parties set up under the Wood panel and ACAS. All six unions, the employers and representatives from the DES joined together to bargain over salary levels and structure, conditions of service, appraisal and training, and negotiating machinery. Throughout the summer these talks continued with the NUT and Labour majority among the employers urgently seeking a deal in the knowledge that the DES under instructions from Kenneth Baker were seeking the excuse to abandon the process altogether (ACAS, Teachers' Dispute: Report of the Working Group of Future Negotiating Machinery, 1987).

On 28th July all the unions bar the NAS/UWT signed the Coventry accords with the employers. The NAS/UWT refused to agree on the grounds that too much was asked for too little (NAS/UWT, The Coventry Agreement, 1986). The NUT, in contrast, backed the deal as the best available (NUT, A New Deal for Teachers, 1986). What worried the DES and Kenneth Baker most was that any agreement was not outside their control, despite efforts to constrain local authorities and the removal of the NUT's Burnham majority. It was this that propelled them forward to remove the negotiating system entirely, and it was this threat that persuaded the NUT to reach an agreement with the employers which fell short of its own policy obligations. This latter point was given emphasis when the negotiators' proposals went through the NUT special conference.

Meanwhile the Main Report (1986) for Scottish teachers recommended some of the reforms wanted by government but resisted by the unions. This extra pressure allowed the Cabinet to underline its threat of abolition in the Queen's Speech (Weekly Hansard, 12.11.86, Col. 4). The talks resumed in November in

Nottingham with the political intention of
government plain, and the parties seeking agreement
in order to convince the public of their responsible
efforts to resolve long standing differences and
hence end school disruption. The NUT and AMMA held
successful membership ballots in support of the
final agreement, but the government was unmoved. By
now even the education establishment was urging
caution on the Secretary of State. The Economist
(15.11.86: 21) noted that 'the teachers, indeed most
of the employers, were united in condemning Mr.
Baker's centralist cane-swishing'.

On 2nd March the Teachers' Pay and Conditions
Act became law, and Kenneth Baker then announced his
imposed settlement of 16.4 per cent and his list of
contractual duties (Weekly Hansard, 2.3.87, Cols.
588-97). Since the March 1987 act the NUT and
NAS/UWT have held a series of half-day strikes in
protest against the abolition of their negotiating
rights.

Thus the teachers had staggered from Clegg to
Wood to the 1987 act in the eight years of the
Thatcher governments, and had seen three Secretaries
of State announce a belief in the standards of state
education and then proceed to undermine the system
through financial cuts, a remarkable series of
schemes to privatise the state system, attacks on
the teaching profession allied with deliberate
attempts to divide teacher from teacher, and with a
level of incompetent and insensitive management from
local and central government rarely witnessed in the
post-war world. Even if lack of clarity and
confusion of purpose infused the employers the real
outcome has been a terrible deterioration in the
schools, a loss of confidence among teachers and
parents, and an inadequate education for the
children of the 1980s (Report of Her Majesty's
Inspectors on the Effects of Local Authority
Expenditure Policies on Education Provision in
England 1985, DES, 1986).

In terms of industrial relations the mirage of
deals secured through a modified Burnham and/or
through arbitral inquiries under any other name
remained a false and wishful illusion. The reality
was that low pay, unreformed structures and
conditions, unfair treatment and unsubstantiated
attacks on the qualities and commitment of the
profession as a whole moved a generation of teachers
to use their trade unions as defence organisations
for themselves, their trade and their service. This
resulted in the end of the old system, which

received its first push in the 1970s (Coates, 1972b)
and the final development of the new system of
strikes, the end of national negotiating machinery,
court actions and workplace industrial relations.

The Conservative government of 1979-87 pushed
the majority of teachers in the state sector to
ditch any final associations with professionalism as
a form of defence against government policies and
whole-heartedly towards trade unionism, perhaps more
than all the arguments and struggles of left-wing
activists.

LOCAL INDUSTRIAL ACTION AND THE DEVELOPMENT OF SCHOOL INDUSTRIAL RELATIONS

While pay and national conditions of service were
the targets for control by central government in the
1980s the situation in local authorities and at
school level was less easy to contain. As a result
of government policy, and as a consequence of the
changing nature of British labour markets and
therefore of the demand for the products of state
schooling, there developed new systems of LEA-based
and school-based collective bargaining. This shift
in the focus of negotiations has important
repercussions for the management of schools, the
organisation of the trade unions, and the power of
teachers over their working lives. This section
provides a general account of the local industrial
action that followed from cutbacks, and of how those
actions speeded up the process of the establishment
of school industrial relations. In particular the
experience in many schools of teachers taking strike
action and withdrawing goodwill vitally altered
head/staff relations, and helped to create a
permanent shift towards a more formal and systematic
resolution of school issues through industrial
relations mechanisms.

Throughout the period of the Conservative
government's two terms of office school teachers in
England and Wales have faced severe cuts in the
funding of their pay and their workplaces. This has
varied somewhat according to LEA fashion, but has
been seen in every state school in the country.
These cuts have reduced the conditions of service of
the profession through, for example, deteriorating
buildings and equipment, inadequate books, the half-
hearted introduction of information technology, and
curtailment of the curriculum.

At the same time, and for broadly the same

reasons, the teachers have been asked to increase disciplinary control, maintain the quality of educational standards, work harder, take more orders, and deal with more intervention from local and central government and from parents. There has been a clear pattern of response from the two largest unions in terms of persistent and consistent industrial action in many parts of the country (Seifert, 1987), and this in turn has been met by a varied management response including recourse to the courts, docking of pay, and a mixture of threats on closures and dismissals.

Late in 1979 Mark Carlisle stated the government's belief that cuts in expenditure would not harm standards or pupils because inefficiencies in the operation of the school system allowed new cash strictures without real-life penalties. This position unleashed a wave of unrest and confusion within schools unseen in this country since just after the Great War (Ozga and Lawn, 1981). The NUT and NAS/UWT both held special conferences and both decided to strike if faced with compulsory redundancies. As the Scottish secretary of NAS/UWT wrote: 'Responsible trade unions do not shrink from the possible use of strike action . . . to achieve legitimate ends . . . but . . . only as a last resort' (Schoolmaster and Career Teacher, February 1980: 10). One popular form of action by the teachers was a refusal to cover for absent colleagues since it caused great inconvenience to the LEA at little cost to union members and highlighted inadequate staffing levels.

Early in 1980 the extent and speed of the cuts in education had surprised even the harshest of the government's opponents. £360 million or three per cent had gone from budgets with a further 3.5 per cent next year. During 1980 the pattern became clearer: on the one hand a call to rid the system of inadequate teachers from both employers and some unions, and on the other pupils sent home due to refusal by teachers to undertake duties which had increased through staff cuts.

In Avon, for example, the authority announced cuts of over £4 million in July 1979, and one immediate consequence was a reversal of an earlier decision to admit 'rising fives' in September thus breaching part of an agreement with the NUT. The action committee of the union sanctioned no-cover action in response, and the authority in turn announced its intention to make 406 teachers redundant. The union then called a half-day protest strike and balloted on extended strike action (<u>NUT Annual Report 1980</u>: 147). A group of NUT members on strike in Avon kept a four-day diary which was published in the <u>Times Educational Supplement</u> (7.3.80). The story is of reluctant strikers forced to act to protect their schools from cuts, 'empty store cupboards, decaying buildings, an impoverished curriculum, strained morale and the growing bewilderment of youngsters . . . remedial groups dispersed, options dropped' (p. 24).

Another example of local management strategy was when in January 1980 Mrs. Eileen Crosbie refused to teach her class of 40 children because it exceeded the recognised maximum class size. She was immediately suspended by her LEA. Her action in a Nottingham nursery led to the first NUT strike in this round of action against cuts. After her disciplinary hearing in April the county sacked her which led to an indefinite strike by NUT members. By September the union called off its 20-week-old action during her hearing before an industrial tribunal. At the hearing several important mistakes by the management emerged: for example, the county's senior adviser on nursery education had not visited Mrs. Crosbie at her unit. Despite these failings and the attempt to settle out-of-court the decision of the tribunal was to uphold her dismissal. The NUT's Law and Tenure Committee thought that the decision 'is a denial of common sense justice in so far as it has resulted in a teacher losing her job, having made a stand for educational principles' (<u>NUT Annual Report 1981</u>: 111). This decision led to a rally in November 1980 in Nottingham attended by over 5,000 teachers in support of Mrs. Crosbie and a commitment from the NUT to fight for her reinstatement (NUT, <u>The Case of Mrs. Eileen Crosbie</u>, 1980). After further campaigning the Labour Party won the local elections in May 1981, reinstated Mrs. Crosbie, and made improvements in the education service.

The catalogue of cuts, job losses, union action and management counteraction continued throughout 1980 with all the disruption, bitterness and loss of direction associated with massive dislocation and a power struggle between central government, local authorities and teacher trade unions.

As 1980 neared its end it became apparent from the announcement of the 1981/82 rate support

R. V. Seifert

> grant settlement, that even more serious damage
> is likely to be inflicted upon the education
> service by the Government's determination to
> further reduce public expenditure, regardless
> of the consequences for vital services. (NUT
> Annual Report 1981: 66)

So the largest teachers' union gloomily reported and
saw no respite from the round of local industrial
action and fiercer management responses creating
great damage to children and their education for the
next decade. These actions also changed the
attitudes of many teachers to their line managers
and to their employers, and in so doing introduced
on a wide scale the imperative of union protection
at the place of work as well as in the locality of
employment.

> Every member of the NUT and, indeed, every
> teacher should be aware of the damage inflicted
> on the education service in 1981. As a result
> of the Government's determination to impose
> further cuts in public expenditure, and the
> compliance, willing or unwilling, of many local
> education authorities, with the demands of the
> Government, there was no improvement at any
> point, only a further deterioration in the
> level of resources and the range of educational
> opportunities provided. (NUT Annual Report
> 1982: 62)

Such an uncompromising statement tells a story of
disenchantment and opposition unparalleled in the
history of English education. Most industrial
action in schools continued to be local and mainly
against the cuts, and often enjoyed support from
parents and the wider labour movement.
   When Sir Keith Joseph took over as Secretary of
State the state system for which he had so little
regard was already in a dire situation. The Second
Report from the Education, Science and Arts
Committee of the House of Commons (HMSO, December
1981) reported that nearly one in five local
authorities were 'falling short in overall
performance' (para. 8.2) due to government financial
constraints. The Committee also pointed out with
some vigour that 'a pro-rata reduction of teaching
staff is in effect a cut' (para. 8.8) and that 'the
maintenance of pupil/teacher ratios in a period of

232

falling rolls is tantamount to a cut' (para. 8.11).

The end of 1981 saw industrial action by teachers in 27 LEAs, more cuts announced and implemented, and a hardening of attitudes from all participants. The new year brought no hope of amelioration or a replacement for the hand-to-mouth conflicts between teacher unions and employers. The drip, drip, drip, of eroding confidence and disappearing resources had not yet turned into any coherent stream of rejection and opposition.

The most important local strike was in Barking early in 1982. All NUT members in secondary schools struck from 16th-19th February and an indefinite strike of all NUT members was called from the 25th which lasted six weeks (Jones, 1985; NUT Annual Report 1983: 141). This strike in Barking was the longest local strike since the 1920s, and resulted in a notable victory for the NUT based on strong local union organisation, national union support, and an alliance with the local labour movement and parents' organisation. This victory against a Labour authority showed both the greater unity among teachers at local level than at national level, and how the Labour Party's failure to control their own councils made the relationship between employers and unions so poor as to allow a Conservative government to exploit this vital weakness in the labour movement. The White Paper on expenditure (Cmnd. 8494) issued in March created more gloom as it underlined the Labour Party's inability to prevent cuts, and this was allied to a get-tough policy of LEAs which claimed that refusal to supervise midday meals and out-of-class activities was in breach of contract.

By April elections to the NUT executive had brought a left shift with some local strike leaders winning places; for example, Ken Jones in Barking. This fuelled the militant response of the union against short-term contracts, in reaction to the HMI report, and against the increasingly competitive NAS/UWT. At the NUT Scarborough conference the president, Alf Budd, urged the government to recognise that there never had been enough teachers in the maintained sector, to remove the threat of redundancies, and to reduce class size (NUT Annual Report 1982: 59). He might have added to his list the restoration of proper conditions of work in schools. The HMI's (Report of Her Majesty's Inspectors on the Effects of Local Authority

Expenditure Policies on Education Provision in
England 1985) had already noted the difficulty of
studying in cold and badly equipped classrooms, and
more and more examples now came to the fore.

In the summer and autumn after the 1983 general
election the pattern re-emerged of threats of
redundancies (Devon, Sefton and Ealing), and the
reality of compulsory redeployment in Southwark.
The NUT and NAS/UWT stepped up their action in
response, and in Sefton such was management's
insensitive handling of the issues that AMMA, NAHT
and SHA joined in the dispute. The trouble within
the NUT of official action by rank and file and STA
reappeared in one of the far left's strongholds
(Southwark) and again it resulted in internal
disciplinary action against the leaders of such
action (Seifert, 1984). The year ended, as so many
did in the early 1980s, with more cuts and a major
dispute in Durham over supply cover.

More cuts and job losses were now announced,
and this catalogue of dismantling of the schools was
used by the NUT president, Don Winters, in his
presidential address to conference:

> . . . and local authorities, far from being
> encouraged to advance and improve, are being
> coerced into cutting, closing down and
> destroying. And those among them with merely
> the modest target of simply maintaining
> services at their present level, are branded by
> the Government as outrageous overspenders.
> (NUT Annual Report 1983: 56)

The rest of 1983 saw many more local disputes
including one in Durham which brought out strong
antagonisms between the NUT and NAS/UWT much to the
enjoyment of the government and local press.

1984 saw the government win and lose its
greatest pitched battle of a long and costly war.
The miners' strike dominated the year and ended in a
proclaimed and technical victory for government.
But the political and moral costs inflicted on the
government were so great and the benefits much
smaller than assumed that the decline of Thatcher-
style Toryism can be dated from this time. For the
teachers there was also national strike and
industrial action to force the employers to
arbitration. These events overshadowed the local
disputes against the continuing cutbacks in
education.

Whilst the developments on the salaries front provided the most dramatic events of the year, there were other developments equally serious in their implications for the teaching profession. First among these was the continuing deterioration in the provision of resources for the education service. (NUT Annual Report 1985: 63)

The February White Paper continued with plans until 1987 offering cuts in real terms for education spending of nearly a billion pounds from 1979 to 1985. It was made clear that the service was to be kept in books and equipment by a reduction in teaching staff and pay.

Some local authorities, encouraged by their national organisations and the DES, began to try to outflank the unions and refuse to recognise agreements: in Walsall they ended the collective disputes procedure when the three largest unions invoked it over redeployment (Education, 2.3.84: 175); and Hereford and Worcester refused to recognise a collective dispute jointly called by the unions over redeployment and premature retirement (NUT Annual Report 1985: 141). These employer initiatives were the first steps to stop the development of nationally negotiated conditions of service, and were the storm petrels of the end of national wage bargaining and the imposition of contractual duties.

The HMI report for 1984 received more public attention than usual and contained several passages of great political embarrassment for the government. It tells of 'hardpressed teachers, dilapidated school buildings and tatty textbooks' (NUT, Children Are Suffering Because of Education Cuts, 1984). It continues with the lack of funds to replace books and equipment, teacher shortages in key subjects, conditions of classrooms that adversely affect learning, and that failure to fund education properly has lead to unsatisfactory quality of work. This report helped make education a more important political issue, and over the next three years it became a central theme of attacks on the government's record.

1985 was dominated by the extensive strike action and withdrawal of goodwill by the major teacher unions over their pay claim. It became the decisive battle between teachers and the government, and from its start in early February to the end of

the year it remained unresolved despite local
election defeats for the Tories in May and the loss
of the NUT's majority on the Teachers' Panel by
December. In this way the fight against the cuts
was postponed since the industrial action taken
locally merged into the national pay fight. But the
cuts went on fuelling the determination of the
teachers and politically isolating the government.

The NUT action committee reported 28 local
disputes and noted that their main preoccupation
'has once again been the defence of employment,
conditions of service and working conditions of
members' (NUT Executive Report 1986: 9). The White
Paper (Cmnd. 9426) projected the loss of another
five per cent of posts from 1984/85 to 1987/88, and
this followed the loss of 32,000 jobs since 1979/80.
It was felt that:

> . . . schools and education have become
> scapegoats for the broader failings of
> governmental policy. Education has thus become
> an easy pray for expenditure cutbacks and has
> laid itself open to the introduction of
> specious tests of effectiveness and
> performance. (Hughes, 1985: 4)

This political perspective allowed government to cut
education spending in real terms despite bogus
statistics provided by official sources (see Maclure
and Travers, 1985, on diseconomies of declining
scale and the appropriate deflator). In 1973/74
expenditure on education and science was 13 per cent
of total public expenditure, 11 per cent by 1983/84
and a planned 10 per cent by 1987/88. The
conclusion is that 'education has become the victim
of recession. Its resources have been cut
disproportionately and even its basic facilities are
being allowed to deteriorate' (Hughes, 1985: 23).

Three unconnected but related events occurred
later in the year to highlight this issue of the
political role of schooling, and unintentionally and
indirectly helped rocket education up the political
agenda and sustain the teachers on strike. The
first was the Tottenham riots. The second was the
suspension of teachers followed by strikes in a
Manchester school (see The Career Teacher, May 1986:
5-6, on Poundswick) over the 'graffiti' affair.
Although this began as a dispute over the
disciplining of pupils, the reaction of the LEA
turned it into a row over the respective authority
of teachers, heads, governors and the LEA. The

suspension of teachers by the LEA against the will
of most staff, governors and parents lead to a
strike throughout Manchester's 350 schools. The
third incident was the disciplinary action taken by
an employer against a local headmaster in Bradford
after he had proclaimed his opposition to local
policy on multi-racial education. In Bradford 25
teachers went on strike in support of parents
calling for the dismissal of Ray Honeyford in a day
of action against his reinstatement by order of the
High Court. Later he resigned from post with full
compensation. Late in 1986 another case of a head
disciplined by her employers for making an allegedly
racist comment created great public concern.
Maureen McGoldrick was suspended from her post in
Brent, but later she was reinstated after court
action and the threat of strikes. All these three
cases involved teachers suspended by their employers
after incidents with racist elements.

While that in itself is an important issue and
one that will come increasingly to the fore over the
next few years, the wider issue was one of the
authority and power relations between teachers,
their unions, school governors, the local employer,
the courts, and the Secretary of State; a situation
which remains unclear. This lack of clarity has
encouraged the development of local industrial
relations at school level, and has helped it to take
a traditional workplace form.

The start of 1986 had a depressingly familiar
ring to it: a White Paper (Cmnd. 9702) announcing
more cuts in education, large scale job losses in
the secondary sector (Audit Commission, 1986), a
national pay strike, and several important local
strikes. But this familiarity was deceptive. The
government was on the defensive and the real
situation in state schools was of more and more
public concern.

In February the NAHT announced that 60 per cent
of its members had voted for a one-day strike over
government plans on midday supervision, and by
Easter the main union conferences restated their
opposition to cuts and the government. The
ideological battle over privatising schools and
state funding of education had reached its high
point. Parents' organisations had evidence to show
that 72 per cent of secondary schools have 'badly
dilapidated buildings' and that 82 per cent of
pupils are 'sharing essential textbooks'; and the
inspectorate reported that 'only 11 out of 97
authorities are providing satisfactory resources'.

This situation was well documented by Margaret Jay in Panorama and she concluded that 'it's hard for even the most cost-efficient authority to maintain standards in the face of such a reduction in its resources' (The Listener, 20.3.86: 2).

The local election results in May had sounded an ominous knell for the government and Kenneth Baker was brought in to replace Sir Keith Joseph in order to stop the political rot (although not the rot in the schools). The courts also had their say at this time with a High Court judgement ruling that teachers must cover for absent colleagues as part of their contractual duties.

In May 1986 the NUT took the cases of four of their members to the High Court after their respective LEAs had taken action over their refusal to cover for absent colleagues. Mr. Justice Scott concluded his judgement:

> For my part, the right approach to these and any other questions as to the ambit of teachers' contractual obligations is to ask whether the obligation in question is a part of the professional obligations owed by a teacher to pupils or to his or her school. If the answer is 'yes' then, in my view, a person who is employed as a teacher prima facie owes that obligation . . . it follows that, in my judgement, each of the plaintiffs had a contractual obligation to comply with the request to cover . . . in each case the refusal was, in my judgement, a breach of contract. (Transcription of the High Court (Chancery Division) decision of Mr. Justice Scott in the cases of Sim v Rotherham MBC; Townend v Doncaster MBC; Barnfield v Solihull MBC; Rathbone v London Borough of Croydon, 23.5.86: 37-8)

This judgement helped the employers to put more pressure on the unions to agree to contractually defined duties, and it also aided the government's intention to impose duties on teachers. The industrial relations outcome was clearly linked with the impressive series of local campaigns undertaken by the teacher unions with increasing public support throughout the country. In so doing the parties to bargaining created the conditions for the existence of an extensive system of school industrial relations.

Towards school-based industrial relations: union responses to staff losses, performance appraisal and management control
A minimal amount of research has been completed into school-based union stewards and school industrial relations (Cole, 1969, has outlined some of these developments for American teachers). More recently, Johnson (1983) has studied the impact of collective bargaining on schools in the USA. She quotes from Bailey (1981) in a passage that would now apply with equal vigour to the situation in the United Kingdom:

> Few issues in the field of American education have been more controversial in the past two decades than the rise of teachers' unions. Struggles over appropriate bargaining agents, what issues are negotiable, grievance procedures, the right to strike, and even the underlying compatibility of unions and the educating profession have divided faculty, outraged administrators, politicised schools and colleges, entangled the courts, and roiled public opinion. (p. ix)

The majority of state schools in Great Britain have faced cuts in the level of resources since 1979, increased management control and attempts to introduce tighter definitions of conditions of service especially merit pay systems based on performance appraisals. The 1984/86 strikes by school teachers in England, Wales and Scotland were about relatively low pay and against government and employer initiatives to tie pay increases to changes in performance and duties. CLEA/ST had begun to lay down national conditions through the Burgundy Book, but its slow progress was overtaken by the imposition of duties in 1987. The issues covered included maternity leave, early retirement, redeployment and working duties (NUT Executive Report 1985: 48-51), and under the direction of government policy and legislation these issues and their implementation have been increasingly the subject of negotiations at local and school levels.
The government has two stated major objectives: to save money and to improve standards. The first is part of their well-documented strategy of reducing state expenditure, while the second is based on the argument that much of our industrial decline (Worswick, 1985), lawless tendencies among the young and the moral crisis of work and authority

is due to failure by teachers and the education system. Sir Keith Joseph has often made this argument and tied it explicitly to changes in the pay system (including the introduction of merit pay). In a major statement to the House of Commons he said:

> Our objective is to improve the standard of teaching in schools and the quality of our education system. That is why we have agreed to the commitment of such substantial additional resources towards improving teachers' salaries. But we are not prepared to release the resources without simultaneous action on teachers' duties and the pay structure to ensure that the nation receives a fair return for the extremely large investment. (Weekly Hansard, 22.10.85: 87)

On the same day Mr. George Younger, the Secretary of State for Scotland, spoke of the teachers' dispute in Scotland with a more direct comment:

> . . . the public have the right to expect that one element in a settlement should be a firm clarification of teachers' duties so that they cannot again inflict such chaos and demoralisation on our schools at so little cost to themselves. (Ibid., 91)

The Prime Minister has frequently backed them up as with this reply to a question in the House of Commons from Martin Flannery:

> . . . in dealing with teachers' pay it is vital to set out a statement of their contract of service so that there can be no other argument about it. It is also vital to have a pay structure that means that the better teachers will be paid more. (Weekly Hansard, 10.12.85: 396)

The logic of this position is that national decline can be traced to poor educational standards and that poor educational standards are due to the poor standard of teachers. This line of debate leads to a solution which requires performance appraisal with merit pay for better teachers. This policy of the British government is paralleled by the concern of other governments who also blame

teachers for their relative economic decline.
President Reagan speaking at Seton Hall University
in May 1983 declared: 'Teachers should be paid and
promoted on the basis of their merit and competence.
Hard-earned tax dollars should encourage the best.
They have no business rewarding incompetence and
mediocrity' (quoted in Johnson, 1984: 175).

This crisis in education is mediated in
practice through social and institutional mechanisms
downward to the workplace. Such mechanisms include
the budgets of local education authorities, the
media portrayal of the failures of the school system
to teach 'relevant' and therefore useful subjects,
the Burnham system geared to expansion not
contraction, cash limits, and the school management
(both governors and heads). It is this last
category that concerns this section: the ways in
which head teachers pass on, willingly or
unwillingly, the ideological and financial attacks
on education to classroom teachers.

The main ways in which this has operated is
through staff reductions, performance appraisals
with merit pay, and through an increase in
management control despite protestations from heads
themselves to the contrary. In the introduction to
the government's White Paper, Teaching Quality
(Cmnd. 8836, March 1983), the logic of the argument
flows from 'the government's aim is to make the best
use of available resources to maintain and improve
standards in education; (para. 1) through 'school
rolls are falling' (para. 2) and 'a substantial
decline in demand for newly-trained secondary
techers' (para. 4) to the need for local authorities
'to make full use of management tools such as
premature retirement, redeployment, and, if
necessary, compulsory redundancy' (para. 8).

These initiatives by managers to the crisis
that was thrust upon them were met with a trade
union counter. The NUT considered that:

> The White Paper gives little thought to the
> professional integrity and responsibility of
> teachers: instead, it views teachers as a
> number of units, totally subject to the control
> of central government and their employers, the
> local authorities. (NUT, Teaching Quality –
> The Union's Response to the White Paper, June
> 1984: 7)

It further attacks the notion of moving 'teachers

from post to post and in the last resort dismissing those who fail to fit the tasks allocated to them' (p. 7). The NUT goes on bitterly to reject the overall rhyme and reason of government policy:

> The instruments of management recommended include the increased use of short-term contracts, regular and systematic assessment of teachers' performance and the threat of dismissal for those teachers deemed unsatisfactory. Contraction of the teacher force is given paramount importance . . . special emphasis is placed on using redeployment. (Ibid., 27)

It is the union's school representative who mediates between individual teachers involved in these processes of change and head teachers involved in the implementation of the policies of change. The creation of a set of school-based industrial relations agreements comes from this process of bargaining.

To recap the logic of the argument so far: financial cutbacks and the redefinition of standards are the general strategic objectives of the government (Tolliday and Zeitlin, 1985), these lead in the end to the creation of a set of industrial relations issues in schools. This generation of issues which are formally resolvable within traditional trade union/management relations provides the basis for more school and local bargaining and hence enhances the role of the school-based union representative (Perry and Wildman, 1970). Three particular issues are now examined: staff losses, merit pay, and management control.

Staff losses. These come from falling rolls (Walsh et al., 1984), school closures and mergers, subject rationalisations, and adjustments to new financial targets. This aspect of the management of the cuts is resolved into five related union negotiating areas: redeployment, tenure, redundancy, early retirement and temporary contracts. The main concern of government is not just the reduction in the number of teachers, but also the match of supply to demand and the greater flexibility of teacher labour time. The premature retirement compensation scheme is seen as neutral in this respect (Teaching Quality, op. cit., para. 78), but redeployment is granted the status of 'the most

powerful single instrument available to authorities'
(para. 79). Other planned methods for fitting
existing supply to demand include short-term
contracts (para. 80), dismissals (para. 81), and
part-time teachers (para. 82). Needless to say, the
NUT is 'totally opposed to compulsory redundancy'
(Teaching Quality, op. cit., 31), and supports
genuinely voluntary and carefully planned early
retirements. The NUT objects to redeployment of the
kind already undertaken and to the widespread abuse
of fixed-term contracts (pp. 32-4).

A major task of the 1980s for many head
teachers is to reduce the number of staff in their
schools. Their job, whether they like it or not
(and most do not), is to implement the selection
processes within local authority policy guidelines
and to meet the target numbers set. There are
several options open to the school managers to
achieve these reductions, and there are also
additional but secondary objectives which can be
achieved apart from the main one of reducing staff
numbers. The general purpose of the exercise is to
reduce 'the total stock of teachers and its
distribution between sectors and schools' (Thomas,
1984: 1). This reflects the fall in England and
Wales in the maintained sector of 38,000 primary
teachers between 1978 and 1985, and of 10,000
secondary teachers in the same period (DES
Statistics of Education, Schools 1985).

Some heads see falling rolls and the subsequent
management of decline as a positive chance to alter
the curriculum (Reid, 1983). Through the use of
specially selected redeployment policies for
individual teachers within schools or for groups of
teachers between schools the management can restrict
the choice of subjects and specialisms considered
unpopular and/or unworthy and/or damaging to the
school. This process creates more discretionary
powers for the head and greater control over the
remaining staff fearful for their own futures, as
Walsh et al., (1984: 145) concluded redeployment
creates 'a general atmosphere of apprehension and
uncertainty'. If schools are closed then 'spreading
the pain and diffusing the blame' (Zerchykov, 1983:
183) is a strategy for the avoidance of open
conflict. In general the appearance (although often
not the reality) of ad hoc policies on the
contracting of school systems, reducing funds,
removing staff and eroding facilities may allow
local politicians in the educational sub-government

243

R. V. Seifert

to avoid the political consequences (although not
the real ones) of the detrimental neighbourhood
effects of closures (Andrews, 1983). The ease with
which this can be achieved may depend on the methods
used: early retirements, for example, are often a
soft option but themselves depend for success on the
age profile of the teachers in the area. In
contrast redundancies and the ending, and not
renewing, of fixed-term contracts are a tougher
prospect and raise fundamental questions about the
selection of those to go.

Many head teachers when faced with the need to
reduce staff by any of the methods discussed are
aware of the fine line in practice between voluntary
and compulsory lay-offs. In these circumstances
heads will seek to rationalise their decisions by
reference to the quality of the staff involved.
Seniority and subject are seen as secondary
considerations to the chance of ridding the school
of poor performers. Such performance-related lay-
offs, however, have important unintended
consequences for those who remain: they compromise
the autonomy of the local school; they alter the
positively held views of the role of the head; they
jeopardise co-operative relations among staff; and
they diminish the effectiveness of teacher
supervision and assessment of other teachers. All
these factors 'call into question their educational
worth' (Johnson, 1980: 216).

Heads will often have mixed motives in getting
rid of staff and therefore will treat the unions in
different ways (see NAS/UWT's Curriculum Related
Staffing Levels, 1983). Nonetheless the existence
of a web of local understandings, general agreements
about the ethos of professional comradeship, and the
strength of teacher trade unions in many schools
combine together to force heads to deal with school-
based union representatives and hence to be party to
(even if unwillingly and unwittingly) the
strengthening of school industrial relations
systems.

Merit pay. The basic thinking behind private
enterprise virtues and market forces holds that good
teachers of needed subjects should and will receive
greater pecuniary rewards than bad teachers of less
favoured subjects. The judgements required to
implement this reward system will be made through
performance appraisal schemes. The government has
stressed often enough its emphasis on 'the
connections between the structure of the salary
scales on which teachers are paid and policies for

244

promoting commitment and high standards of professional performance amongst teachers' (Teaching Quality, op. cit., para. 90). In particular the government believes that 'employers can manage their teacher force effectively only if they have accurate knowledge of each teacher's performance' (para. 92). The NUT reject the tone and substance of this approach. They feel that it is 'top-down' and they find unacceptable policies that 'link assessment of experienced teachers to greater financial rewards' (Teaching Quality - The Union's Response, op. cit., 40). This point is made more forcibly in a later NUT statement where the union opposes 'proposals within the salary structure talks that assessment should be linked to merit pay or conversely to the withholding of annual increments' (NUT, Teaching Appraisal and Teaching Quality, February 1985: 1). The argument is widened to incorporate merit pay and performance appraisal within a battery of 'management tools aimed at identifying and dismissing "unsatisfactory" teachers'.

The government is increasingly attracted to merit pay systems based on performance appraisal and borrowed from an ideal type of structure said to exist (and operate successfully) within private industry (Everard, 1982). Such schemes are also being introduced into the NHS for nurses, managers and other staff, and the Civil Service for managers.

From the perspective of the head teacher performance appraisal allows an apparently rational and acceptable method of discarding bad teachers and of rewarding good teachers. One survey found that heads overwhelmingly preferred teacher evaluations rather than seniority as the criteria for lay-offs (Phelan, 1983: 192). Not surprisingly in the same survey teachers themselves rejected evaluation as the basis for sackings and the trade unions involved would only negotiate redundancy agreements based on seniority.

The arguments in favour of merit pay based on assessment that are marshalled by some heads, school governors and local and national politicians include the recognition of public demand for taxpayers' money to be spent on good teachers only, that merit pay ensures the efficient use of resources, that it encourages individual effort, that it makes the profession in general more self-critical and therefore helps all teachers to improve, and it enables exceptional teachers to get quick promotion to senior positions within the profession. The debate on this became more intense after the

publication of the CIPFA consultative paper by
Ramsdale (see for example the views of Graham,
Gould, Springett, Hinds, and Esp). As Stenning and
Stenning (1984: 77) say:

> Against a background of financial stringency,
> the issue of educational standards has led to a
> public demand for schools to be more
> accountable to the communities they serve and
> to society generally. Here the question of
> teacher competence is of prime concern.

The main arguments against include the basic
lack of a definition of and measuring instrument for
an efficient teacher, it lowers morale, it spoils
normal relationships between senior and junior
staff, it hampers the work of teachers, it leads to
the ostracism of those who benefit from the system,
it is not an effective incentive, and it inhibits
experimentation (Johnson, 1984). Opposition comes
from various quarters: the NUT argues these days
that:

> There is a place for the assessment and
> appraisal of experienced teachers where the aim
> is to promote professional development . . .
> the Union is wholly opposed to linking this
> type of assessment to that which is essentially
> a management tool aimed at identifying and
> dismissing 'unsatisfactory' teachers. (Para. 8
> of <u>NUT Evidence to the Education, Science and
> Arts Committee of the House of Commons</u>, minutes
> of 18.12.84)

A British HMI visiting American schools concluded:

> I found little evidence that the procedures
> encouraged flexible, sensitive, interactive
> teaching in the classrooms. The emphasis on
> demonstrating specific competencies may well
> encourage the rather 'safe', static and
> didactic teaching which is common to many
> schools. (Peaker, 1986)

Lawn (1985a: 29) has warned that 'regular assessment
of teachers is intended to make them more
'productive' but it will also intensify the controls
upon them'.

Detailed accounts of actual schemes and
measurements abound (Stenning and Stenning, 1984),
but none of them addresses the central issues: the

resolution of a general low pay problem by a scheme aimed at increasing the pay of some, and the criteria upon which the payments are made. The strategic objective for school managers is a tighter control of the internal labour market, while the task for workplace trade unionists is to resist individual solutions to low pay and mechanisms to control the quality and quantity of teacher labour time.

In the absence of a teachers' register and therefore of no direct professional control over teacher numbers it is left to the unions to control labour market forces and the dictates of management inspired control over the teachers' pay and hence of teacher labour time. The primary mechanism for this is control over duties, promotions and standard negotiated earnings. Merit payments systems threaten all this. Since 1980 the government and the management panel of both Burnham and CLEA/ST have pushed hard for a definition of a teacher's pay and duties, and for a link between conditions of service and pay and pay structure. Merit pay based on appraisal is favoured by management while the NUT prefers a new pay structure which combines a main professional scale with pay comparability.

One example of the ways in which unions will have to negotiate safeguards against the use of merit pay is the granting and use of leave (see the NUT's A Fair Way Forward: Memorandum on Appointment, Promotion and Career Development, June 1981). The need for study leave to improve standards and/or to claim new skills and knowledge may influence the ability of any individual teacher to achieve the levels of performance necessary to receive the extra financial rewards. The head has discretion over who gets such leave and for how long, and therefore can effectively give a helping hand to aspiring high performers. In addition an important number of women teachers take maternity leave and then return to work. The attitude to this leave and to promotion already discriminates against women: merit pay will underscore that discrimination.

Management control. The greater the power and authority given to head teachers to control individual members of staff the easier it becomes to impose management definitions of professionalism and excellence on classroom teachers. This development in schools parallels those in the NHS (Long and Harrison, 1985) and Civil Service (Lloyd and Blackwell, 1985) where the aim is to secure the most

flexible management control over units of available
labour time. The union response to this new
management revolution included the definition of
duties, in loco parentis duties and their legal
interpretations, some conditions of employment, and
industrial relations procedures on grievances and
discipline. In May 1984 the HMIs reported that
'poor management not only affects teaching quality
but also the level, appropriateness and effective
use of available resources' (DES, Report by Her
Majesty's Inspectors on the Effects of Local
Authority Expenditure Policies on Education
Provision in England, May 1984: 17). This claim is
made after an analysis based on the primary
assumption that 'the right teachers in the right
numbers are the most important requirements of the
education service' (p. 11).

This echoes the central contention of the 1983
White Paper on Teaching Quality that:

> Head teachers, and other senior staff with
> management responsibilities within the schools,
> are of crucial importance. Only if they are
> effective managers of their teaching staffs and
> the material resources available to them, as
> well as possessing the qualities needed for
> effective educational leadership, can schools
> offer their pupils the quality of education
> which they have a right to expect. (Para. 83)

The choice of language, couched as it is in
traditional managerial terms, signals more truly
than the operational details the objectives and
attitudes of government policy-makers. The NUT
response here is limited to the proposition that
heads cannot be 'effective leaders' if they do not
have the resources and if they have to cover in the
classroom for lack of staff (Teaching Quality - The
Union's Response, op. cit., 35). The weight of
policy and opinion is at present irresistible and
therefore shows itself increasingly in school
practice.
    The head teacher exercises control over staff
in several ways: influencing their hiring and
firing; promotion; task selection; the extent of
participation in decision-making (Gaziel, 1983);
and the creation of power relations with key members
of staff (Barnet, 1984). Recent developments have
put more pressure on heads in terms of the
allocation of diminishing resources, a reduction in

staffing levels, parental rights, and a national and public concern for standards. These new pressures have resulted in heads experiencing a felt loss of authority to the politicians particularly at central government and DES level (Taylor, 1983). But the situation has so altered as to also provide a chance for heads to exert more authority through the control of lay-offs, pay and performance links, and the discretionary decision-making over the priorities for expenditure within schools. Although elected members, administrators, advisers, inspectors, parents and unions all expect a greater say in running schools (Partington, 1981) the heads have fought back through their own unions and as workplace managers have more power than before.

One major area in which this is apparent is in the terms of employment teachers enjoy through their duties and legal responsibilities. The conditions of employment affected by these changes in the power and authority relationships within schools include health and safety, facilities, holidays and travel allowances. All affect teachers' abilities to do their job and to do it properly.

This concern with duties has a long history, a complicated series of ad hoc arrangements, and no realistic permanent solution despite the 1987 imposition of some duties. Often during industrial disputes this grey area of duties, the thin line between professional conscience and professional status, is taken to be a legitimate target for teachers, for example, withdrawal of lunch cover, no meetings with parents, a cessation of additional activities outside normal school hours.

The duties carried out by teachers and their hours of work have been a constant source of confusion, argument and exploitation. The Burgundy Book notes in paragraph 11 that 'there are no existing national collective agreements on these matters' (p. 11) except for the midday lunch break where a working party report is included in Appendix VII, and which notes that:

> Among the more important of the educational and social developments has been the increasing tendency of teachers to engage in voluntary extra-curricular activities between the morning and afternoon sessions and after the school day has finished. This has been accompanied by an increasing tendency for children to spend the midday break at school. (p. 45)

R. V. Seifert

Most teachers are employed to teach, to supervise and to prepare their work. Many also now have managerial functions, extra-curricular activities and must spend time and effort on responsibilities endured by all professionals which are governed by self-imposed standards and large areas of self-regulation.

There exists within this pattern scope for a variety and dimension of limits on hours and duties only just made explicit in a legal contract, frequently not recognised in any collective agreement or monetary reward, and not readily appreciated by the outside world. As a result, there is a continuous occurrence of arguments, potential disputes and inevitable disagreements between staff of all grades and in particular between management and union members.

The implementation and interpretation of the new contracts and of the new powers of school-based managers will bring into sharper focus those industrial relations issues which entail the classic conflicts between management and worker, and those specifically mediated through the local workplace representative (the rep). This underlines both the need for a workplace trade union for teachers and the main purpose of the reps as figures of pivotal contact in the conduct of school power relations.

Even though most problems are dealt with informally they persist in such a way as to maintain the long standing commitment of classroom teachers to unions beyond both ideological and professional reservations. The Burgundy Book provides a model grievance procedure in Appendix II (pp. 23-8) which allows for grievances within the school to be decided through a mixture of informal and formal stages, or for a direct approach to be made to the chief education officer if the grievance is with management other than staff members. Coping with member grievances is the bread and butter of workplace industrial relations and provides both a genuine channel for discontent and a series of examples of the need for a proper brokerage system between the power centres of classroom, staff room and senior staff based on the school rep system. The existence of the procedures (itself a product of union organisation and success over the years) and the ability of the school rep to activate it on behalf of a member are positive developments for school industrial relations.

For many school reps formal industrial

250

relations and the process of bargaining with management remain remote, unusual and probably unacceptable. Their prime task is to recruit, disseminate information and chat informally to members about a range of employment topics located in the school. In the vast majority of cases they become the rep through a marginal political system that provides continuity in office and no electoral contest (in an earlier study, 1983, of NUT reps in the Midlands I found that only 13 per cent stood for election). In these circumstances, particularly found in primary schools, reps are seen as, and see themselves as, the passive and empty vessels for member expression and wish.

The trade union realities for teachers are negotiations with undemocratic employers, strikes against unjust methods of allocating rewards, and defensive actions to protect members from arbitrary decisions by managers. This harsh experience tends to make the active trade union member in schools adopt a more instrumental approach (Allen, 1954) in contrast with the liberal democratic ideals of the majority of members (Pateman, 1970). Whatever else happens the rep must deal effectively with both management strategies (Purcell and Sissons, 1983) and with hostile competitive unions (Poole, 1974). As school reps bargain more with head teachers over industrial relations issues so these imperatives of effectiveness may lead them to seek support from local association side rep networks (Terry, 1982) and hence to a more developed industrial relations system.

This tendency to abide by formal elements of school industrial relations is further supported by the overwhelming response in favour of sticking to the agreed rules of industrial relations and the heavy reliance put on local and regional officials to help out in local negotiations. In July 1981 the NUT issued circular 268 with a model constitution for local joint negotiating committees based at divisional level, and has recently reviewed its regional services (NUT Executive Report 1985: 6-8) in order to strengthen school and local bargaining on conditions of service issues.

Workplace industrial relations take on a formal existence when there exists a trade union organisational framework with members, representatives and local and regional back-up; and when the management can and will negotiate the most important issues facing their staff. Until now the basic pay award

has been subject to national agreements and formulas
with some elements of local and head discretion.
Any move, as the one proposed by the government,
towards a merit payment system associated with
performance appraisal will locate the centre of pay
disputes at local education authority and school
level. This tendency will be increased if plans for
regional pay structures are implemented.

In the case of conditions of service there has
been a series of ad hoc and often unclear national
and local agreements; but with budget cutbacks, and
with standards and performance being forced to the
centre of the school stage then many terms and
conditions of service will de facto be settled at
school and local level which is why the government
is seeking to tie up national definitions of duties
with the merit pay system.

Both of these trends when allied to the labour
market position of teachers will result in more
regular and more formal negotiations and this in
turn will lead to the strengthening of the workplace
trade union representative. In the USA there has
been a marked spread in collective bargaining at
school site levels between principals and unions.
Many conditions of work such as hours, work
schedules, workloads, free time, extra duties and
promotions are negotiable (Kerchner and Mitchell,
1981). Even so the impact in American schools
varies considerably and only some of the major
concerns of teachers are resolvable through
collective bargaining such as pay, job security,
redeployment, consultation and participation, and
fewer non-teaching duties. The overall consequence
has been to increase union membership in schools and
the number of collective agreements, but there is no
evidence that this has so restricted heads as to
prevent them managing nor has it damaged standards
(Johnson, 1983).

Industrial relations in schools, as far as the
NUT and its members are concerned, have depended
traditionally upon the informal interactions of
members with their reps and the reps with school-
based management. This indicates, along with the
findings on the attitudes and lines of argument used
by reps, that most NUT reps at present simply pass
on from member to manager articulated queries and
worries. This process has become more significant
with changes in the role of school-based managers,
with the devolving of some negotiable issues to
school level, and with the widespread involvement of
so many teacher trade unionists in industrial

action: hence we are witnessing the early stages in the development of a traditional workplace industrial relations system.

Thus the major developments of two terms of Thatcher government are the dismemberment of national pay bargaining, the dislocation of state schooling, the weakening of national teacher trade unions, the contraction of local authority powers, the central control over school life in both curriculum and teacher duties, and the increased divisions among teachers themselves. The outcomes of these policies have been large scale industrial action by teachers, the growth of the left in the main teacher unions, attempts to forge new bonds of unity between teachers, parents and the wider labour movement, and the growth of school-based industrial relations. There is no evidence that the future will be better for children, teachers or parents as a result of the immense upheavals of these years, and there is no evidence that the country will receive a higher quality service at lower unit costs as a result of the new management initiatives. The 1980s have been years of perpetual crisis for state education, and the only lasting outcome is that the main teacher trade unions and the majority of their members are now firmly embedded in the traditions and methods of the British trade union movement.

REFERENCES

Allen, V. (1954) Power in Trade Unions, Longman

Andrews, R. (1983) 'Managing Contracting Systems: Three Policy Alternatives', Education and Urban Society, 15(2), pp. 199-210

Audit Commission (1986) Towards Better Management of Secondary Education, HMSO, London

Bailey, S. (1981) 'Foreword', in Angell, G. (ed.) Faculty and Teacher Bargaining, Heath, Lexington, Mass.

Barnet, B. (1984) 'Subordinate Teacher Power in School Organisations', Sociology of Education, 57, pp. 43-55

Benford, M. (1985) 'The Structure Proposals - A Recipe for Conflict', Education, 19th January, p. 58

Clark, R. (1984) Review Body on Doctors' and Dentists' Remuneration, Cmnd. 9256, HMSO, London

Clegg, H. (1980) Standing Commission on Pay Comparability, Cmnd. 7880, HMSO, London

R. V. Seifert

Coates, R. (1972a) Teachers' Unions and Interest Group Politics, Cambridge University Press, Cambridge

Coates, R. (1972b) 'The Teachers' Associations and the Restructuring of Burnham', British Journal of Educational Studies, 20, pp. 192-204

Cockcroft, W. (1982) Committee of Inquiry into the Teaching of Mathematics in Schools, HMSO, London

Cole, S. (1969) The Unionisation of Teachers: A Case Study of the UFT, Praeger, New York

Cook, M. and Barnbaum, G. (1983) 'Unemployed Graduates: The Case of Student Teachers', Employment Gazette, 91(6), pp. 223-9

David, T. (1983) 'The Teacher Unions: Their Friends and Enemies', Education, 1st April, p. 255

Esp, D. (1984) 'Measure for Measure', Education, 7th September, p. 191

Everard, K. (1982) Management in Comprehensive Schools - What Can Be Learned From Industry?, Centre for the Study of Comprehensive Schools, University of York, York

Gaziel, H. (1983) 'Staff Participation in Elementary School: Decision-Making and Job Satisfaction', School Organisation, 3(2), pp. 139-51

Gosden, P. (1972) The Evolution of a Profession, Blackwell, Oxford

Gould, G. (1984) 'Measuring Teacher Performance', Education, 20th April, p. 328

Graham, D. (1984) 'Will Teacher Assessment Ever Get Off The Ground?', Times Educational Supplement, 23rd November, p. 4

Greenborough, J. (1984) Review Body for Nursing Staff, Midwives, Health Visitors and Professions Allied to Medicine, Cmnd. 9258, HMSO, London

Hall, S. and Jacques, M. (eds.) (1983) The Politics of Thatcherism, Lawrence & Wishart, London

Hinds, T. (1984) 'A Case for Performance Indicators' Education, 20th April, p. 329

Houghton, D. (1974) Report of the Committee of Inquiry into the Pay of Non-University Teachers, Cmnd. 5848, HMSO, London

Hughes, J. (1980) 'Repeat Performance: Clegg and Houghton', Times Educational Supplement, 2nd May, p. 4

Hughes, J. (1985) Education: Investment or Impoverishment, NUT, London

Jay, M. (1986) 'The Crisis in Education', The
Listener, 20th March, pp. 2-3

Johnson, S. (1980) 'Performance Based Staff Lay-
Offs in the Public Schools: Implementation and
Outcomes', Harvard Educational Review, 50(2),
pp. 214-33

Johnson, S. (1983) 'Teacher Unions in Schools:
Authority and Accommodation', Harvard
Educational Review, 53(3), pp. 309-26

Johnson, S. (1984) 'Merit Pay for Teachers: A
Poor Prescription for Reform', Harvard
Educational Review, 54(2), pp 175-185

Jones, K. (1985) 'The National Union of Teachers
(England and Wales)', in Lawn, M. (ed.) The
Politics of Teacher Unionism, Croom Helm,
London

Kerchner, C. and Mitchell, D. (1981) Dynamics of
Public School Collective Bargaining and its
Impact on Governance, Administration and
Teaching, Institute of Education, Washington DC

Latta, G. (1969) The NAS: A Historical Analysis,
MA thesis, University of Warwick, Warwick

Lawn, M. (1985a) 'Teachers' Hard Lessons', Marxism
Today, 29(12), pp. 29-32

Lawn, M. (ed.) (1985b) The Politics of Teacher
Unionism, Croom Helm, London

Leopold, J. and Beaumont, P. (1986) 'Pay
Bargaining and Management Strategy in the NHS',
Industrial Relations Journal, 17(1), pp. 32-45

Lloyd, P. and Blackwell, R. (1985) 'Manpower
Economies, Management and Industrial Relations
in the Civil Service', Industrial Relations
Journal, 16(4), pp. 25-37

Long, A. and Harrison, S. (eds.) (1985) Health
Services Performance, Croom Helm, London

Maclure, S. and Travers, T. (1985) 'Damned Lies
and Statistics?', Times Educational Supplement,
8th February, pp. 12-3

Main, P. (1986) Committee of Inquiry Report into
the Pay and Conditions of Service of School
Teachers in Scotland, Cmnd. 9893, HMSO, London

Manzer, R. (1970) Teachers and Politics,
Manchester University Press, Manchester

Megaw, J. (1982) Report of an Inquiry into Civil
Service Pay, Cmnd. 8590, HMSO, London

Morris, M. (1984) 'Separating the Boss from His
Cash', Education, 30th November, pp. 446-7

Ozga, J. (1985) 'Teacher Contracts and Teacher
Professionalism: The Educational Institute in
Scotland', in Lawn, M. (ed.) The Politics of
Teacher Unionism, Croom Helm, London

Ozga, J. and Lawn, M. (1981) Teachers, Professionalism and Class, The Falmer Press, London

Partington, J. (1981) 'Heads You Win, Heads You Lose?', Times Educational Supplement, 30th November, p. 4

Pateman, C. (1970) Participation and Democratic Theory, Cambridge University Press, Cambridge

Peaker, G. (1986) 'Teacher Management and Appraisal in Two School Systems in the Southern USA', Journal of Education for Teaching, pp. 77-83

Perry, C. and Wildman, W. (1970) The Impact of Negotiations in Public Education: the Evidence from the Schools, C. A. Jones, Worthington, Ohio

Phelan, W. (1983) 'Governing Staff Reductions: The Use and Abuse of Teacher Evaluations', Education and Urban Society, 15(2), pp. 189-98

Poole, M. (1974) 'Towards a Sociology of Shop Stewards'. The Sociological Review, 22, pp. 57-82

Preston, M. (1985) 'Is Another Houghton the Answer?' Times Educational Supplement, 5th April, p.4

Purcell, P. and Sissons, K. (1983) 'Strategies and Practices in the Management of Industrial Relations', in Bain, G. (ed.) Industrial Relations in Britain, Basil Blackwell, Oxford

Ramsdale, P. (1984) Performance Indicators in Education, CIPFA, London

Reid, K. (1983) 'The Management of Decline: A Discussion Paper', School Organisation, 3(4), pp. 361-70

Rhodes, R. (1985) 'Corporatism, Pay Negotiations and Local Government', Public Administration, 63, pp. 287-307

Roy, W. (1968) The Teachers' Union - Aspects of Policy and Organisation in the NUT 1950-1966, Schoolmaster Publishing, London

Roy, W. (1983) Teaching Under Attack, Croom Helm, London

Saran, R. (1985) The Politics Behind Burnham: A Study of Teachers' Salary Negotiations, Sheffield Papers in Education Management No. 45, Sheffield City Polytechnic, Sheffield

Seifert, R. (1984) 'Some Aspects of Factional Opposition: Rank and File and the NUT 1967-1982', British Journal of Industrial Relations, XXII(3), pp. 372-90

Seifert, R. (1987) Teacher Militancy: A History of Teacher Strikes 1896-1987, The Falmer Press, London

Simon, B. (1986) 'Crisis in Education', Marxism Today, 30(5), p. 5

Springett, J. (1984) 'Making Professional Judgements', Education, 31st August, p. 169

Stenning, W. and Stenning, R. (1984) 'The Assessment of Teachers' Performance: Some Practical Considerations', School Management and Organisation Abstracts, pp. 77-90

Stewart, J. (1981) 'Recipe for Irresponsibility', Times Educational Supplement, 12th June, p. 4

Taylor, K. (1983) 'Heads and the Freedom to Manage', School Organisation, 3(3), pp. 273-86

Terry, M. (1982) 'Organising a Fragmented Workforce: Shop Stewards in Local Government', British Journal of Industrial Relations, XX(1), pp. 1-19

Thomas, H. (1984) 'Teachers in Decline? The Quality Consequences of the Management of Changing Rolls', Educational Management and Administration, 12, pp. 1-14

Thomson, A. and Beaumont, P. (1978) Public Sector Bargaining, Saxon House, London

Tolliday, S. and Zeitlin, J. (1985) Shop Floor Bargaining and the State, Cambridge University Press, Cambridge

Tropp, A. (1957) The Schoolteachers, Heinemann, London

Walsh, K. (1981) 'Centralisation and Decentralisation in Local Government Bargaining', Industrial Relations Journal, 12(5), pp. 43-54

Walsh, K., Dunne, R., Stoten, B. and Stewart, J. (1984) Falling School Rolls and the Management of the Teaching Profession, NFER-Nelson, Windsor

Walton, R. and McKersie, R. (1965) A Behavioural Theory of Labour Negotiations, McGraw Hill, New York

Way, P., Duncan, J. and McCarthy, W. (1981) 'Official Pay Inquiries: The Houghton Committee on Teachers' Pay', Industrial Relations Journal, 12(1), pp. 27-45

Winchester, D. (1983) 'Industrial Relations in the Public Sector', in Bain, G. S. (ed.) Industrial Relations in Britain, Blackwell, Oxford

Worswick, G. (ed.) (1985) Education and Economic

R. V. Seifert

Performance, Gower, London
Zerchykov, R. (1983) 'Closing Schools and Managing Conflict', _Education and Urban Society_, 15(2), pp. 175-88

Chapter 7

SOME CONCLUSIONS

R. Mailly, S. J. Dimmock and A. S. Sethi

The introduction to this book put forward the proposition that, although the growth of public expenditure was reappraised and to an extent checked in the mid 1970s, it was the coming to power of the Conservative government in 1979 that marked a fundamental change in policy towards the public sector. The analysis provided in the chapters has only served to underline how important the change of direction has been for industrial relations in the public services. Although there have been undoubted changes in the economic policy followed by the Conservatives such changes have only touched the periphery of their policy towards the public sector. Control of the money supply as a principal method of regulating the economy was finally rejected in 1982, and the privatisation of major areas of the public sector became a central element within Conservative policy, as the realisation that public expenditure could not be reduced without terminally damaging the welfare state appeared to exercise an influence on the minds of ministers it would have to be controlled.

These developments, however, have little effect on the fact that a most important influence upon industrial relations in the public services is that of the 'political contingency'. Equally, there is no question that this influence was heightened following the election of the Conservative government in 1979. This conclusion attempts to draw together some of the principal developments in the three services since 1979. It aims to analyse such developments within the framework of a 'continuum' of state influence as postulated by Ferner (1985). The dynamics of managements' and trade unions' response to the implementation of radically different policies within the public

R. Mailly, S. J. Dimmock and A. S. Sethi

services will be assessed. Tentative judgements
will then be made concerning likely policy
developments within the public services and their
probable impact upon industrial relations. The
concluding chapter is structured along the following
lines: first, developments in bargaining structure
are analysed; second, bargaining outcomes and
finally the impact of government policy on local
industrial relations is discussed.

BARGAINING STRUCTURE

Perhaps the most profound development in bargaining
structure since 1979 has been the eclipse of
collective bargaining as a principal method of
determining terms and conditions of employment for
approximately one million employees. As stated in
the introduction, support for collective bargaining
by government, management and trade unions has been
one of the keynotes of public services industrial
relations since the establishment of the Whitley
model throughout the Civil Service in the 1920s. In
two distinct areas of the public services, large
groups of employees now have their terms and
conditions of employment settled by other means. In
January 1983 the Secretary of State for Health and
Social Services announced the establishment of a pay
review body for nurses, midwives and the professions
supplementary to medicine. These employees
constitute just under half of all staff employed in
the NHS. Taking into account the already
established Doctors and Dentists Review Body, the
pay of over half NHS employees is now decided
outwith the Whitley bargaining machinery. The
establishment of the review body was hardly a
strategic attempt to deprive these employees of
their collective bargaining rights; rather, an
expedient and ideologically inspired solution to a
long-running and politically embarrassing dispute.
Realising that the support of the nurses was crucial
to any dispute in the NHS and that only a minority
had been directly involved, the government appeased
the profession by appearing to offer them separate
treatment. The offer was made on the promise that
the body representing the nurses had not pursued
industrial action. The non-TUC affiliated RCN was
willing to agree to the terms, having a clause
within its constitution forbidding involvement in
direct industrial action. The nurses, midwives and
most of the professions supplementary to medicine

accepted involvement in the review body as the best way to maintain their professional status and improve their conditions of employment. So far, they have only been proved partially correct.

The abrogation of bargaining rights for teachers took place in a rather different context and may have markedly different implications from those of the Nurses Pay Review Body. The abolition of the Burnham Negotiating Committee took place in the context of a long and bitter dispute between the teachers, education authorities and the government. The immediate background to the Teachers Act 1987 was increasing disillusionment on the part of the Secretary of State over progress in negotiations within Burnham. The 'Concordat' agreed in 1965 between the DES and education authorities had been torn up by the management side (the Concordat stated that, although the DES had only two members on the Burnham panel, they would have the right to veto any agreement reached within Burnham which did not meet with their approval). The abolition occurred at a time when education authorities and teacher unions were about to settle the two-year dispute on terms which did not meet with the Secretary of State's approval. The Teachers Act, abolishing Burnham and setting up an interim advisory panel to the Secretary of State, has as one purpose the centralisation of power into the government's hands; power which the Secretary of State was only willing partially to relinquish after opposition from within and outside his own party. The Conservative government has indicated that during 1988 the 'interim' advisory panel will be replaced by 'effective' machinery which may or may not mean a pay review body. Any dilution of the bargaining rights of teachers will be implemented in the teeth of opposition from the TUC affiliated teacher unions, who are now far more 'unionate' than two decades ago. If a pay review body is established then it is likely that recommendations on pay will be marginally above the 'going rate' for the public services. Moreover, rather than reject the recommendations of a review body, the Prime Minister is likely to stage settlements and may only partially fund them. Education authorities in such circumstances will be placed in a similar situation to health authorities over the under-funding of its employees' pay awards. It is a prospect teachers and education authorities will not relish.

R. Mailly, S. J. Dimmock and A. S. Sethi

THREAT TO NATIONAL BARGAINING?

The second important development has been in the bargaining structures in the public services with the incremental weakening of national agreements on pay and conditions. As stated in the introduction, centralised bargaining has been a feature of industrial relations in each of the public services in the post-war period. Although sometimes criticised for its rigidity (McCarthy, 1976) it was still intact at the end of the 1970s. However, Conservative monetarist philosophy held that pay and conditions of employment should respond to the employment market and there was a growing realisation that the labour market was becoming geographically differentiated with particularly large differences existing between north and south. Developments recently have started to produce cracks in seemingly impregnable edifices of national bargaining.

In the Civil Service an agreement recently reached with the IPCS does not preclude the possibility of regional variations in pay being agreed in the future. Moreover, the fact that IPCS have agreed to a payment system independently of other Civil Service unions portends the break-up of one bargaining unit at national level. In the NHS, general managers' pay is now decided outwith the Whitley negotiating machinery and one important element within their pay depends upon locally related factors such as restructuring or 'development' activities to be carried out within the manager's region, district or unit. There is also increasing pressure upon the present payment structure for administrative and clerical staff to have more flexibility within it, so allowing for regional variations (King's Fund/NAHA, 1987).

More far reaching developments are taking place in education. The imposed pay settlement of 1986 allowed for greater flexibility on a 'local' level and the Teachers Act 1987 allows the Secretary of State to vary any award: 'An order may make different provision for different cases, including different areas' (para. 3.4).

The national bargaining machinery for local authority staff has so far remained unchanged. However, as Kessler points out (Chapter 5), the national agreement for white collar staff allows reasonable flexibility. In the case of manual staff, there have been attempts to move outside the more rigid boundaries of the national agreements.

262

Examples include movements outside the national agreement by certain authorities on the conditions for school dinner ladies and local agreements to tackle low pay, as for example in Sheffield. There have been exhortations for authorities to act further to loosen the hold of national agreements. The Secretary of State for the Environment has called for authorities not to stick to national agreements and pay what the market will bear (Financial Times, 11.9.86) and this was echoed by Nigel Lawson in the forum of NEDC and Kenneth Clarke in a more wide-ranging speech directed at both private and public sectors (Personnel Management, December 1986).

It is unlikely that the government wishes to see an end to national bargaining; if it did, its aims would be unrealistic for a number of reasons. More likely, it wishes to see more local flexibility within what would become national enabling agreements similar to the 'partial agreements' described by Sissons and Brown (1983), operating in some parts of the private sector.

PAY AND CONDITIONS OUTCOMES 1979-87

Broadly speaking, the government has been able to hold down wages in the public sector particularly the public services, to within set pay provisions. Its policy of allowing market forces to control pay in the private sector has been less successful (Hatchett and White, 1985). The gap between public and private has therefore grown wider since 1979. Within this broad picture, however, differences between groups do appear. Government ideology has influenced bargaining outcomes also. In the NHS, those employees who by and large forsook industrial action during the 1982 dispute - nurses, midwives and the professions supplementary to medicine - were 'rewarded' with an independent pay review body. Review body recommendations have tended to take into account recruitment and comparability factors as well as 'affordability'. Pay increases have averaged two to four per cent above those offered to other groups in the public services and have been weighted towards the qualified nurse and student nurses with auxiliaries receiving lower awards. Other groups in the NHS have been less favoured, receiving awards marginally above the government's norm for central government employees. In the Civil Service, pay awards have again been remarkably close

to the advised limits, with the important exception
of senior civil servants, senior members of the
armed forces, and judges who received an award of
12-17.5 per cent in 1985 on the recommendation of
the Top Salaries Review Body. Equally, in local
government the pay policy has held together until
recently. Pay awards in excess of the suggested pay
limits have been made to manual workers as Labour-
controlled authorities formed a majority on the NJC
and negotiated agreements involving the
restructuring of grades incorporating equal pay
principles.

To the surprise of some, the government has
been able to make its pay policy stick in the public
services (Hatchett and White, 1985). The
discrepancy between private sector and public sector
wages has led some analysts to suggest that a pay
explosion was inevitable (op. cit.). The predicted
explosion has not happened, although the teachers
have put the policy under severe pressure. The
reasons for the 'success' of the government's policy
have been explored in the individual chapters, but
perhaps there are some common developments across
the public services which suggest it may hold for
the foreseeable future.

For some time now the government has been aware
of the discrepancy of the two aspects of their
policy on the public services; i.e. holding down
pay, and the achievement of efficiency and cost
effectiveness in the management of the public
services. Thus Hatchett and White comment:

> While Whitehall maintains strict controls over
> pay and conditions in the public sector, it
> also expects them to achieve the same kind of
> success in winning union agreements to change
> and in motivatng employees, that is happening
> in the private sector. (op. cit., 21)

There have been recent initiatives attempting to
bridge this gap between payment methods in the
private and public sectors through the introduction
of performance pay and greater flexibility in
national agreements mentioned earlier.

One initiative has been the introduction of pay
schemes for middle to senior civil servants. In the
first scheme introduced for staff in grades 3 to 7
(formerly under-secretary to principal) annual cash
bonuses of up to 20 per cent are awarded to staff at
the discretion of individual departments. The
scheme was reviewed by Hay-MSL, who found that it

was having no perceptible effect upon performance (Brindle, 1987). Since then, more sophisticated schemes have been introduced for both grades 2 and 3 and a separate scheme for grades 5, 6 and 7. Moreover, a third and most important scheme has been introduced for scientists and engineers and agreed with the IPCS. The government won the unions' agreement to the scheme by offering a 10 per cent pay award and a long-term pay determination system based largely on the principles of comparability.

Performance related pay has gained a foothold in the NHS in which general managers' pay is linked to performance. Similar developments are taking place in education. Taken together, with moves to increase the flexibility within national agreements, these policy changes are responding to public service managers' concerns over the recruitment and motivation of employees. It is unlikely that such changes are assuaging all the concerns of such managers; however, the increased flexibility may be enough to stall any major public sector pay revolt. Although regional and merit pay may be introduced in the face of union opposition, once introduced it may prove to be a divisive and corrosive influence on union solidarity.

Finally, although the government has weakened the force of comparability as a principle for deciding pay in the public services, it has not eradicated it. The system of pay determination established after Megaw (1982) in the Civil Service contains a diluted form of comparability and the government has accepted awards of pay review bodies largely based upon the principles of comparability with the private sector - most notably the Top Salaries Review Body.

THE POLITICAL CONTINGENCY AND LOCAL INDUSTRIAL RELATIONS

The impact of government policies in the years 1979-87 in the public services has broadly reflected the position of each of the services on the 'continuum' of state influence put forward by Ferner (1985) and discussed in Chapter 1. The Civil Service has acted as a test bed for policies later implemented (sometimes in diluted form) in the NHS and local authorities. As the authors of Chapter 3 state: 'Changes in policy and practice have, therefore, been less diluted and felt more quickly and more sharply in the Civil Service than in some other

R. Mailly, S. J. Dimmock and A. S. Sethi

areas' (see page 73). Perhaps the policy initiative
which most clearly exemplifies this point is the
Financial Management Initiative. The FMI, as
Blackwell and Lloyd argue, was crucial to the
decentralisation of management decision-making in
the Service. The FMI epitomised the paradox of
simultaneous moves to decentralise and centralise in
the public services. As the authors state:

> The specific approach adopted has been to
> d e v o l v e   a n d   d e l e g a t e   managerial
> responsibilities wherever possible to the
> lowest level of line management practicable,
> allowing greater discretion and autonomy within
> clear and absolute budgetary limits. Central
> control and direction is retained through
> b u d g e t a r y   m e c h a n i s m s ;   development of
> sophisticated monetary systems at central and
> departmental levels, allowing scrutiny of line
> manager cost-effectiveness and the development
> and transmission of management skills, beliefs
> and values appropriate to the strategy (through
> training, publications, management seminars and
> gatherings).

This policy has been replicated in the NHS and
local authorities but less sharply and with weaker
central control. Although accountability is
somewhat clearer in the NHS, following the introduction of general managers, the decentralisation of
budgets is dependent upon acceptance by clinicians
which has not always been forthcoming (Long and
Harrison, 1985). Moreover, government policy is
mediated by regional health authorities which, in
the person of the regional general manager, act as
reviewers of the district health authorities'
performance. It is perhaps for this reason, the
multi-professional structure of the NHS, and the
fact that demand for certain health services is
expanding, that the decentralisation of management
decision-making in the NHS has not had the pervasive
impact it has in the Civil Service, particularly in
the form of manpower reductions.
    In local authorities, cash limits, rate
capping, pressures to contract out services, and the
role of the Audit Commission, have all served to
heighten concern over budgets and raised the
importance of ability to pay as a factor in pay
determination (see Chapter 5). The response of
authorities to their situation has been varied. In
this sector, and in other areas of the public

services, it has been policy initiatives other than a translated FMI that have had the most direct impact upon industrial relations. For example, in the NHS the imposed programme of contracting out ancillary services has had a considerable effect upon industrial relations locally. Although it was a centrally imposed policy, the nature of its introduction; its impact upon manpower levels; hours worked; and terms and conditions of employment, were to be determined locally. Consultation and negotiation over the implementation of such policies has taken place to varying degrees in both the NHS and local authorities.

It is this ability to interpret and modify central government policy initiatives that has resulted in the tightening of some central controls. The abolition of the Burnham negotiating machinery for teachers is one example of this, as is the legislation (promised in the Queen's Speech opening the Conservatives' third term) requiring local authorities to put certain services out to tender. This is likely to lead to heightening of the conflict between management, unions and central government. It is possible that on the issue of the contracting out of services some local authorities and trade unions will form alliances against a centrally imposed policy.

A direct assault upon the traditional support for trade unions in the Civil Service was noted by the authors of Chapter 3. The most public action was the barring of trade unions at GCHQ in January 1984 on the grounds of national security. The fact that the ban was maintained despite the offer of a no-strike deal by the unions, supported by the TUC, raised widespread suspicions that the ban was indicative of a government that wished where possible to eradicate trade union influence more generally. Blackwell and Lloyd point to other initiatives that have not attracted as much publicity but may be equally important. During the 1981 dispute in the Civil Service, the unions were informed that the check-off arrangements for union subscriptions could not be guaranteed for the duration of the action. In 1982 the Facilities Agreement, providing rights to time off with pay for trade union representatives, was tightened up and controls strengthened. Management has stressed that participation in industrial action by civil servants is a factor which will be taken into account when assessing fitness for promotion to managerial posts. Finally, it is reported that the positive

encouragement of union membership in the Civil
Service handbook has been revised. All these
factors indicate an undermining of one of the
principal elements within the concept of the 'good
employer' (Beaumont, 1981).

These direct moves to undermine support for
trade unions have not taken place in the other
public services. Rather, it is argued, such moves
as the contracting-out of services to private
contractors have been, to an extent, motivated by
the desire to weaken trade unions. However, there
are indications that there will be pressure from
central government for more direct measures to be
taken if the trade unions prove to be obstacles in
the way of implementing radical policies in
education and health discussed below.

In general during this period the trade unions,
in terms of membership density, have held up well in
the public services as compared to the private
sector. However, if the theory that employer
support and encouragement of trade unions in the
public sector as a major reason for their high
density is valid (Bain, 1970), then trade unions are
in for their severest test yet in the public
services, as indicated in Chapter 2.

THE NATURE OF INDUSTRIAL RELATIONS IN THE PUBLIC SERVICES AND PROSPECTS FOR THE FUTURE

At the time of writing there is no sign that the
importance of the 'political contingency' as an
influence on industrial relations will diminish as
the Conservatives enter a third successive term in
government. Rather, it seems the position of some
sectors of the public services on the 'continuum' of
state influence is to be shifted and the balance
between management autonomy and central control
changed. Education is the area in which the
political contingency is likely to be heightened in
importance. The Conservative manifesto pledges,
repeated in the Queen's Speech of 1987, to allow
state schools to 'opt out' of local authority
control and to introduce a national 'core'
curriculum, are policies which are likely to meet
concerted opposition from teacher unions. Equally,
the decentralisation of budget management to the
heads of schools - in line with the FMI (Burgess,
1986) - will further increase industrial relations
activities at workplace level in schools, already
noted by Seifert (Chapter 6).

A second area of radical change in the public services is likely to be the NHS. Despite consistent Conservative protestations that the NHS is safe in their hands, an increasing section of opinion believes the NHS is being underfunded, as the volume of reports about health authorities in financial difficulties grows. It seems likely that one element in this process, the underfunding of national pay awards, is to continue. Simultaneously, in the years since 1983, health authorities have been increasingly involved in money-raising activities, including offering services funded by themselves to other health authorities and supporting commercial ventures on the sites of hospitals. In addition, the NHS has commenced a process of collaboration with private health care. These activities are likely to intensify in the coming years as further pressure is placed upon the resources allocated to the NHS. One sign that such developments are anticipated is the decision of the IHSM and the King's Fund Centre to establish study groups to examine alternative ways of funding the NHS and means of collaboration with the private sector. Although as yet the concept of equity in national health care provisions remains unchallenged these decisions are an indication of the success of the Thatcher government in changing the climate sufficient to encourage discussion of some of the main tenets of the NHS.

The 'politicisation' of trade unions in the public services will only be further underlined by the developments mentioned above. The role of education and health services in capitalist society, and the function of the state, will be contested between trade unions, community groups and perhaps representatives of the local state with a central government wishing further to reduce the role of the state in Britain. Industrial relations both locally and nationally will be shaped in the context of such disputes as we move into the 1990s.

PUBLIC SECTOR - MIRRORING THE PRIVATE SECTOR?

In an interesting review of industrial relations in the public sector, Fogarty and Brookes state that: 'In a number of ways, what has been happening in the public sector in the 1980s has followed the same lines as the private sector' (1986: 178). What are the ways in which the public sector has been mirroring the private sector and is this trend

R. Mailly, S. J. Dimmock and A. S. Sethi

PUBLIC SECTOR - MIRRORING THE PRIVATE SECTOR?

In an interesting review of industrial relations in
the public sector, Fogarty and Brookes state that:
'In a number of ways, what has been happening in the
public sector in the 1980s has followed the same
lines as the private sector' (1986: 178). What are
the ways in which the public sector has been
mirroring the private sector and is this trend
likely to continue? Management in the private
sector has been reacting in different ways to the
collapse of manufacturing industry and the change in
the balance of power between management and unions
accompanying high unemployment. In general,
however, it is believed that the anti-union,
authoritative management style (i.e. macho-
management) is not prevalent in the private sector
(Edwards, 1985). However, the direction followed by
the majority of British firms, although it would be
a mistake to label it a 'strategy', has been based
on a number of principles. Firstly, there has been
a perceived need to attract and retain workforce
commitment by direct and indirect employee
involvement and concessions to core workers. This
has involved simultaneously supporting trade
unionism whilst fostering consultative methods of
communication, such as briefing sessions, and
quality circles. In addition, a flexible response
to employment has been increasingly developed as
part-time, temporary and casual staff have been
employed as a means of enabling the firm to operate
competitively and efficiently (Atkinson, 1984).
Fogarty and Brookes suggest that, if anything, the
move to a 'tougher' or more authoritarian style of
management has been more prevalent in the public
sector (op. cit.) than the private. They cite
examples from the public enterprises, but it could
be said that this may be equally relevant to certain
parts of the public services in the sense of the
introduction of outside contractors and temporary
and fixed term staff. Examples of this type may
increase or proliferate in future years as pressure
on resources becomes greater, whilst simultaneously
areas such as community health services are required
to expand. Moreover, it seems probable that
struggles may ensue over managerial requirements for
a greater skill mix of staff in the public services
with the result that the distinction between
trained, multi-skilled, but less costly staff and
more costly professionals becomes blurred. By
comparison, this move will be strongly resisted by

270

professional groups concerned to heighten the distinction between qualified staff and unqualified 'helpers' as, for example, is currently envisaged in the proposals contained in Project 2000 on the future of the nursing profession. Factors such as these are likely to have profound implications for industrial relations.

Fogarty and Brooke suggest (1986: 178) that, although the day-to-day management of industrial relations in the public sector may follow the pattern of the private sector, important differences will remain. In this context it seems that the most crucial difference emanates from the fact that the government is the employer either directly or indirectly in the public services and therefore industry-made bargaining is of great significance relatively compared with enterprise bargaining. This, together with the pervasive importance of the political contingency, remain significant factors differentiating industrial relations in the public sector from the private. This last factor, particularly, will ensure that industrial relations in the public services will remain as unstable in the next five years as they have in the past eight.

REFERENCES

Atkinson, J. (1984) 'Manpower Strategies for Flexible Organisations', Personnel Management, August 1984

Bain, G. S. (1970) The Growth of White-Collar Unionism, Oxford University Press, London

Beaumont, P. (1981) Government as Employer - Setting an Example?, Royal Institute of Public Administration, London

Brindle, D. (1987) 'Will Performance Pay Work in Whitehall', Personnel Management, August

Burgess, T. (1986) Public Money, June, pp. 21-4

Edwards, P. (1985) 'The Myth of the Macho Manager?', Personnel Management, April

Ferner, A. (1985) 'Political Constraints and Managerial Strategies: The Case of Working Practices in British Rail', British Journal of Industrial Relations, XXIII(1), March

Fogarty, M. and Brookes, D. (1986) Trade Unions and British Industrial Development, Policy Studies Institute, London

Hatchett, A. and White, W. (1985) 'Public Sector Pay Limits: How Long Can Managers Take The Strain?', Public Money, June

R. Mailly, S. J. Dimmock and A. S. Sethi

King's Fund/NAHA (1987) NHS Pay: Achieving
    Greater Flexibility, King's Fund, London
Long, A. and Harrison, S. (eds.) (1983) Health
    Services Performance, Croom Helm, London
McCarthy, W. C. (1976) Making Whitley Work, HMSO,
    London
Megaw, J. (1982) Inquiry into Civil Service Pay,
    HMSO, London
Sissons, K. and Brown, W. (1983) 'Industrial
    Relations in the Private Sector: Donovan Re-
    Visited', in Bain, G. (ed.) Industrial
    Relations in Britain, Basil Blackwell, Oxford

INDEX

ability to pay, 69, 167,
  179
absence: teachers'
  refusal to cover,
  54, 230, 238; unpaid
  leave of, 210
ACAS, 34, 143-4, 223,
  225-7
administrative, profes-
  sional, technical
  and clerical workers
  (APT&C), 156, 162-3,
  167, 172-4, 177-8;
  settlements in local
  government, 17, 176
AEUW, 23
affordability, 8, 10,
  80-2, 120-1, 263
AGSRO, 25, 95, 96
  (table)
ambulancemen, 119, 120,
  127, 145; strike
  (1974), 48
AMMA, 203 (table), 204,
  206-7, 211, 213,
  217, 220, 225, 228
apprenticeships, 57
arbitration, 52-3, 78,
  80, 123, 204-5, 209,
  211-12, 216-7
armed forces, 20
  (table); use of, in
  NHS, 145
ASLEF, 19
Association of County
  Councils (ACC), 166,

202, 203 (table),
  205, 211, 221-2, 226
Association of District
  Councils (ADC), 166
Association of Municipal
  Authorities (AMA),
  164 (table), 166,
  203 (table), 205,
  210-11, 221-2
ASTMS, 27, 144
Asylum and Poor Law In-
  stitution Workers,26
ATCDE, 24
ATTI, 24, 46
Audit Commission, 13,
  191, 266
Austin Rover Group, 55
AUT, 22 (table)

Baker, Kenneth, 227, 238
ballots, 80, 100, 103,
  120, 204, 228
black minorities, 37-8
BMA, 27, 115, 117, 129
bonus schemes, 33-4, 57,
  137, 141, 157,
  162-3, 169-70, 182,
  186, 191, 192
breakaway unions, 98
British Gas, 19, 55
British Shipbuilders, 19
British Telecom, 19,
  54-5, 95, 135
Britoil, 55
Broad Left, 37, 97,
  100-1

273

Burgundy Book, 239, 250
Burnham Negotiating
    Committee, 247, 261;
    reform of, 202-29,
    267; structure of,
    203 (table)

care assistants, 182
caretakers, 40, 43
Carlisle, Mark, 205, 230
cash limits, 73, 82,
    120, 125, 160, 175
casual workers, 89, 192,
    270
catering, 136, 187, 190
CCMA, 136, 138
CCSU, 71, 78, 82-3, 90,
    97-8, 103
central control over
    schools, 253
centralisation, 31,
    92-3, 107, 123, 157,
    187-8, 191, 199,
    202, 205, 266
check-off arrangements,
    102, 267
childbearing, 44
civil servants, 49, 54,
    61; industrial, 21;
    industrial action
    by, 267; inquiry
    into, 50; non-
    industrial, 21
Civil Service, 1, 6, 7,
    9, 12-13, 21, 24-9,
    32-3, 41, 43, 46,
    55, 57, 68-113, 120,
    130, 209, 218, 245,
    247, 260, 262, 263,
    265, 267; disputes
    (1973), 48; disputes
    (1977), 48; disputes
    (1979), 30, 48;
    disputes (1981), 30,
    54; efficiency in,
    90-2; new mana-
    gerialism in, 68-
    113; pay in, 81
    (table); union
    membership in, 268
CLEA/ST, 203, 205,
    209-12, 220, 225-6,
    239, 247
cleaning, 40, 44, 57,
    136, 139, 161, 182,
    190
Clegg Commission, 50,
    119, 167, 207-9, 211
clerical staff, 24,
    40-1, 43, 121-2,
    133, 162, 262
COCSU, 52
COHSE, 22 (table), 26,
    32, 35-6, 41, 42
    (table), 45 (table),
    60, 115, 127, 139-
    41, 144, 164 (table)
collective bargaining,
    12, 44, 49, 57, 61,
    68-70, 105-6, 117,
    129, 167, 219, 239,
    252, 260; structure
    of, in local
    government, 161-7
comparability, 7-9, 50,
    68-71, 78, 81-2,
    120-1, 158, 180, 204
    209, 215-16, 263
Comparability Commission
    see Clegg Commission
Computer Centre, DHSS,
    100
computer workers, 54,
    79, 93
Concordat in education,
    205-6, 221, 261
conditions of service,
    103, 190, 227, 229,
    252
Conservative councils,
    55, 166, 190, 193,
    203, 205, 211
Conservative government,
    8, 10-11, 13, 46,
    48, 50, 55, 60, 62,
    77, 99, 118-21, 130-
    6, 145, 147-8, 175,
    201, 204, 206, 212,
    229, 233, 259, 267-9
Conservative Party, 61,
    71, 188, 236, 262
construction work, 40,

187
contracting out, 14, 60,
    87, 90, 133, 135-8,
    189, 193, 267, 268
contracts: fixed-term,
    210, 244; short-
    term, 233, 242, 243
CPSA, 21, 22 (table),
    24-5, 32, 35, 37-41,
    42 (table), 45
    (table), 72 (table),
    79, 87, 89, 95, 96
    (table), 97, 100,
    103
crowding-out thesis, 12,
    71, 135
CSD, 86, 99, 106
CSU, 21, 22 (table), 25,
    32, 41, 42 (table),
    72 (table), 81, 90,
    95, 96 (table), 97
curriculum, national,
    213
Customs and Excise, 21,
    25
cuts campaigns, 95, 138

Daylight group, 97, 100
decentralisation, 76,
    82, 93, 101, 122,
    135, 187, 266, 268
Defence, Ministry of,
    25, 56, 79, 98, 135
democracy, in trade
    unions, 27-35
deregulation of public
    transport, 135
direct labour organisa-
    tions, 187, 192
Dirty Jobs Dispute
    (1970), 30, 48, 157
disabled, employment of,
    70
disciplinary control by
    teachers, 230
disciplinary issues, 34,
    53, 141, 146
disputes procedure, 209,
    210
dock industry, 46
doctors, 27, 127

Doctors' and Dentists'
    Review Body, 128,
    132, 260
domestic assistants, 43
Donovan Commission, 33,
    157

education, 2, 8, 16, 21,
    41, 43, 53, 61, 161,
    199-258; spending,
    cuts in, 235
Education Act (1980),
    189
Education and Science,
    Department of, 203
    (table), 205-6,
    211-12, 218-22, 227,
    235, 261
EETPU, 102
efficiency initiatives,
    Civil Service, 90-2
EIS, 22 (table)
electricians, 52, 120
electricity industry, 1,
    23, 26, 36, 54;
    strike (1972), 48
emergency services,
    withdrawal of, 49
Employment, Department
    of, 25
Employment Act (1980),
    12; (1982), 12, 104
employment practices in
    local government,
    188-94
employment rights, 103,
    200
engineering industry,
    46, 52
equal pay, 46, 169
ethnic minorities, 37,
    38

facility time, 102
Fair Wages Resolution,
    136
FBU, 22 (table), 24, 41
FDA, 21, 22 (table), 25,
    42 (table), 71, 72
    (table), 74, 85,
    101, 103

Index

FDA/AIT, 96 (table)
Financial Management
    Initiative (FMI),
    13, 75-6, 91-5, 97,
    266-7
fire service, 49, 50,
    156; strike (1977),
    48
five per cent norm, 7,
    46, 119
flat rate increases,
    132, 172
flexibility, 58, 77, 84,
    169, 171, 174, 188,
    192, 264, 265, 270
flying pickets, 49
Fowler review, 77, 122

gas industry, 1, 23, 26,
    36, 50, 54
gas workers, strike
    (1973), 48
GCHQ, 54, 61; union ban
    at, 83, 95-9, 101,
    103-4, 267
GLCSA, 22 (table), 24,
    42 (table)
GMBATU, 23-4, 127, 164
    (table), 165, 169
grading structures, 162,
    169, 172
grave diggers, 49
grievance procedures,
    141, 239, 250
Griffiths Report, 128,
    147

harmonisation, 171
HCSA, 27
head teachers, as
    management, 248
Healey, Dennis, 9, 46
health and safety, 34,
    35, 141, 249
Health and Safety at
    Work Act, 34
Health and Social
    Security, Department
    of, 21, 79, 87, 89,
    93, 95, 98, 100,
    102, 128, 137-8, 145

health visitors, 27, 127
Heath, Edward, 10, 46,
    115
holidays, 44, 57, 141,
    163, 190, 249
home helps, 40, 43, 182
hospitals, 28, 36, 49
Houghton inquiry, 207-8,
    211, 214
hours of work, 34, 171,
    177, 195, 210, 267
HVA, 22 (table), 27, 41,
    42 (table)

ICPS, 21
IFF, 35
incentive schemes, 50,
    51
incomes policy, 6-7, 46,
    48, 50, 68, 70-1,
    77, 98, 115, 157,
    158, 175
index-linking, 76, 208
industrial action: in
    Civil Service, 73;
    in local government,
    173, 183; in NHS,
    127, 140, 141, 148;
    in public services,
    46; by teachers,
    199, 201, 214, 233
industrial relations:
    in local government,
    180-94; management
    of, 32, 51; in NHS,
    114-55; in public
    services, 1-16; role
    of government in,
    130-41; school-
    based, 239-42; in
    school sector, 199-
    258;
Industrial Relations Act
    (1971), 26
inflation, 9-10, 71,
    77-8, 158, 222, 224
Inland Revenue, 21
IPCS, 22 (table), 25-6,
    32, 42 (table), 72
    (table), 84, 95, 96
    (table), 97, 103,

262, 265
IRSF, 21, 22 (table),
    25, 34-5, 39, 42
    (table), 72 (table),
    78, 81, 96 (table),
    101, 103

Jarvis, Fred, 218, 226
job evaluation, 43, 82,
    169
joint consultation, 105,
    184
Joint Staff Consultative
    Committees (JSCC),
    115
Joseph, Sir Keith, 205,
    207, 210, 212,
    218-23, 226-7, 232,
    238, 240

King's Fund Group, 123,
    124, 128

Labour councils, 55,
    189-90, 193, 203,
    205, 211, 213, 218,
    221, 227, 231, 233
Labour government, 7, 9,
    68-9, 119, 145, 158,
    207-8
Labour Party, 39, 60,
    136, 166, 169, 173,
    179, 188, 201, 207,
    213, 218, 226
Labour Research
    Department, 60
LACSAB, 165-6, 170-1,
    177
laundries, 55, 56, 136
left movement, 101, 200,
    201, 253
lobbying by unions, 103,
    107
local authorities, 1, 7,
    9, 20 (table), 41
    120, 135, 266
local authority
    craftsmen, strike
    (1975), 48
local authority manual
    workers, 57, 120,

159, 161, 168-72,
    178 (table), 179,
    194; settlements,
    17, 176; strike see
    Dirty Jobs Dispute
local bargaining, 33, 51
local government, 16,
    23, 26, 28, 33, 36,
    39, 50, 52, 61, 156-
    98; bargaining
    strategies in, 156-
    98; reorganisation
    of, 185
Local Government Act
    (1982), 186
Local Government Plan-
    ning Act (1980), 187
London weighting, 158
low pay, 50, 58, 82, 98,
    168-9, 189, 200,
    239, 246;
    supplements, 189

McCarthy, Lord, 122,
    124, 126, 129
maintenance work: local
    authority, 187; NHS,
    133
management: in local
    government, 185,
    191, 193; in NHS,
    124-6, 130, 137-8,
    143, 146-8; in
    schools, 247
manpower cuts, 68, 70,
    73, 75, 87, 90-1,
    192
manpower levels, NHS,
    133-5
Manpower Services
    Commission, 89
manual workers, 23, 24,
    28-9, 41, 53, 156,
    177, 262; see also
    local authority
    manual workers
market forces, 80, 82
maternity leave, 210,
    239, 247
measured day work, 51
Megaw Inquiry, 68, 78,

80-1, 83-5, 97, 123, 209, 265
merit pay, 84, 103, 130, 200, 212-3, 217, 240-1, 244-7, 252
midwives, 122, 124, 127, 129, 132, 260, 263
militancy: in Civil Service, 98, 100, 101; local, 52; in public service, 46
Militant Tendency, 97, 100
miners, 49; inquiry into, 50; strike (1974), 48; strike (1984), 234
minimum wage, 158
monetarism, 10-4, 262
MPU, 27

'N Minus One', 46
NAHT, 203 (table), 207, 213, 222, 237
NALGO, 22 (table), 23, 26, 29, 32, 35, 41, 42 (table), 44, 45 (table), 46, 60, 120, 157-8, 163, 164 (table), 172-3, 177, 181, 183-4, 193
NAS/UWT, 22 (table), 24, 42 (table), 46, 203 (table), 204-14, 220-8, 230, 233, 234
NATFHE, 22 (table), 24, 42 (table), 46
national agreements, 162, 174, 179; undercutting of, 190
National Association of Health Authorities (NAHA), 123, 131
national bargaining, 160; threat to, 262
National Board for Prices and Incomes (NBPI), 50-1, 115, 157, 162
National Health Service Act (1946), 114

National Joint Councils, 156, 161, 163, 165, 170, 173, 180; composition of, 164 (table)
national negotiating systems, 229; for teachers, 253
National Power Loading Agreement (1966), 51
National Savings, Department of, 100
national security, 103-4
nationalised industry sector, 52
NCSA, 27
NCU, 22 (table), 24, 41, 42 (table)
new managerialism: in Civil Service, 68-113; development of, 86-95
new realism, 100
new technology, 95, 193, 216
NHS, 1, 2, 5, 7, 9, 20 (table), 21, 23, 26, 29, 31, 33, 38-9, 46, 56-7, 60-1, 73, 79, 168, 190, 204, 218, 245, 247, 260, 263, 266-7, 269; ancillary services in, 56, 59, 267; ancillary staff in, 26, 40, 115, 118-22, 127, 130-3, 137, 139, 140, 144-5 (strike (1972), 48; strike (1973), 30, 48); consultants in, 27; engineers, strike (1974), 48; industrial relations in, 114-55; restructuring of pay determination in, 119-30; strikes in (1982), 204
non-manual workers, 95, 99; employed by gov-

ernment, 94 (table)
non-unionism, 98, 136
NUPE, 22 (table), 23,
    26-8, 32, 34-5, 38,
    41, 42 (table), 44,
    45 (table), 60, 115,
    117, 127, 137,
    139-41, 144, 158,
    164 (table), 165,
    181, 184, 193
NUR, 19
nurses, 26, 41, 43, 119,
    121-2, 124, 127,
    129-30, 132, 146,
    148, 260, 263, 270;
    strike (1974), 48
Nurses' Pay Review Body,
    261
NUT, 22 (table), 24, 42
    (table), 45 (table),
    46, 203-36, 203
    (table), 241-52

office cleaning, 44, 55
Office of Manpower
    Economics, 83, 127
officials, full-time
    union, 37, 71, 95,
    101, 137, 182
ordnance factories, 54,
    56, 90
overtime, 34, 43; bans
    on, 54, 79, 89, 145

parks workers, 162
part-time teachers, 243
part-time workers, 13,
    39-46, 118, 161,
    163, 167, 177, 178
    (table), 181, 192,
    270
party politics in local
    government, 165,
    169, 173-4
PAT, 203 (table), 204-5
pay: in Civil Service,
    81 (table); in NHS,
    118, 126, (under-
    funding of, 132-3)
pay bargaining, in Civil
    Service, 76-86

pay based on
    performance, 264-5
pay cuts, 177, 211
Pay (Relativities)
    Board, 50
pay research system, 71;
    abolition of, 68,
    73, 75, 78, 97
Pay Research Unit (PRU),
    48, 50, 78
pay review bodies, 127,
    129, 132, 260
payment by results, for
    teachers, 212
pensions, 44, 52; in
    Civil Service, 76-86
personnel management,
    32; in local gov-
    ernment, 158, 187;
    in NHS, 143, 144
physiotherapists, 119;
    Chartered Society
    of, 117, 119
Planning and Land Act
    (1980), 57, 160
POA, 22 (table), 84, 93,
    96 (table), 97
political fund, 103
Ponting, Clive, 74
Post Office, 1, 4, 16,
    21
postal workers, 49;
    strike (1971), 48
Priestly Commission,
    6-7, 50
private contractors,
    56-8, 140
private medicine, 49
privatisation, 1, 14,
    38, 48, 52-3, 55-60,
    73, 87, 89, 97-8,
    135, 189, 228, 237,
    259
procedure, in NHS, 143
productivity, 11, 50,
    57, 157, 162, 171,
    191
productivity bargaining,
    34, 186
professional workers, 36
Property Services Agency

Index

(PSA), 56
Public Expenditure
Survey Committee
(PESC), 10
public ownership, 49, 52
public sector borrowing
requirement (PSBR),
8
public sector, employ-
ment in, 20 (table)
public service conflict,
nature of, 49-55
public spending, 8-10,
52, 105; cuts in, 9,
10, 23, 33, 54, 68,
199, 232, 235, 236,
239, 259; restric-
tions on, 38, 48

quality circles, 270

racism, 237
radiographers, 119
railways, 1, 19, 46
rate support grant, 231
Rayner, Sir Derek, 90,
91, 131
RCN, 22 (table), 30, 37,
115, 117-18, 121,
129, 138-9, 144,
148, 260
redeployment, 33, 93,
210, 234-5, 239,
241-2, 252
redundancy, 33-4, 52-3,
58, 87, 137, 139,
141, 231, 233, 241-
5; voluntary, 192
re-employment on new
contracts, 189
refuse collection, 40,
48, 55, 57, 157,
161, 163, 182, 187,
190, 192
Remuneration of Teachers
Act (1965), 204
residential homes, 36,
182
Resource Allocation
Working Party
(RAWP), 131-2

restructuring of NHS pay
system, 119-30
retirement, early, 235,
239, 241-2, 244
Ridley plan, 73
road sweepers, 44
roadmen, 163
rolling industrial
action, 49
rolls, school: falling,
209, 242, 243
Royal College of
Midwives, 117
Royal Navy Dockyards, 56

Scamp Committee, 157
school meals, 40, 54,
182, 187, 189, 214;
supervision of, 210,
222, 233, 237, 249;
workers, 161, 185,
189, 193, 263
school sector, indus-
trial relations in,
199-258
Scott, Sir Bernard, 76
SCPS, 21, 22 (table),
25-6, 32, 34, 42
(table), 46, 72
(table), 80-1, 83,
87, 95, 96 (table),
97, 100, 102
secretarial workers,
162, 182
sexual harassment, 44
sexual segregation of
labour, 43
SHA, 203 (table), 207,
213, 217
shipbuilding industry,
46
shop stewards, 27-9,
117, 137, 139, 144,
181-2, 184, 239,
252; growth of, 31,
38, 51, 163, 188;
training of, 95
shop stewards
committees, 183
sick leave, 34, 44, 140,
190

sickness benefits, 190
Social Contract, 9, 46
social security, 8, 58
social services, 8, 40, 43, 161, 183, 192
social workers, 162, 182; strike of (1978), 48
Socialist Teachers' Alliance, 224
Socialist Workers' Party, 37
Society of Radio- graphers, 117, 119
Special Pay Additions (SPA), 84
speech therapists, 119
staffing levels, 87, 137
steel workers, 49
street cleaning, 187
strike action: all-out, 54, 78; in Civil Service, 79; in DHSS, 87; local, 97; among manual work- ers, 53; national, 49, 53, 79, 101, 141, 199, 237; na- tional, in NHS, 145- 7; in NHS, 118, 121, 145, 204; official, 46, 49, 53, 99; se- lective, 49, 54, 97; among teachers, 201, 206-7, 213, 219-20, 222, 229, 231, 233, 235-7, 239, 251; unofficial, 46, 48, 49; among white collar workers, 99
strike pay, 146
superannuation, 190

Tavistock Institute, 34
teachers, 24, 41, 46, 49, 54, 61; appraisal of, 210, 241-2, 245-6, 252; defined duties of, 217, 238, 240; div- isions among, 253; extra-hours activity of, 214; inquiry into, 50; reduction of numbers, 232, 242; register, 247; salaries, structure of, 214; in Scotland, 206, 218, 223, 227; shortages of, 235; strike (1973), 48; strike (1974), 48; strike (1984), 204; strike (1985-6), 201, 204; terms of employment, 249; work, purpose of, 201
Teachers' Pay and Condi- tions Act (1987), 200, 228, 261-2
telecommunications, 16, 21, 24
temporary workers, 192, 270
tendering, competitive, 56-8, 133, 187, 189, 192, 267; in NHS, 134 (table), 136-7, 139, 140-1, 147
TGWU, 23, 24, 117, 127, 164 (table), 165
Thatcher, Margaret, 10, 12-13, 48-9, 53, 60- 1, 68-113 passim, 184, 213, 225, 228, 240, 253, 269
Tottenham riots, 236
Trade Union Act (1984), 12, 37, 39, 80, 101, 103
trade unionism, 229; growth of, 16, 70, 101, 114
trade unions, 12, 27-35, 61, 213, 225; attack on, 268; ban on GCHQ, see GCHQ; branches, 32, 35, 184; changes within, 51; in Civil Service, 72 (table),

95-104, 96 (table),
268; decline of, 98;
democracy in, 27-35;
density in NHS, 116
(table), 118; in
education sector,
200; in local gov-
ernment, 163-7, 181;
in NHS, 126, 138-41,
142 (table); politi-
cisation of, 269; in
public services, 17-
67, 95; reform of,
12; sectional dif-
ferences between, 98
training, 35, 57, 95
Transport Act (1985),
57, 135
travel allowances, 210,
249
Treasury department, 9,
56, 80, 82, 90
TSSA, 19
TUC, 11, 16, 19, 23, 26,
37, 44, 51-2, 54,
60, 71, 123, 127,
130, 139, 157, 158,
168, 171, 194, 267;
affiliation to, 22
(table), 30, 46,
121, 126, 127, 130,
144, 148, 201, 204,
260
TUC Health Services
Committee, 121
TUC Public Services
Committee, 52, 59

UCW, 22 (table), 23, 42
(table)
unemployment, 11, 12,
71, 200, 216, 270;
among teachers, 212
universities, 23, 26, 36

value for money, 171,
186, 194, 211
Vehicle Licensing
Centre, 100
voluntary nature of
teachers' duties,
206, 207, 210
volunteers, use of in
NHS, 146, 147

wage cuts, 139, 158
wage payment, methods
of, 169
Warwick University, 34
water, 1, 23, 26, 36,
50, 54, 79
water workers, dispute
(1983), 48
Westland Helicopters, 74
white collar workers, 5,
23, 26, 28-30, 35-6,
99, 156, 158-9, 162-
3, 172-4, 177, 179,
181-2, 192, 194, 262
Whitley Council system,
51, 59, 69, 70-1,
76-7, 103, 105, 118,
121-3, 124-30, 136-
7, 156-7, 163, 260
Winter of Discontent
(1979), 7, 30, 46,
48-9, 53, 60, 158
women, 37, 38, 163; dis-
crimination against,
247; in industrial
action, 49; member-
ship of public
service unions, 41-
2; pay patterns of,
43, 51; as shop
stewards, 28, 29,
44; in trade unions,
44; as union
officials, 44; as
workers, 13, 39-46,
118, 161, 167, 177,
178 (table), 181
work study, 34, 186
working days lost
through strikes, 47
(table)
working practices, 87,
177
working to rule, 54
Workplace Industrial
Relations Survey,
28, 29, 30

For Product Safety Concerns and Information please contact our
EU representative GPSR@taylorandfrancis.com Taylor & Francis
Verlag GmbH, Kaufingerstraße 24, 80331 München, Germany